First Workshop on Insights from Negative Results in NLP (Insights 2020)

Online
19 November 2020

ISBN: 978-1-7138-1996-7

Insights 2020

First Workshop on Insights from Negative Results in NLP

Proceedings of the Workshop

November 19, 2020
Online

Introduction

Publication of negative results is difficult in most fields, and the current focus on benchmark-driven performance improvement exacerbates this situation and implicitly discourages hypothesis-driven research. As a result, the development of NLP models often devolves into a product of tinkering and tweaking, rather than science. Furthermore, it increases the time, effort, and carbon emissions spent on developing and tuning models, as the researchers have little opportunity to learn from what has already been tried and failed.

Historically, this tendency is hard to combat. ACL 2010 invited negative results as a special type of research paper submissions[1], but received too few submissions and did not continue with it. *The Journal for Interesting Negative Results in NLP and ML*[2] has only produced one issue in 2008.

However, the tide may be turning. The first iteration of the *Workshop on Insights from Negative Results* attracted 35 submissions and 11 presentation requests for papers accepted to "Findings of EMNLP". Moreover, we are not alone: an independent workshop *"I can't believe it's not better!"* is held at NeurIPS 2020[3].

We invited submissions with many kinds of negative results, with the hope that they could yield useful insights and provide a much-needed reality check on the successes of deep learning models in NLP. In particular, we solicited the following types of contributions:

- broadly applicable recommendations for training/fine-tuning, especially if X that didn't work is something that many practitioners would think reasonable to try, and if the demonstration of X's failure is accompanied by some explanation/hypothesis;

- ablation studies of components in previously proposed models, showing that their contributions are different from what was initially reported;

- datasets or probing tasks showing that previous approaches do not generalize to other domains or language phenomena;

- trivial baselines that work suspiciously well for a given task/dataset;

- cross-lingual studies showing that a technique X is only successful for a certain language or language family;

- experiments on (in)stability of the previously published results due to hardware, random initializations, preprocessing pipeline components, etc;

- theoretical arguments and/or proofs for why X should not be expected to work.

In terms of topics, 15 papers from our submission pool discussed "great ideas that didn't work", 12 dealt with the issues of generalizability, 5 were on the topic of "right for the wrong reasons", and 2 more papers focused on reproducibility issues. We accepted 18 short papers (51.4% acceptance rate) and granted 5 presentation requests for Findings papers.

We hope that this event will be the first of many reality-check discussions on progress in NLP. If we do not talk about things that do not work, it is harder to see what the biggest problems are and where the community effort is the most needed.

[1] https://mirror.aclweb.org/acl2010/papers.html
[2] http://jinr.site.uottawa.ca/
[3] https://i-cant-believe-its-not-better.github.io/

Organizers:

Anna Rogers, Univeristy Copenhagen (Denmark)
João Sedoc, Johns Hopkins Univeristy (USA)
Anna Rumshisky, University of Massachusetts Lowell (USA)

Program Committee:

Emily Alsentzer, MIT (USA)
Amittai Axelrod, DiDi Labs (USA)
William Boag, MIT (USA)
Anneke Buffone, Facebook (USA)
Aleksandr Drozd, RIKEN (Japan)
Allyson Ettinger, University of Chicago (USA)
Stefan Evert, Friedrich-Alexander-Universitäat Erlangen-Nürnberg (Germany)
Jason Alan Fries, Stanford (USA)
Leibny Paola Garcia, Johns Hopkins University (USA)
Matt Gardner, Allen AI (USA)
Sharath Chandra Guntuku, University of Pennsylvania (USA)
Constantine Lignos, Brandeis University (USA)
Tal Linzen, Johns Hopkins University (USA)
Kyle Lo, Allen Institute for Artificial Intelligence (USA)
Ana Marasović, Allen Institute for Artificial Intelligence (USA)
Matthew B. A. McDermott, MIT (USA)
Neha Nayak, University of Massachusetts Amherst (USA)
Mark Neumann, Allen Institute for Artificial Intelligence (USA)
Denis Paperno, Université de Lorraine (France)
Ellie Pavlick, Brown University (USA)
Masoud Rouhizadeh, Johns Hopkins University (USA)
Jordan Rodu, University of Virginia (USA)
Neville Ryant, University of Pennsylvania (USA)
Djamé Seddah, Université Paris-Sorbonne (France)
Andy Schwatz, Stony Brook University (USA)
Emma Strubell, University of Massachusetts Amherst (USA)
Ekaterina Vylomova, University of Melbourne (Australia)
Chris Welty, Google Research (USA)
Matthijs Westera, Universitat Pompeu Fabra (Spain)
Mark Yatskar, Allen AI (USA)

Invited Speakers:

Rada Mihalcea, University of Michigan (USA)
Byron C. Wallace, Northeastern University (USA)

Table of Contents

Program

Thursday, November 19, 2020

7:00–7:15	*Opening remarks*
7:15–8:15	*Invited talk: Rada Mihalcea (University of Michigan)* *The ups and downs of word embeddings*
8:45–9:15	*Thematic session: representation learning*
8:15–8:45	*Thematic session: dialogue*
9:15–10:00	*Social break / meal time*
10:00–11:00	*Invited talk: Byron C. Wallace (Northeastern University)* *Negative results yield interesting questions, or: a bunch of stuff that didn't work*
11:00–11:30	*Thematic session: question answering*
11:30–12:00	*Thematic session: natural language inference*
12:00–12:30	*Thematic session: lessons learned the hard way*
12:30–13:00	*Social break / meal time*
13:00–14:00	*Interactive orals*
14:00–14:45	*Panel discussion*
14:45–15:00	*Breakout*
15:00–15:15	*Closing remarks*
15:15–16:00	*Happy hour*

The program is subject to change, please check the EMNLP 2020 virtual conference website for the final program and schedule in different time zones. The program will also be available at `https://insights-workshop.github.io`. All times above are specified in PST.

Domain adaptation challenges of BERT in tokenization and sub-word representations of Out-of-Vocabulary words

Anmol Nayak, Hari P. Timmapathini, Karthikeyan Ponnalagu, Vijendran Venkoparao
ARiSE Labs at Bosch
{Anmol.Nayak, HariPrasad.Timmapathini, Karthikeyan.Ponnalagu,
GopalanVijendran.Venkoparao}@in.bosch.com

Abstract

BERT model (Devlin et al., 2019) has achieved significant progress in several Natural Language Processing (NLP) tasks by leveraging the multi-head self-attention mechanism (Vaswani et al., 2017) in its architecture. However, it still has several research challenges which are not tackled well for domain specific corpus found in industries. In this paper, we have highlighted these problems through detailed experiments involving analysis of the attention scores and dynamic word embeddings with the BERT-Base-Uncased model. Our experiments have lead to interesting findings that showed: 1) Largest substring from the left that is found in the vocabulary (in-vocab) is always chosen at every sub-word unit that can lead to suboptimal tokenization choices, 2) Semantic meaning of a vocabulary word deteriorates when found as a substring in an Out-Of-Vocabulary (OOV) word, and 3) Minor misspellings in words are inadequately handled. We believe that if these challenges are tackled, it will significantly help the domain adaptation aspect of BERT.

1 Introduction

BERT is one of the prominent models used for a variety of NLP tasks. With the Masked Language Model (MLM) method, it has been successful at leveraging bidirectionality while training the language model. The BERT-Base-Uncased model has 12 encoder layers, with each layer consisting of 12 self-attention heads. The word representations are context-dependent 768 dimensional dynamic embeddings. In order to leverage the learnings of such pre-trained networks, fine tuning is commonly done while building NLP applications in industries.The BERT-Base-Uncased vocabulary has a size of 30522 with only 994 unused slots (in comparison, BERT-Base-Cased has only 101 unused slots). While the unused slots in the vocabulary can be used to include domain specific words, the representations of these will have to be fine tuned with domain specific corpus before they can be utilized. Hence, it is essential that the tokenization algorithm performs well to handle domain specific OOV words.

BERT relies on the WordPiece algorithm (Schuster and Nakajima, 2012) to create the vocabulary, that chooses those sub-word units for the vocabulary towards maximising the language model likelihood. However, the tokenization using this vocabulary is not done semantically. This leads to a poor tokenization that induces a semantic information loss in terms of dealing with OOV words for domain centric downstream tasks. While the largest substring tokenization problem can be alleviated to a large extent by integrating recent algorithms like BPE-Dropout (Provilkov et al., 2019) or SentencePiece (Kudo and Richardson, 2018), that use frequency and/or language model based tokenization, the remaining aforementioned challenges still persist. In the following section, we discuss these challenges with respect to two categories: Tokenization and Sub-word representations.

2 Experiments

The experiments we performed are using the pre-trained BERT-Base-Uncased model without any domain specific fine tuning as the examples were chosen with the purpose of highlighting the challenges with BERT across various domains. The 12th encoder layer dynamic embeddings were used for all the analysis tasks. In case a word was OOV, the average of its sub-word units embeddings was considered as its embedding. Otherwise, the embedding for the word was considered as it is. In all cases, we ignore the [CLS] and [SEP] embeddings while computing the embedding of a par-

Proceedings of the First Workshop on Insights from Negative Results in NLP, pages 1–5
Online, November 19, 2020. ©2020 Association for Computational Linguistics

Input	Tokenized
deconstructed	[CLS], deco, ##nst, ##ru, ##cted, [SEP]
deactivated	[CLS], dea, ##ct, ##ivated, [SEP]
unequal	[CLS], une, ##qual, [SEP]
ccabbage	[CLS], cc, ##ab, ##bag, ##e, [SEP]
cababge	[CLS], cab, ##ab, ##ge, [SEP]
cabbagee	[CLS], cabbage, ##e, [SEP]']
unsaturated	[CLS], un, ##sat, ##ura, ##ted, [SEP]
saturated	[CLS], saturated, [SEP]
pork has saturated fat	[CLS], pork, has, saturated, fat, [SEP]
pork has ##sat ##ura ##ted fat	[CLS], pork, has, ##sat, ##ura, ##ted, fat, [SEP]

Table 1: BERT tokenized representations.

Cosine similarity	$Count_{beg}$	$Count_{mid}$	$Count_{end}$
0.0-0.1	0	1	0
0.1-0.2	6	1	1
0.2-0.3	39	44	19
0.3-0.4	160	232	113
0.4-0.5	368	562	232
0.5-0.6	264	442	213
0.6-0.7	96	145	179
0.7-0.8	15	60	145
0.8-0.9	0	0	23
0.9-1.0	0	0	1
Avg. similarity:	**0.474**	**0.49**	**0.552**

Table 2: Cosine similarity score count for words vs misspelled versions in the TOEFL-Spell corpus when the error occurs at the beginning, middle or end of the word.

ticular word. The ## counterpart of a word is ## prefixed to the word. For example, the ## counterpart of the word *active* is *##active*. We also made a subtle change to the tokenizer to leave untouched any word beginning with ##.

2.1 Tokenization problems

BERT always picks the largest substring from the left that is in-vocab at every sub-word unit for the tokenized output. While this performs reasonably well for words where the root (or stem) are suffixed, prefixed words are vulnerable to a poor tokenization.

Taking *deconstructed*, *deactivated* and *unequal* as examples, even though the vocabulary had the prefixes *de* and *un* as well as the words *constructed*, *activated* and *equal*, the tokenizer chose the substrings *deco*, *dea* and *une* (see Table 1). In comparison since SentencePiece is a likelihood based tokenization algorithm, it has managed to generate better tokenizations (*deconstructed*: _de, con, struct, ed; *deactivated*: _de, activated; *unequal*:

_unequal). We believe that if the BERT tokenizer correctly separates the prefixes while the model is being trained, it can help the model to learn better representations for the prefix as well as the sub-word units since the attention mechanism would understand the influence of the different categories of prefixes. Further it can be seen in Section 2.2 how a poor tokenization can lead to weaker semantic representations for the word.

Domain specific corpus often contain a large amount of jargons that can be misspelled frequently. Taking the in-vocab word *cabbage* as an example, *ccabbage*, *cababge* and *cabbagee* were chosen as the misspelled versions. The cosine similarities of *cabbage* with *ccabbage*, *cababge* and *cabbagee* were 0.33, 0.44 and 0.63 respectively. To verify that the low cosine similarity scores in the misspelled versions were not due to lack of surrounding context, we checked the cosine similarity score between *cabbage* and *onion* (in-vocab) and found it to be 0.88.

To analyze the extent of this problem and the im-

Cosine similarity	$\text{Count}_{L=4}$	$\text{Count}_{L=5}$	$\text{Count}_{L=6}$	$\text{Count'}_{L=4}$	$\text{Count'}_{L=5}$	$\text{Count'}_{L=6}$
0.0-0.1	0	0	0	0	0	0
0.1-0.2	6	8	13	0	0	1
0.2-0.3	25	86	134	4	0	2
0.3-0.4	198	404	556	5	2	2
0.4-0.5	573	975	1159	21	17	7
0.5-0.6	622	933	1133	8	3	14
0.6-0.7	176	340	398	172	54	23
0.7-0.8	4	17	32	127	58	28
0.8-0.9	0	0	1	51	23	8
0.9-1.0	0	0	0	0	0	0
Avg. similarity:	**0.496**	**0.487**	**0.484**	**0.665**	**0.669**	**0.652**

Table 3: Cosine similarity score count for word vs OOV ## counterpart ($\text{Count}_{L=4,\,5,\,6}$) and word vs in-vocab ## counterpart ($\text{Count'}_{L=4,\,5,\,6}$).

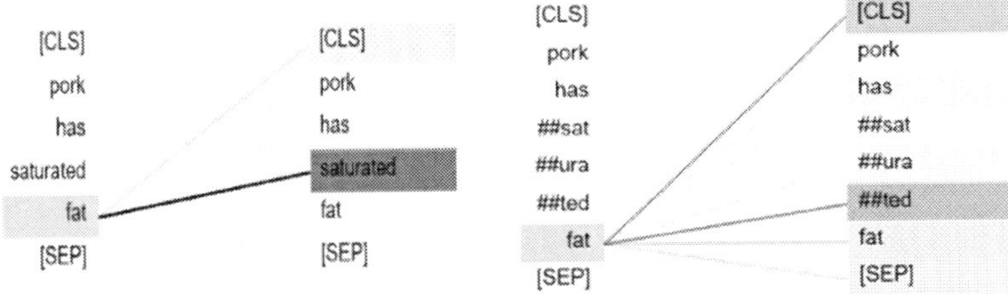

Figure 1: Inward Attention visualization for *fat* in Encoder layer 1 - Attention head 3.

pact of the position of the error in the word on the tokenization, we chose the TOEFL-Spell corpus that contains over 6000 common spelling errors.[1] We took the intersection of the common words between the TOEFL-Spell corpus and the BERT vocabulary words. The corpus was segregated depending on whether the spelling error occurred in the word within the starting 33% of the letters, in the middle or at the end. As we can see in Table 2, since the BERT tokenizer has the largest substring problem, the penalty of a spelling error earlier in the word is more harmful as it leads to subsequent sub-word tokenization choices to be suboptimal.

2.2 Semantic meaning deterioration from sub-word representations

For a model to handle OOV words well, it should learn strong representations of a words constituents. While OOV words that begin with an in-vocab root (or stem) will retain its semantic meaning when tokenized, they become vulnerable in other cases as the root (or stem) will be broken down into smaller constituent sub-word units.

To see how BERT handles this, we created two sets of words from the vocabulary of length 4,5 and 6 that were consisting of: 1) Words whose ## counterparts were OOV and 2) Words whose ## counterparts were in-vocab. We chose these particular words since a word with length less than 4 would be commonly be found as a sub-word across many words, while a word with length larger that 6 would be rarer to be found as a sub-word. The cosine similarity between a word and its ## counterpart was computed (see Table 3). This problem is not a concern when the ## counterpart is in-vocab as the average cosine similarity was around 0.66, which can be improved if supplied with a context in a sentence. However, when the ## counterpart is not part of the vocab, the average cosine similarity drops to a low value of 0.48, which makes it difficult for the network to recover from.

To further analyze this problem, we compared the embeddings of the words *unsaturated* (OOV but *un* and *saturated* are in-vocab) with *saturated*. The cosine similarity between *unsaturated* and *saturated* was only 0.30. In comparison, the cosine similarity between *un saturated* and *saturated* is 0.81. To verify that this low similarity was being

[1]https://github.com/
EducationalTestingService/TOEFL-Spell

3

Layer	Influence	[CLS]	pork	has	fat	[SEP]
1	Outward	-0.00905915	0.06523646	0.06099863	**0.18786138**	0.03023722
	Inward	-0.01837084	0.04225173	0.01648326	**0.18937206**	0.01520266
2	Outward	-0.0004705	0.00843187	-0.00484527	0.02482779	0.01454217
	Inward	**0.17178166**	-0.01259612	-0.03369101	0.01195145	0.01798595
3	Outward	0.00184171	0.01289389	**0.12865019**	0.08927301	0.00345621
	Inward	0.03889459	0.01265209	-0.01004721	**0.15340301**	-0.00876677
4	Outward	-0.00047312	-0.00136977	0.03939556	0.03750715	-0.00168958
	Inward	0.04355699	0.00727928	0.04730521	0.04906496	0.01223874
5	Outward	0.0048245	-0.00982189	-0.02644702	0.02499489	-0.00251921
	Inward	0.00937152	-0.00695391	-0.01893955	0.05315585	**0.16019171**
6	Outward	-0.00265443	-0.01301921	0.0342003	0.01597476	-0.00048893
	Inward	-0.00409265	0.01658719	0.01285958	0.02900258	0.05893058
7	Outward	-0.00125295	0.00154607	-0.01132394	0.01854416	0.00031497
	Inward	0.00937736	-0.04564465	0.04480758	0.01291878	**0.11453587**
8	Outward	-0.00527599	-0.01248677	0.00545111	0.00576302	-0.00044466
	Inward	0.00128797	0.00911033	0.06117178	-0.02267864	0.06066525
9	Outward	-0.01058492	0.00061043	0.03902156	0.03468442	0.00406067
	Inward	0.0006195	0.01115873	0.03967107	-0.00104411	0.02020252
10	Outward	0.01764568	0.00554455	0.02936521	0.03989781	0.01815606
	Inward	0.03199076	0.03799912	0.01782591	-0.00910724	0.02136517
11	Outward	0.02042433	0.0195443	0.01784758	0.02018948	0.00963123
	Inward	-0.03223545	0.08976553	0.04230637	0.04836676	-0.10472655
12	Outward	0.02328578	0.00367201	0.00402358	0.03388398	0.00260962
	Inward	0.01822337	0.0257406	0.02513322	0.03337914	-0.0509001

Table 4: Difference in inward and outward attention scores between *saturated* and *##sat ##ura ##ted*.

Word	Nearest neighbours
saturated	bacon, nutrition, cereal, obesity, flour, tobacco, humidity, mustard, cigarettes, vitamin
##sat ##ura ##ted	destruction, egypt, erosion, malaria, morphology, concussion, organ, topography, aroused, sample

Table 5: Top 10 cosine similar nearest neighbours in the vocabulary for *saturated* and *##sat ##ura ##ted* as found in the sentences.

caused by the poor representation learning of the constituents of *saturated*, we compared the average embedding of *##sat, ##ura, ##ted* (since *unsaturated* was tokenized into sub-word units) with *saturated* and found their cosine similarity to be only 0.35.

Further, to rule out the possibility that it was being caused due to lack of surrounding context, we compared the average embedding of *##sat, ##ura, ##ted* with *saturated* as found in the following sentences: *pork has saturated fat* and *pork has ##sat ##ura ##ted fat*.

The cosine similarity even in this case was found to be only 0.57. For the above sentences, we wanted to see the impact of this problem by an-

alyzing the attention scores in each encoder layer. The multi-head (12 heads) attention score matrix across the 12 encoder layers is of size 12 x 12 x 6 x 6 for the first sentence and 12 x 12 x 8 x 8 for the second sentence. Within each layer, we averaged the attention scores across the 12 heads. This resulted in 12 x 6 x 6 and 12 x 8 x 8 sized attention scores matrices for the two sentences respectively. We wanted to observe the inward influence of other words on *saturated* as well as outward influence of *saturated* towards the other words in both sentences. For the first sentence, the attention score matrix was hence reduced to a size of 12 x 5 x 5. In the second sentence, we averaged the inward and output influence for *##sat ##ura ##ted*, leading to a reduced matrix of size 12 x 5 x 5. The two matrices were then subtracted to see the difference in the inward and outward influences for the word *saturated* (see Table 4).

Since the difference was taken, a positive value means *saturated* as found in the first sentence had a larger inwards or outwards attention influence compared to the second sentence. Clark et al. (2019) previously showed that a large number of attention heads in the early layers of BERT put >50% of their attention on previous and next tokens. As we can see in Table 4, the values in bold show a significant difference in attention scores, especially in the case for the neighbouring words of *saturated*, which we believe has caused the loss of semantic meaning between *saturated* and when tokenized to *##sat, ##ura, ##ted*. The inward attention visualization for *fat* in Encoder layer 1 - Attention head 3 generated using BertViz (Vig, 2019) can be seen in Figure 1. Further, we checked the top 10 cosine similar neighbours in the BERT-Base-Uncased vocabulary (using their dynamic embeddings) for the embeddings of *saturated* and *##sat ##ura ##ted* from the above sentences. We found that while *saturated* as found in the first sentence had semantically similar neighbours, its occurrence in the second sentence had neighbours which had a completely irrelevant semantic meaning (see Table 5). This confirmed that such a challenge can lead to cascading problems in the network.

3   Conclusion

In this paper we highlighted various challenges in the BERT model which if solved could significantly boost the models accuracy, especially in domain specific applications. These are mainly due to BERT lacking a semantic tokenization algorithm and its semantic information loss from sub-word representations in OOV scenarios.

References

Kevin Clark, Urvashi Khandelwal, Omer Levy, and Christopher D. Manning. 2019. What does BERT look at? an analysis of BERT's attention. In *Proceedings of the 2019 ACL Workshop BlackboxNLP: Analyzing and Interpreting Neural Networks for NLP*, pages 276–286, Florence, Italy. Association for Computational Linguistics.

Jacob Devlin, Ming-Wei Chang, Kenton Lee, and Kristina Toutanova. 2019. BERT: Pre-training of deep bidirectional transformers for language understanding. In *Proceedings of the 2019 Conference of the North American Chapter of the Association for Computational Linguistics: Human Language Technologies, Volume 1 (Long and Short Papers)*, pages 4171–4186, Minneapolis, Minnesota. Association for Computational Linguistics.

Taku Kudo and John Richardson. 2018. SentencePiece: A simple and language independent subword tokenizer and detokenizer for neural text processing. In *Proceedings of the 2018 Conference on Empirical Methods in Natural Language Processing: System Demonstrations*, pages 66–71, Brussels, Belgium. Association for Computational Linguistics.

Ivan Provilkov, Dmitrii Emelianenko, and Elena Voita. 2019. Bpe-dropout: Simple and effective subword regularization. *arXiv preprint*, arXiv:1910.13267.

Mike Schuster and Kaisuke Nakajima. 2012. Japanese and korean voice search. In *2012 IEEE International Conference on Acoustics, Speech and Signal Processing (ICASSP)*, pages 5149–5152. IEEE.

Ashish Vaswani, Noam Shazeer, Niki Parmar, Jakob Uszkoreit, Llion Jones, Aidan N Gomez, Łukasz Kaiser, and Illia Polosukhin. 2017. Attention is all you need. In *Advances in neural information processing systems*, pages 5998–6008.

Jesse Vig. 2019. A multiscale visualization of attention in the transformer model. *arXiv preprint arXiv:1906.05714*.

Q. Can Knowledge Graphs be used to Answer Boolean Questions?
A. It's complicated!

Daria Dzendzik[*]
ADAPT Centre
Dublin City University
`daria.dzendzik`
`@adaptcentre.ie`

Carl Vogel
School of Computer
Science and Statistics
Trinity College Dublin
The University of Dublin
`vogel@tcd.ie`

Jennifer Foster
School of Computing
Dublin City University
`jennifer.foster`
`@dcu.ie`

Abstract

In this paper we explore the problem of machine reading comprehension, focusing on the BoolQ dataset of Yes/No questions. We carry out an error analysis of a BERT-based machine reading comprehension model on this dataset, revealing issues such as unstable model behaviour and some noise within the dataset itself. We then experiment with two approaches for integrating information from knowledge graphs: (i) concatenating knowledge graph triples to text passages and (ii) encoding knowledge with a Graph Neural Network. Neither of these approaches show a clear improvement and we hypothesize that this may be due to a combination of inaccuracies in the knowledge graph, imprecision in entity linking, and the models' inability to capture additional information from knowledge graphs.

1 Introduction

Clark et al. (2019) explore the difficulty of Yes/No questions and introduce the BoolQ dataset which contains 16k questions based on real Google user queries, paired by crowdworkers with passages from Wikipedia. They establish a strong baseline using $BERT_{large}$ (Devlin et al., 2019) and transfer learning from the Multi-Genre Natural Language Inference (MNLI) task (Williams et al., 2018).

In this work, we carry out an error analysis of 200 samples from the $BERT_{large} + MNLI$ baseline model and find out that 77% constitute genuine model errors, almost 6% of samples contain an incorrect answer tag, and 8% do not contain enough evidence to answer the question. The remaining 9% we classified as difficult questions as they involve deep understanding, reasoning, specific knowledge, and sometimes depend on opinion. Due to the unstable behaviour of the model, error samples vary

from run to run, where a run refers to the pipeline of MNLI pre-training, BoolQ fine-tuning, and evaluation of the model. We introduce a *stable accuracy* metric to evaluate a system across multiple runs with the same hyperparameters. Stable accuracy over n runs refers to the proportion of questions that are always correctly answered. We observed a 3.3% and an 11% drop of stable accuracy over 2 and 10 runs respectively.

Next we turn our attention to improving machine reading comprehension (MRC) system performance. We hypothesize the system might benefit from additional information about entities and/or relations between the entities, in the question and passage. Consider, for example, (1) where *pei* is an abbreviation of *Prince Edward Island*.

(1) **Question:** *is anne with an e filmed on pei*
Passage: *The series is filmed partially in Prince Edward Island as well as ...*
Gold Answer: Yes **Predicted Answer:** No

A number of works including Mihaylov and Frank (2018); Bauer et al. (2018); Lin et al. (2019); Qiu et al. (2019); Thayaparan et al. (2019); Talmor et al. (2019); Zhao et al. (2020) show successful usage of knowledge graphs (KGs) in several MRC settings.

We propose and evaluate two approaches for augmenting questions and answers with KG information: (1) concatenating the model input with sentences constructed from ConceptNet triples[1] (Speer et al., 2017); and (2) encoding KG entities and relations with the Graph Neural Network (GNN) proposed by Shaw et al. (2019), a model suited to graph-based input. Neither approach shows a significant improvement over the baseline.

---

[*]A significant part of this work was done during an internship at Google Research Switzerland in September-December 2019 in collaboration with Massimo Nicosia.

[1]`https://conceptnet.io/` − last verified (l.v.) 07/2020

Proceedings of the First Workshop on Insights from Negative Results in NLP, pages 6–14
Online, November 19, 2020. ©2020 Association for Computational Linguistics

Category	#	%	Category	#	%
Factual Reasoning	12	6.0	Paraphrasing	97	48.5
Missing Mention	28	14.0	By Example	7	3.5
Other Inference	16	8.0	Implicit	39	19.5

Table 1: BoolQ errors anlysis by reasoning type.

2 A Closer Look at the BoolQ Baseline

2.1 Error Analysis

We manually analyse 200 errors made by one run of the baseline system (33% of one-run errors) and discover that 6% of them involve an incorrect answer tag and another 8% involve confusing passages which do not give enough support for the answer (see Appendix B for examples).

Table 1 shows a categorization of the errors according to the reasoning types provided by Clark et al. (2019). The majority of errors belongs to the *Paraphrasing* type (48.5%). In these cases, the answer is in the passage and only a minimum amount of extra knowledge and reasoning is required to answer the question. The *Implicit* and *Missing Mention* types account for 19.5% and 14% of errors respectively. Only about 3.5% of incorrectly answered questions require an understanding of examples given in the passage, 6% requrie factual reasoning, and 8% require other inference.

2.2 Stable Accuracy

We reproduce the results of the baseline $BERT_{large} + MNLI$ model released by Clark et al. (2019).[2] Its accuracy is between 80% and 82% (Fig. 1 (a) ●) with an average 81.41% accuracy over 10 runs (vs. 82.2% reported in Clark et al. (2019)). Our error analysis shows that a significant portion of the correctly answered questions varies from run to run together with around 40% of errors.

We define the ratio of the number of correctly answered questions across n runs to the total number of questions as *stable accuracy*. Formally, if Q is the set of all questions and $Q^i_{correct}$ is the set of correctly answered questions at the ith run, the *stable accuracy* after n runs is defined as (2):

$$StableAccuracy_n = \frac{|\cap_{i=0}^{n} Q^i_{correct}|}{|Q|} \quad (2)$$

The stable accuracy over 10 runs drops to 71% (see Fig 1 (a) ⋆). Ensembling with a majority voting for

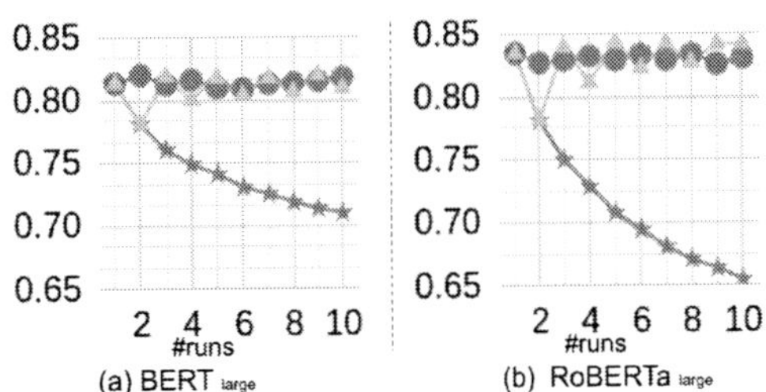

(a) BERT large   (b) RoBERTa large

Figure 1: Accuracy (●), stable accuracy (⋆), and majority voting accuracy (▲) over up to 10 runs of (a) BERT and (b) RoBERTa baselines.

up to 10 runs (Fig. 1 (a), ▲) does not outperform the baseline: the values are within the range of 78.09% and 81.77%.[3]

We repeat the experiment using the robustly optimized $RoBERTa_{large}$ model (Liu et al., 2019) implemented by Wolf et al. (2019) and fine tuned on the MNLI task. This model has a better average accuracy (83.7)% but it is also more unstable: the stable accuracy drops to 64.0% (see Fig. 1 (b)). As with the $BERT$ model, ensembling over 10 runs does not give a performance boost.

This observed behavior means that the system performs well on each run but every time it performs well on a different set of questions. This might be related to the notion of "forgettable" examples described by Toneva et al. (2019). The difference is that they discovered the ability of models to forget the learned examples during the training phase, while we examine stable and unstable examples when the training is finished.

3 Modeling Knowledge Graph Data

Our manual inspection of the results of one baseline system run reveals that approximately 20% of erroneous cases are questions involving some property of an entity or concept, or some hierarchical relationship between entities. An example of the former is (3) and the latter is (4).

(3) *is i 80 in indiana a toll road*

(4) *is college of william and mary an ivy league school?*

We hypothesize that adding knowledge graph data could help in answering such questions, as well

---

[3] Note that the ensemble performs slightly better with an odd numbers of runs as only the samples with strictly more votes for the correct answer are considered to be answered correctly. This is a very strict evaluation. Alternatively, in the case of a tie, the majority answer (*Yes*) can be selected, but we aim to provide the evaluation with the maximum certainty.

as examples such as (1) and (5) below where the entity in the question is referred to using a different name in the passage.

(5) **Question:** *does smeagol die in lord of the rings* **Passage:** *... Gollum finally ... but he fell into the fires of the volcano, where both he and the Ring were destroyed.* **Answer:** Yes

We use the CloudAPI[4] to annotate text with tokens, part of speech tags, named entities with Freebase[5] KG identifiers (MIDs), numbers, dates and VerbNet[6] roles which can be used for establishing relations between entities.

3.1 Extending Passages with ConceptNet

ConceptNet (Liu and Singh, 2004; Speer et al., 2017) is an open semantic network based on DBPedia, Wiktionary, WordNet, and other resources. It captures common-sense knowledge and was created for computers to understand words and concepts in the same way people do. It was particularly designed to be used by NLP applications and widely used in MRC (Weissenborn et al., 2017; Bauer et al., 2018; Mihaylov and Frank, 2018; Lin et al., 2019; Qiu et al., 2019). Partly inspired by Weissenborn et al. (2017), we convert ConceptNet relations into sentences but instead of embedding them independently, we concatenate them to the baseline model input.

3.1.1 Sentence Extraction and Filtering

ConceptNet has 34 relation types.[7] Each relation has start and end entities and a strength of relation (relevance weight). We look up every annotated entity from questions and passages in ConceptNet. We extract the top 100 relations according to the relevance weight, and select those where both the start and end entities are in English. We remove relations that are not useful, such as *"External URLs"*, or too broad such as *"FormOf"*. Then we transform ConceptNet relations into simple sentences based on the relation description or, if there is no description, we create a string: `[entity1] [relation] [entity2]`, e.g. the *"panda is*

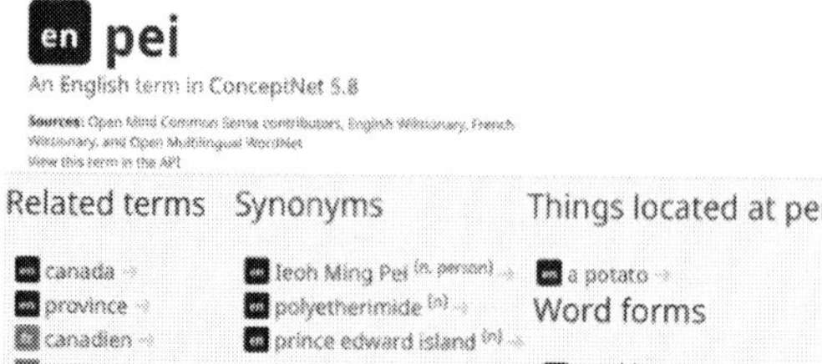

Figure 2: An example of usage ConceptNet entities for answering a Boolean question.

near a bamboo forest" string is created from entites: *"panda"*, *"bamboo forest"* and the relation *"LocatedNear"*. Fig. 2 shows a ConceptNet entity from example (1). The verbalized triples such as *"pei is a synonym of Prince Edward Island"* are prepended to the text passage.

Since such new sentences can add noise (see *polyetherimide* examples in Fig. 2) and a long input might confuse the model (Thayaparan et al., 2019), we aim to add extra sentences to the passages only if it is relevant and can better "explain" the nature of entities. To select those, we rank all extracted sentences S according to the sum of their similarities with the question q and passage p as shown in (6):

$$\forall s \in S : score(s) = g(k(s), k(q)) + g(k(s), k(p)) \tag{6}$$

where $g \in \{correlation, cosine\}$ are similarity measures, k is a semantic embedding function. We use the semantic textual similarity model[8] proposed by Yang et al. (2018). To filter more examples, we add an empirically tuned threshold for similarities[9] and select only those sentences which were ranked as the most similar to the question and passage by both correlation (inner product) and cosine similarity, and each score is higher than the established thresholds. Another method of selecting relevant sentences is to consider only the relations which connect an entity in the question to an entity in the passage. We then combine these two strategies: we add sentences only to the examples which meet both criteria (Intersection) or all that meet at least one of the criteria (Union).

3.1.2 Results

Table 2 shows the results averaged over 5 runs. With threshold filtering we add sentences to 21.84%

---

[4] `https://cloud.google.com/apis/docs/overview` – l.v. 07/2020

[5] `https://en.wikipedia.org/wiki/Freebase_(database)` – l.v. 07/2020

[6] `http://verbs.colorado.edu/~mpalmer/projects/verbnet.html` – l.v. 07/2020

[7] Based on `https://github.com/commonsense/conceptnet5/wiki/Relations` – l.v. 07/2020. We found a few more like *"language"* or *"occupations"*.

[8] Available via TensorFlowHub (Cer et al., 2018): `https://www.tensorflow.org/hub/` – l.v. 07/2020

[9] We used: correlation > 220; cosine similarity > 1.38.

of passages, obtaining an average accuracy of 81.23% (see Table 2: SentEmb). Using entity relations from questions and answers, 22.58% of QA pairs are affected but the performance is slightly worse (see Table 2: Q&P Match).

The intersection gives the best performance. By affecting only 1.23% of the data, we obtain 81.46% average accuracy and 82.05% accuracy for the ensemble majority voting scenario. The Union criterion does not show any improvement on accuracy. The Intersection improvement, as well as the dis-improvement of SentEmb, Q&PMatch, and Union, are not statistically significant with respect to the baseline.[10]

	Base line	Sent Emb	Q&P Match	Intersection	Union
Data Coverage (%)	-	21.84	22.58	1.23	38.57
AVG	**81.26**	81.23	80.86	81.23	**81.46**	80.72
Stable	73.84	73.19	72.61	73.25	73.74	72.40
Ensemble	81.62	81.89	81.37	**81.92**	**82.05**	81.10

Table 2: Percentage of data changed and accuracy over 5 runs: average (**AVG**), **Stable**, and **Ensemble**.

3.2 Modeling Knowledge Graphs with GraphNNs

Facing instability of the BERT-based baseline and low coverage of ConceptNet (see Section 4) we experiment with a new architecture and knowledge graph. To better model graph-based input, such as entities and their relations, we tried a transformer-based seq2seq GNN (Shaw et al., 2019). Entities, relations and input tokens are embedded and fed to a GNN sub-layer that incorporates edge representations extending the self-attention mechanism. The encoder-decoder attention layer considers both encoder output token and entity representations, jointly normalizing attention weights over tokens and entities. In our case, the GNN decoder simply outputs our expected answers: "Yes" or "No" (see Fig. 3). In this case, we initialize the GNN with a pre-trained $BERT_{large}$ model and only fine tune on BoolQ.

As an alternative to ConceptNet we also tried the Google Knowledge Graph. It has more than 500 billion facts about 5 billion entities.[11] The entities describe real-world objects and concepts like

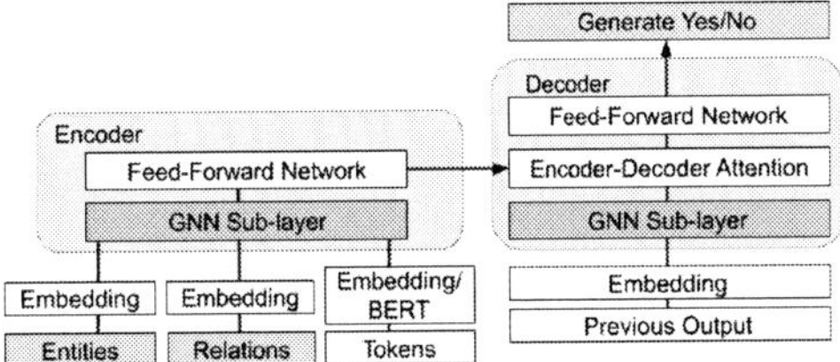

Figure 3: The GNN architecture based on Shaw et al. (2019) without action selection and copy mechanism.

people, places, events, and things. Entities are represented as nodes and connected by relations. The latter can simply indicate that a relation is present, or they may encode the type of relation. We try the first three of the following possible experiments:

1. adding a relation between different entities which have the same MID;

2. only adding connections between entities across the QA pair, as in the ConceptNet Q&P Match experiment;

3. distinguishing different types of relations;

4. adding a relation between different mentions of the same entity;

5. adding entities not mentioned in the text but linked to the mentioned entities.

3.2.1 Results

The results are presented in Table 3. The first row shows the baseline $BERT$ model with no KG data and the remaining rows show the $BERT + GNN$ system with no KG data, with ConceptNet or with the Google Knowledge Graph. Adding KG information does not outperform the baseline result. None of the differences between the baseline are statistically significant.

	No KG	+ConceptNet	+GKG
$BERT_{large}$	**78.09**	-	-
GNN + BERT	77.37	77.4	76.80
+ Same MID	-	-	77.60
+ Relation Type	-	-	77.75
+ Q&AMatch	-	-	76.95

Table 3: **GNN** accuracy results on a development set using ConceptNet or Google KG (**GKG**).

4 Analysis

ConceptNet Even after the filtering described in Section 3.1.1, we observe that often the relations from ConceptNet are too general and do not add new information, e.g. *"cookie jar is a type of jar"*.

---

[10]According to the two sample proportion Z-Test the maximum difference: $z = -1.3674, p = 0.17068$

[11]`https://blog.google/products/search/about-knowledge-graph-and-knowledge-panels/` — l.v. 07/2020

Such relations are already part of the language model. Petroni et al. (2019) show that $BERT$ contains relational knowledge and has a strong ability to recall factual knowledge without fine-tuning.

Furthermore, some entities are missing, e.g. there is a *"Tom Hanks"* entity but no *"Meg Ryan"* entity, or the entity *"dragon ball"* contains only non-English connections, confirming the general coverage issue of KGs. [12]

Sensitivity   We observe that the GNN is sensitive to the learning rate and hyper-parameters. Better tuning may compensate for the difference in performance wrt to the $BERT$ baseline.

Entity recognition and linker   We found issues with the entity linker. Named entities are often not covered or the MID is missing. In some cases, the entity has a wrong MID, e.g. in (7) the entity *"northern ireland"* is not recognised but the entity *"ireland"* (Republic of Ireland) is mentioned instead, while the entity *"great britain"* is recognised with the MID of *"United Kingdom"*.

(7)   **Question:**   *is northern ireland part of the great britain* **Passage:** *... Great Britain is part of the United Kingdom of Great Britain and Northern Ireland ...* **Answer:** No

The questions in the BoolQ dataset are lowercased, and this may have affected the entity recognition.

Do KGs affect stable accuracy?   We observe a positive tendency towards stable correct answers in the ConceptNet experiments (Table 4). The number of new stable correct answers is higher than the number of new stable errors for all settings except Q&AMatch. Also, for all scenarios except Intersection, the number of questions where the predicted answer fluctuates from incorrect to correct is higher than the number of questions where the predicted answer fluctuates from correct.

Is a KG necessary?   The BoolQ dataset was not originally created to be used with a KG, and the passages were selected such that they contain the information required to answer a question. For some questions, such as (1) the additional information provided by a KG is helpful, and for questions like (7), even though the passage has all the

[12] https://conceptnet.io/c/en/jar, https://conceptnet.io/c/en/tom_hanks – An English term in ConceptNet 5.8, https://conceptnet.io/c/en/meg_ryan – 'meg ryan' is not a node in ConceptNet, https://conceptnet.io/c/en/dragon_ball,– l.v. 07/2020

New		Sent Emb	Q&P Match	Inter section	Union
Stable	Correct	27	27	4	54
	Error	18	28	0	32
Fluct.	Err→Corr	34	44	1	65
	Corr→Err	19	23	5	42

Table 4: **New Correct (Error)** corresponds to the number of new stable (wrt to baseline) correct (incorrect) predictions, **New Fluct.** is the number of new questions where answer fluctuates: **Err→Corr (Corr→Err)** is the number of questions where answer was a stable error (correct), becoming correct (error) sometimes.

required information, a KG could highlight the relation between entities and help answer the question. However, there are also cases where a KG is not needed or cannot be applied, e.g. (8) and (9).

(8)   **Question:**   *do all ni numbers have a letter at the end* **Passage:** *The format of the number is two prefix letters, six digits, and one suffix letter. The example used is typically QQ123456C. ...* **Answer:** Yes

(9)   **Question:** *was the movie insomnia based on a book* **Passage:** *Robert Westbrook adapted the screenplay to novel form, which was published by Alex in May 2002.* **Answer:** No

In (8) a question is asked about a number format and the information about the specific last symbol is unlikely to be a part of a KG. (9) contains a very short passage explicitly saying there is a book but it was adapted from the screenplay. In this case, a KG could provide potentially confusing information simply stating that there is a book.

5   Conclusion

In this work, we take a closer look at a $BERT$ baseline system on the BoolQ dataset, which reveals some inconsistencies in the data and some instability in the model. We try two approaches to integrating knowledge graph information, one based on augmenting the passage text and another using a Graph Neural Network. Neither are successful. One culprit is the lack of coverage of ConceptNet and another is related to accuracy of the entity recognition. We also suggest that the number of questions where suitable KG data is needed and could be found might just not be enough for the models to learn from.

Acknowledgments

We are extremely gratefully to Massimo Nicosia from Google Research Switzerland without whom this work would not be possible. We thank the anonymous reviewers for their constructive and helpful feedback. Finally, a big thank you to Andrew Dunne, Lauren Cassidy, and Meghan Dowling.

This research is partly supported by Science Foundation Ireland in the ADAPT Centre for Digital Content Technology, funded under the SFI Research Centres Programme (Grant 13/RC/2106) and the European Regional Development Fund.

References

Lisa Bauer, Yicheng Wang, and Mohit Bansal. 2018. Commonsense for generative multi-hop question answering tasks. In *Proceedings of the 2018 Conference on Empirical Methods in Natural Language Processing*, pages 4220–4230, Brussels, Belgium. Association for Computational Linguistics.

Daniel Cer, Yinfei Yang, Sheng-yi Kong, Nan Hua, Nicole Limtiaco, Rhomni St. John, Noah Constant, Mario Guajardo-Cespedes, Steve Yuan, Chris Tar, Brian Strope, and Ray Kurzweil. 2018. Universal sentence encoder for English. In *Proceedings of the 2018 Conference on Empirical Methods in Natural Language Processing: System Demonstrations*, pages 169–174, Brussels, Belgium. Association for Computational Linguistics.

Christopher Clark, Kenton Lee, Ming-Wei Chang, Tom Kwiatkowski, Michael Collins, and Kristina Toutanova. 2019. BoolQ: Exploring the surprising difficulty of natural yes/no questions. In *Proceedings of the 2019 Conference of the North American Chapter of the Association for Computational Linguistics: Human Language Technologies, Volume 1 (Long and Short Papers)*, pages 2924–2936, Minneapolis, Minnesota. Association for Computational Linguistics.

Jacob Devlin, Ming-Wei Chang, Kenton Lee, and Kristina Toutanova. 2019. BERT: Pre-training of deep bidirectional transformers for language understanding. In *Proceedings of the 2019 Conference of the North American Chapter of the Association for Computational Linguistics: Human Language Technologies, Volume 1 (Long and Short Papers)*, pages 4171–4186, Minneapolis, Minnesota. Association for Computational Linguistics.

Tom Kwiatkowski, Jennimaria Palomaki, Olivia Redfield, Michael Collins, Ankur Parikh, Chris Alberti, Danielle Epstein, Illia Polosukhin, Jacob Devlin, Kenton Lee, Kristina Toutanova, Llion Jones, Matthew Kelcey, Ming-Wei Chang, Andrew Dai, Jakob Uszkoreit, Quoc Le, and Slav Petrov. 2019. Natural questions: A benchmark for question answering research. *Transactions of the Association for Computational Linguistics*, 7(0):452–466.

Bill Yuchen Lin, Xinyue Chen, Jamin Chen, and Xiang Ren. 2019. KagNet: Knowledge-aware graph networks for commonsense reasoning. In *Proceedings of the 2019 Conference on Empirical Methods in Natural Language Processing and the 9th International Joint Conference on Natural Language Processing (EMNLP-IJCNLP)*, pages 2829–2839, Hong Kong, China. Association for Computational Linguistics.

Hugo Liu and Push Singh. 2004. Conceptnet — a practical commonsense reasoning tool-kit. *BT Technology Journal*, 22(4):211–226.

Yinhan Liu, Myle Ott, Naman Goyal, Jingfei Du, Mandar Joshi, Danqi Chen, Omer Levy, Mike Lewis, Luke Zettlemoyer, and Veselin Stoyanov. 2019. Roberta: A robustly optimized BERT pretraining approach. *arXiv:1907.11692*.

Todor Mihaylov and Anette Frank. 2018. Knowledgeable reader: Enhancing cloze-style reading comprehension with external commonsense knowledge. In *Proceedings of the 56th Annual Meeting of the Association for Computational Linguistics (Volume 1: Long Papers)*, pages 821–832, Melbourne, Australia. Association for Computational Linguistics.

Matthew Peters, Mark Neumann, Mohit Iyyer, Matt Gardner, Christopher Clark, Kenton Lee, and Luke Zettlemoyer. 2018. Deep contextualized word representations. In *Proceedings of the 2018 Conference of the North American Chapter of the Association for Computational Linguistics: Human Language Technologies, Volume 1 (Long Papers)*, pages 2227–2237, New Orleans, Louisiana. Association for Computational Linguistics.

Fabio Petroni, Tim Rocktäschel, Sebastian Riedel, Patrick Lewis, Anton Bakhtin, Yuxiang Wu, and Alexander Miller. 2019. Language models as knowledge bases? In *Proceedings of the 2019 Conference on Empirical Methods in Natural Language Processing and the 9th International Joint Conference on Natural Language Processing (EMNLP-IJCNLP)*, pages 2463–2473, Hong Kong, China. Association for Computational Linguistics.

Delai Qiu, Yuanzhe Zhang, Xinwei Feng, Xiangwen Liao, Wenbin Jiang, Yajuan Lyu, Kang Liu, and Jun Zhao. 2019. Machine reading comprehension using structural knowledge graph-aware network. In *Proceedings of the 2019 Conference on Empirical Methods in Natural Language Processing and the 9th International Joint Conference on Natural Language Processing (EMNLP-IJCNLP)*, pages 5896–5901, Hong Kong, China. Association for Computational Linguistics.

Peter Shaw, Philip Massey, Angelica Chen, Francesco Piccinno, and Yasemin Altun. 2019. Generating logical forms from graph representations of text and entities. In *Proceedings of the 57th Annual Meeting of the Association for Computational Linguistics*, pages 95–106, Florence, Italy. Association for Computational Linguistics.

Robyn Speer, Joshua Chin, and Catherine Havasi. 2017. Conceptnet 5.5: An open multilingual graph of general knowledge. In *Proceedings of the Thirty-First AAAI Conference on Artificial Intelligence*, AAAI'17, page 4444–4451. AAAI Press.

Alon Talmor, Jonathan Herzig, Nicholas Lourie, and Jonathan Berant. 2019. CommonsenseQA: A question answering challenge targeting commonsense knowledge. In *Proceedings of the 2019 Conference of the North American Chapter of the Association for Computational Linguistics: Human Language Technologies, Volume 1 (Long and Short Papers)*, pages 4149–4158, Minneapolis, Minnesota. Association for Computational Linguistics.

Mokanarangan Thayaparan, Marco Valentino, Viktor Schlegel, and André Freitas. 2019. Identifying supporting facts for multi-hop question answering with document graph networks. In *Proceedings of the Thirteenth Workshop on Graph-Based Methods for Natural Language Processing (TextGraphs-13)*, pages 42–51, Hong Kong. Association for Computational Linguistics.

Mariya Toneva, Alessandro Sordoni, Remi Tachet des Combes, Adam Trischler, Yoshua Bengio, and Geoffrey J. Gordon. 2019. An empirical study of example forgetting during deep neural network learning. In *International Conference on Learning Representations*.

Alex Wang, Yada Pruksachatkun, Nikita Nangia, Amanpreet Singh, Julian Michael, Felix Hill, Omer Levy, and Samuel Bowman. 2019. SuperGLUE: A stickier benchmark for general-purpose language understanding systems. In H. Wallach, H. Larochelle, A. Beygelzimer, F. dAlché-Buc, E. Fox, and R. Garnett, editors, *Advances in Neural Information Processing Systems 32*, pages 3266–3280. Curran Associates, Inc.

Alex Wang, Amanpreet Singh, Julian Michael, Felix Hill, Omer Levy, and Samuel Bowman. 2018. GLUE: A multi-task benchmark and analysis platform for natural language understanding. In *Proceedings of the 2018 EMNLP Workshop BlackboxNLP: Analyzing and Interpreting Neural Networks for NLP*, pages 353–355, Brussels, Belgium. Association for Computational Linguistics.

Dirk Weissenborn, Tomáš Kočiský, and Chris Dyer. 2017. Dynamic integration of background knowledge in neural NLU systems. *arXiv:1706.02596*.

Adina Williams, Nikita Nangia, and Samuel Bowman. 2018. A broad-coverage challenge corpus for sentence understanding through inference. In *Proceedings of the 2018 Conference of the North American Chapter of the Association for Computational Linguistics: Human Language Technologies, Volume 1 (Long Papers)*, pages 1112–1122. Association for Computational Linguistics.

Thomas Wolf, Lysandre Debut, Victor Sanh, Julien Chaumond, Clement Delangue, Anthony Moi, Pierric Cistac, Tim Rault, R'emi Louf, Morgan Funtowicz, and Jamie Brew. 2019. Huggingface's transformers: State-of-the-art natural language processing. *arXiv:1910.03771*.

Yinfei Yang, Steve Yuan, Daniel Cer, Sheng-yi Kong, Noah Constant, Petr Pilar, Heming Ge, Yun-Hsuan Sung, Brian Strope, and Ray Kurzweil. 2018. Learning semantic textual similarity from conversations. In *Proceedings of The Third Workshop on Representation Learning for NLP*, pages 164–174, Melbourne, Australia. Association for Computational Linguistics.

Chen Zhao, Chenyan Xiong, Xin Qian, and Jordan Boyd-Graber. 2020. Complex factoid question answering with a free-text knowledge graph. In *The Web Conference 2020 (formerly WWW conference)*.

A BoolQ Dataset Details

The BoolQ dataset (Clark et al., 2019) is a part of the SuperGLUE benchmark[13] (Wang et al., 2019). About 3000 question and passages come from NaturalQuestion (Kwiatkowski et al., 2019). The main statistics about the dataset is collected in Table 5.

| Size | Length in Tokens | | | | | |
| | Question | | | Passage | | |
	Min	Max	Avg	Min	Max	Avg
15942	3	21	8.9	6	813	108

Table 5: The basic statistics for the BoolQ dataset.

Clark et al. (2019) showed the $BERT_{large}$ model (Devlin et al., 2019) outperforming recurrent models with attention (Wang et al., 2018), both in their vanilla version and in combination with deep contextualized word representation (Peters et al., 2018).

B Erroneous and Confusing Examples

Some questions in BoolQ are formulated in a certain context which might change given time. For example (10) which is asking about a movie released **this year**. As the dataset was released in 2019 the data could be collected in 2018 so then the answer is *yes* but if this question would be asked in 2015 or today (2020) the answer should be *no*. Another example (11) where a passage provides the information about United States citizens border crossing requirements but the question does not specify what kind of citizenship the person asking the question holds. In contrast with example (12) where the question and passage provide an unconditional outcome as a holder of the Schengen visa (information from question) can enter Montenegro for 30 days (information from the passage). So, in such cases like examples (10) and (11), the passage information is not enough to answer the questions unconditionally.

(10) **Question:** *is there a star wars movie this year*
Passage: *The first film was followed by two successful sequels, The Empire Strikes Back (1980) and Return of the Jedi (1983); ... A prequel trilogy was released between 1999 and 2005, albeit to mixed reactions from critics and fans. A sequel trilogy concluding the main story of the nine-episode saga began in 2015 with The Force Awakens. ... Together with the theatrical spin-off films The Clone Wars (2008), Rogue One (2016) and Solo: A Star Wars Story (2018), Star Wars is the second highest-grossing film series ever.*
Answer: Yes (true)

(11) **Question:** *Can I get into Canada with a military ID?*
Passage: *(Title: American entry into Canada by land) Canadian law requires that all persons entering Canada must carry proof of both citizenship and identity. A valid U.S. passport or passport card is preferred, although a birth certificate, naturalization certificate, citizenship certificate, or another document proving U.S. nationality, together with a government-issued photo ID (such as a driver's license) are acceptable to establish identity and nationality.*
Answer: Yes

(12) **Question:** *Can I go to Montenegro with a Schengen visa?*
Passage: *Nationals of any country may visit Montenegro without a visa for up to 30 days if they hold a passport with visas issued by Ireland, a Schengen Area member state, ...*
Answer: Yes

Some passages looked unrelated or do not contain enough information to obtain the answer, e.g. (13 - 14). The passages are related to the questions but specific information is missing the answer "Yes" cannot be confirmed by the passages. We observe, around 8% of questions we confusing or have certain assumptions.

(13) **Question:** *is daisy the director of shield in the comics*
Passage: *Daisy Johnson, ... The daughter of the supervillain Mister Hyde, she is a secret agent of the intelligence organization S.H.I.E.L.D. with the power to generate earthquakes.*
Answer: Yes

(14) **Question:** *is chicken cordon bleu made with blue cheese*

Passage: *A cordon bleu or schnitzel cordon bleu is a dish of meat wrapped around cheese (or with cheese filling), then breaded and pan-fried or deep-fried. Veal or pork cordon bleu is made of veal or pork pounded thin and wrapped around a slice of ham and a slice of cheese, breaded, and then pan fried or baked. For chicken cordon bleu chicken breast is used instead of veal. Ham cordon bleu is ham stuffed with mushrooms and cheese.*
Answer: Yes

There are a few examples of errors (15 - 17) from the dataset. The first error example is asking if shower gel can be used instead of shampoo in a negative form (*"is it bad to ..."*) and the passage says that they are perfectly substitutable so the answer should be *No (it is not bad)*. In the second example (16) the passage explicitly says India does not have a national language so the answer should be *No*. And in the third example (17) there is nothing that should make the reader believe there were any games outside of Russia, so the answer should be *Yes*. According to our analysis 6% of samples have the wrong answer tag.

(15) **Question:** *Is it bad to wash your hair with shower gel?*
Passage: *... This means that **shower gels can also double as an effective and perfectly acceptable substitute to shampoo**, even if they are not labelled as a hair and body wash.*
Answer: Yes Should be **No**

(16) **Question:** *Is Hindi is our national language of India?*
Passage: *The Constitution of India designates the official language of the Government of India as Hindi written in the Devanagari script, as well as English. **There is no national language as declared by the Constitution of India.** Hindi is used for official purposes ...*
Answer: Yes Should be **No**

(17) **Question:** *are all world cup matches played in russia*
Passage: *The 2018 FIFA World Cup was the 21st FIFA World Cup, an international football tournament contested by the men's national teams of the member associations of FIFA once every four years. **It took place in Russia** from 14 June to 15 July 2018. ...*
Answer: No Should be **Yes**

How Far Can We Go with Data Selection? A Case Study on Semantic Sequence Tagging Tasks

Samuel Louvan
University of Trento
Fondazione Bruno Kessler
slouvan@fbk.eu

Bernardo Magnini
Fondazione Bruno Kessler
magnini@fbk.eu

Abstract

Although several works have addressed the role of data selection to improve transfer learning for various NLP tasks, there is no consensus about its real benefits and, more generally, there is a lack of shared practices on how it can be best applied. We propose a systematic approach aimed at evaluating data selection in scenarios of increasing complexity. Specifically, we compare the case in which source and target tasks are the same while source and target domains are different, against the more challenging scenario where both tasks and domains are different. We run a number of experiments on semantic sequence tagging tasks, which are relatively less investigated in data selection, and conclude that data selection has more benefit on the scenario when the tasks are the same, while in case of different (although related) tasks from distant domains, a combination of data selection and multi-task learning is ineffective for most cases.

1 Introduction

Transfer learning is a common approach for training NLP models that scale across different tasks, domains, and languages. One of the challenges in transfer learning is to deal with the data distribution mismatch between the source ($\mathcal{D}_S$) and the target data ($\mathcal{D}_T$) (Rosenstein et al., 2005). One solution to alleviate the impact of the mismatch is using data selection, a process for selecting relevant training instances from the source data. Data selection (DS) has been applied in the context of domain adaptation to address changes in the data distribution for various NLP tasks, such as sentiment analysis and POS Tagging (Ruder and Plank, 2017; Liu et al., 2019; Blitzer et al., 2007; Remus, 2012), machine translation (Axelrod et al., 2011), dependency parsing (Søgaard, 2011) and Named Entity Recognition (NER) (Murthy et al., 2018; Zhao et al., 2018). To our knowledge, all existing previous works apply data selection to *different* domains, while maintaining the *same* task.

In this work we aim to investigate the benefit of data selection in a more complex setting, where we have not only different domains ($\mathcal{D}_S \neq \mathcal{D}_T$), but also different tasks ($\mathcal{T}_S \neq \mathcal{T}_T$). Intuitively, such setting may bring advantage in situations where large training data are available for a source task $\mathcal{T}_S$, and we want to exploit such data for a different (although related) target task $\mathcal{T}_T$, where much less training is available. We experiment with the situation where $\mathcal{T}_S$ is Named Entity Recognition (NER) on a general domain, where several datasets are available, and $\mathcal{T}_T$ is slot tagging (ST) in the context of utterance interpretation for dialogue systems, where much less data is available. Both of the tasks are rarely investigated in data selection and there is no consensus about the benefit of data selection for them.

We propose an experimental framework where we can compare data selection settings with an increasing level of complexity. First, we consider data selection where NER is both the source and target task, and apply transfer learning from different domains: we call this setting **Same Tasks from Different Domains (STDD)**, $\mathcal{T}_S = \mathcal{T}_T$ and $\mathcal{D}_S \neq \mathcal{D}_T$. In a second, more complex setting, we consider NER as the source task and ST as the target: this is called $\mathcal{T}_S \neq \mathcal{T}_T$ and $\mathcal{D}_S \neq \mathcal{D}_T$, **Different Tasks from Different Domains (DTDD)**. In this scenario, as we have disjoint label space between the source and the target task, we combine the data selection process with multi-task learning (MTL). To our knowledge, this combination has received very little attention in the literature.

We base our work on the data selection framework proposed by Ruder and Plank (2017), and apply it to our experimental settings. Their framework is model-agnostic and has shown significant advantage in sentiment analysis, POS tagging, and

Proceedings of the First Workshop on Insights from Negative Results in NLP, pages 15–21
Online, November 19, 2020. ©2020 Association for Computational Linguistics

parsing. However, it is not obvious to what extent the selection process can actually help on semantic sequence tagging tasks on STDD and DTDD scenarios. The contributions of the paper are the following: (i) we apply previous work to multi-task learning setup to evaluate the effectiveness of data selection in DTDD scenarios; (ii) we systematically compare data selection on settings of increasing complexity, and observe that existing selection metrics do not show clear advantages over baselines in most cases. Nevertheless, data selection has more potential in STDD when source and target are more similar, while *combining* MTL and data selection for DTDD is *ineffective* for most cases in our experimental settings in which we have different but related tasks (NER and ST) from relatively distant domains (news and conversational domains).

2 Data Selection Framework

In general, the goal of data selection is to select an optimal subset of training instances, X_S^*, from all the available data X_S in $\mathcal{T}_S$, to be used for training the model for the target task $\mathcal{M}_{\mathcal{T}_T}$. Given the source data $X_S = \{x_1^S, x_2^S, ..., x_n^S\}$, each instance is ranked according to a score S and the top m examples are then used to train $\mathcal{M}_{\mathcal{T}_T}$.

We apply the data selection approach from Ruder and Plank (2017), based on Bayesian Optimization (BO) (Brochu et al., 2010), to evaluate the effectiveness of data selection on both the STDD and DTDD scenarios. Specifically, for DTDD we *combine* data selection and multi-task learning. Given X_S, the framework performs data selection based on a score S derived from a set of features. The top m examples are then used to train $\mathcal{M}_{\mathcal{T}_T}$. In case of STDD, the $\mathcal{M}_{\mathcal{T}_T}$ is a single task sequence tagging model, where we use a biLSTM-CRF model (Lample et al., 2016). As for DTDD, $\mathcal{M}_{\mathcal{T}_T}$ is a *hard parameter sharing* MTL model, which has been applied to many NLP tasks (Søgaard and Goldberg, 2016; Plank et al., 2016; Changpinyo et al., 2018; Schulz et al., 2018). The performance on the validation set of the target task is then used by the BO optimizer to update the weight of the scoring features.

Following Ruder and Plank (2017), the selection process is based on a score S computed as the linear combination of weighted features, which include both similarity and diversity features: $S_\theta(x) = \theta^\top \cdot \phi(x)$, where θ represents the weight for each feature and $\phi(x)$ denotes the feature values of each instance x. The features are calculated between the representation of X_S instances and X_T. We use term distribution as the representation of the instances. We use the same similarity and diversity measures as Ruder and Plank (2017). The weights θ are learned through BO by taking into account the performance on the validation set when selecting a particular subset of X_S. The score S is computed for each x in X_S, and then the top m examples are selected for training the $\mathcal{M}_{\mathcal{T}_T}$ model. The loss value $\mathcal{L}$ from the $\mathcal{M}_{\mathcal{T}_T}$ in the validation set is used by BO as a feedback to select the next points for θ.

3 Experiments

We systematically investigate how data selection is effective when applied on both the STDD and DTDD scenarios. We address two semantic sequence labeling tasks: Named Entity Recognition (NER) and slot tagging (ST).

3.1 Datasets

For NER we use the OntoNotes 5.0 (Pradhan et al., 2012) dataset, which consists of several sections: newswire (NW), talkshows broadcast (BC), telephone conversation (TC), news broadcast (BN), articles from web sources (WB), and articles from magazines (MZ). We use different OntoNotes sections as different domains in our experiments.

As for ST we use three datasets: ATIS (Price, 1990), MIT-R, and MIT-M (Liu et al., 2013), that are widely used as benchmarks for spoken language understanding. Each dataset contains utterances annotated with domain-specific slot labels, which are typically more fine-grained than NER labels. For example, in the utterance *"show me all **Delta** flights from **Milan** to **New York**"*, the bold words are tagged as *airline_name*, *fromloc*, and *toloc* respectively. The overall statistics of each dataset are shown in Table 1.

3.2 Data Selection Configurations

We make use of the selection framework described in Section 2, and apply three Bayesian Optimization data selection (*BODS*) configurations, according to whether we use features both for similarity and diversity ($\mathrm{DS}_{\mathrm{sim,div}}$), similarity features only ($\mathrm{DS}_{\mathrm{sim}}$), or diversity features only ($\mathrm{DS}_{\mathrm{div}}$). We compare the three configurations with the following baselines:

- All source, which uses all the data from $\mathcal{T}_S$.
- Random, which selects random data from $\mathcal{T}_S$.

Dataset	#train	#dev	#test	#label
Slot Tagging				
ATIS	4478	500	893	79
MIT Restaurant	6128	1532	3385	8
MIT Movie	7820	1955	2443	12
NER				
OntoNotes NW	34970	5896	2327	18
OntoNotes BC	11879	2117	2211	18
OntoNotes TC	12891	1634	1366	18
OntoNotes BN	10683	1295	1357	18
OntoNotes WB	16598	2316	2307	18
OntoNotes MZ	6911	642	780	18

Table 1: Statistics about the datasets used in the experiments. The language of the datasets is English.

- $DS_{map,full}$. We provide a manual mapping from NER labels to ST labels (Appendix A). A sentence from $\mathcal{T}_S$ is selected is if *all* the NER occurrences have a mapping to a slot in $\mathcal{T}_T$.
- $DS_{map,partial}$. A sentence from $\mathcal{T}_S$ is selected if *at least* one of the NER occurrences in the sentence has a mapping to a slot label in $\mathcal{T}_T$.

3.3 Settings

We follow most of the hyperparameters[1] as recommended by Reimers and Gurevych (2018). We train the model for $\mathcal{T}_S$ and $\mathcal{T}_T$ in an alternating fashion. We use early stopping on the dev. performance of $\mathcal{T}_T$. For the model performance evaluation, we calculate the F1-score using the standard CoNLL script[2]. For all experiments, we report the average F1 score results from 10 runs with different seeds.

We follow Ruder and Plank (2017) for most configurations of the optimizer, and run 50 iterations. For both the STDD and DTDD scenarios, we select top 50%[3] examples from X_S. For MTL we adapt the implementation from Reimers and Gurevych (2017), extending the Bayesian Optimization data selection framework from Ruder and Plank (2017) to support MTL.

4 STDD Scenario: $\mathcal{T}_S = \mathcal{T}_T, \mathcal{D}_S \neq \mathcal{D}_T$

This is scenario is the same setup as Ruder and Plank (2017), where we use the same tasks both for the source and the target task from different domains, except that we apply the data selection to a semantic sequence tagging task namely NER. In this scenario, we use NER both for the source and the target task. The target domain is one three

OntoNotes sections namely NW (news), TC (telephone conversation) and BC (mixed of conversation and broadcast) while as source domain ($\mathcal{D}_S$) we use all available sections in OntoNotes except the one used as the target domain. We only use 10% of training data for the target domain to simulate limited data settings. At the end of the data selection process, we select the top 50% sentences from $\mathcal{D}_S$ using the best feature weights learned with the Bayesian Optimizer.

Table 2(a) compares the performance of the baselines with the selection-based approaches. In general, we do not observe clear advantages of data selection methods over the baselines, especially the all source data baseline. Using all source data yields the most competitive results almost in all cases. The only case in which DS surpasses the all source baseline is on the BC domain but only for a tiny gain. For NW and BC domains, some DS methods show clear advantages over the random baseline, but still worse than using all source data.

We want to see whether the distance between domains may characterize the performance of the data selection. For this purpose we quantify the domain similarity between each pair $\mathcal{D}_S$ and $\mathcal{D}_T$ with Jensen Shannon Divergence (JSD) (Lin, 1991). We compute the JSD between the term distribution of $\mathcal{D}_S$ and $\mathcal{D}_T$. The average JSD of each target task with respect to the source tasks are 0.80 (TC), 0.86 (NW), and 0.87 (BC)[4]. We observe that the higher the JSD is, the more beneficial is the data selection for the target task. BC, which has the highest JSD average, benefits the most from the data selection. On the other hand, TC with the lowest average similarity, has the largest gap between the baseline and the best DS methods (-1.7 F1 point).

Based on our experiments, for the STDD scenario we observe that:

1. In most of the cases, DS methods are inferior to the all source baseline. Yet, it is clear that each domain has a different selection metric configuration that performs the best. This observation suggests that the hypothesis from Ruder and Plank (2017) i.e., different tasks or even different domains demand a different notion of selection metric, is also applicable to semantic sequence tagging tasks such as NER.

2. The gap between the best DS method and the baseline for each $\mathcal{D}_T$ can be characterized from the average JSD similarity to its $\mathcal{D}_S$. Being

---

[1] Appendix C reports all used hyperparameters.
[2] https://www.clips.uantwerpen.be/conll2000.
[3] We tune from 10% to 50% on the dev set.

[4] Complete pairwise JSD values are listed in Appendix B.

Method	TC	NW	BC
Baseline			
All source	$\mathbf{63.17}_{4.75}$	$\mathbf{79.08}^{\dagger}_{0.42}$	$\underline{73.42}_{2.13}$
Random	$\underline{62.02}_{4.47}$	$77.93_{0.54}$	$71.39_{2.12}$
BODS			
$DS_{sim,div}$	$61.71_{4.57}$	$76.99_{0.40}$	$72.60_{1.14}$
DS_{sim}	$61.45_{3.80}$	$78.30_{0.41}$	$\mathbf{73.44}_{1.12}$
DS_{div}	$61.65_{3.77}$	$\underline{78.32}_{0.53}$	$71.89_{1.53}$

(a) STDD

Method	ATIS	MIT-R	MIT-M
STL			
biLSTM-CRF	$85.46_{0.25}$	$63.99_{0.77}$	$76.39_{0.57}$
Baseline (MTL)			
All source	$\mathbf{90.05}_{0.34}$	$69.28_{0.40}$	$81.28_{0.23}$
Random	$89.93_{0.26}$	$\mathbf{69.54}_{0.35}$	$\mathbf{81.35}_{0.31}$
$DS_{map,full}$	$89.97_{0.25}$	$68.82_{0.50}$	$79.27_{0.36}$
$DS_{map,partial}$	$89.85_{0.29}$	$69.24_{0.40}$	$80.76_{0.30}$
MTL+BODS			
$DS_{sim,div}$	$89.78_{0.39}$	$69.29_{0.37}$	$81.07_{0.29}$
DS_{sim}	$89.83_{0.31}$	$69.25_{0.41}$	$81.17_{0.25}$
DS_{div}	$89.95_{0.41}$	$69.09_{0.24}$	$81.10_{0.28}$

(b) DTDD

Table 2: Average F1-score and standard deviation on the test set. † indicates significant differences ($p < 0.05$) between the best BODS approach and the best baseline.

more similar to other $\mathcal{D}_S$ is a more suitable situation to get benefit from data selection.

5 DTDD Scenario: $\mathcal{T}_S \neq \mathcal{T}_T, \mathcal{D}_S \neq \mathcal{D}_T$

In this scenario we intend to observe whether data selection adds benefit to MTL. As in the STDD case, data selection is performed on the auxiliary task, where data is assumed to be abundant, and we only use a small portion of data for the target task. We use NER as the auxiliary task and ST as the target task. Prior work from Louvan and Magnini (2019) shows that NER is helpful for ST through MTL, although it is not clear whether adding data selection is beneficial. We follow the setup in Louvan and Magnini (2019), where OntoNotes NW is used as the auxiliary task, and the target task is one of the ST datasets with only 10% of available training data.

Observing the results in Table 2(b), in all the cases the baselines, namely all source data and random selection, perform better than MTL with DS methods. The selection methods based on manual label mapping, DS_{map}, do not bring advantage over all source data. Therefore, given two distant $\mathcal{D}_S$ and $\mathcal{D}_T$, selecting sentences based on the label mapping does not help. Moreover, as random selection gives good results as well for most scenarios, this indicates that data selection is not beneficial in our experimental setting that combines data selection and MTL.

Our findings and lessons learned for DTDD are the following:

1. We observe that MTL performs better than single-task learning (STL) for low-resource slot tagging, confirming the finding from Louvan and Magnini (2019). However, adding data selection for MTL is *ineffective* in our DTDD experimental setup. We hypothesize that MTL learns good common feature representations across tasks, this way inherently helping the model to focus on relevant features even from noisy data in $\mathcal{T}_S$. In addition to that, due to data sparsity in limited training, using all the training data works better because the model may learn a better text representation (sentence encoder). Recent similar work from Schröder and Biemann (2020) which uses information theoretic based for estimating the usefulness of an auxiliary task for MTL also found that for semantic sequence tagging tasks such as NER and argument mining, it is less clear when a particular dataset is useful as an auxiliary task.

2. Data selection typically produces selected sentences with concentrated similarity distribution[5]. Therefore, it is probably ineffective when the sentence similarity distribution between $\mathcal{T}_S$ and $\mathcal{T}_T$ is already concentrated on a very narrow range.

6 Conclusion

In this paper we investigated the benefit of data selection for transfer learning in several scenarios of increasing complexity. We apply an existing model-agnostic state of the art data selection framework, and carried on experiments on two semantic sequence tagging tasks, NER and Slot Tagging, and two transfer learning scenarios, STDD (Same

---

[5]We embed the sentence in source and target with InferSent (Conneau et al., 2017) and compute cosine similarity between the centroid of the target and each of the sentence in source.

Tasks Different Domains), and DTDD (Different Tasks Different Domains).

For the STDD scenario, selection methods show potential when the target domain has the highest similarity to the source domains, based on Jensen Shannon Divergence. As for the DTDD scenario in which we use related tasks (NER and ST) from distant domains (news and conversational domains), using selection does not bring advantage over using all the source data. A possible cause is that, because of data sparsity on the target task, it is only by injecting more source data that we can improve the model. Finally, MTL does not benefit from data selection, as it may already effectively help the model to focus on relevant features even though in the presence of noisy data from distant domains.

References

Amittai Axelrod, Xiaodong He, and Jianfeng Gao. 2011. Domain adaptation via pseudo in-domain data selection. In *Proceedings of the 2011 Conference on Empirical Methods in Natural Language Processing*, pages 355–362, Edinburgh, Scotland, UK. Association for Computational Linguistics.

John Blitzer, Mark Dredze, and Fernando Pereira. 2007. Biographies, Bollywood, boom-boxes and blenders: Domain adaptation for sentiment classification. In *Proceedings of the 45th Annual Meeting of the Association of Computational Linguistics*, pages 440–447, Prague, Czech Republic. Association for Computational Linguistics.

Eric Brochu, Vlad M Cora, and Nando De Freitas. 2010. A tutorial on bayesian optimization of expensive cost functions, with application to active user modeling and hierarchical reinforcement learning. *arXiv preprint arXiv:1012.2599*.

Soravit Changpinyo, Hexiang Hu, and Fei Sha. 2018. Multi-task learning for sequence tagging: An empirical study. In *Proceedings of the 27th International Conference on Computational Linguistics*, pages 2965–2977, Santa Fe, New Mexico, USA. Association for Computational Linguistics.

Alexis Conneau, Douwe Kiela, Holger Schwenk, Loïc Barrault, and Antoine Bordes. 2017. Supervised learning of universal sentence representations from natural language inference data. In *Proceedings of the 2017 Conference on Empirical Methods in Natural Language Processing*, pages 670–680, Copenhagen, Denmark. Association for Computational Linguistics.

Guillaume Lample, Miguel Ballesteros, Sandeep Subramanian, Kazuya Kawakami, and Chris Dyer. 2016. Neural architectures for named entity recognition. In *Proceedings of the 2016 Conference of the North American Chapter of the Association for Computational Linguistics: Human Language Technologies*, pages 260–270. Association for Computational Linguistics.

Jianhua Lin. 1991. Divergence measures based on the shannon entropy. *IEEE Trans. Information Theory*, 37:145–151.

Jingjing Liu, Panupong Pasupat, Scott Cyphers, and Jim Glass. 2013. Asgard: A Portable Architecture for Multilingual Dialogue Systems. In *Acoustics, Speech and Signal Processing (ICASSP), 2013 IEEE International Conference on*, pages 8386–8390. IEEE.

Miaofeng Liu, Yan Song, Hongbin Zou, and Tong Zhang. 2019. Reinforced training data selection for domain adaptation. In *Proceedings of the 57th Annual Meeting of the Association for Computational Linguistics*, pages 1957–1968, Florence, Italy. Association for Computational Linguistics.

Samuel Louvan and Bernardo Magnini. 2019. Leveraging non-conversational tasks for low resource slot filling: Does it help? In *Proceedings of the 20th Annual SIGdial Meeting on Discourse and Dialogue*, pages 85–91, Stockholm, Sweden. Association for Computational Linguistics.

Rudra Murthy, Anoop Kunchukuttan, and Pushpak Bhattacharyya. 2018. Judicious selection of training data in assisting language for multilingual neural NER. In *Proceedings of the 56th Annual Meeting of the Association for Computational Linguistics (Volume 2: Short Papers)*, pages 401–406, Melbourne, Australia. Association for Computational Linguistics.

Barbara Plank, Anders Søgaard, and Yoav Goldberg. 2016. Multilingual part-of-speech tagging with bidirectional long short-term memory models and auxiliary loss. In *Proceedings of the 54th Annual Meeting of the Association for Computational Linguistics (Volume 2: Short Papers)*, pages 412–418, Berlin, Germany. Association for Computational Linguistics.

Sameer Pradhan, Alessandro Moschitti, Nianwen Xue, Olga Uryupina, and Yuchen Zhang. 2012. CoNLL-2012 shared task: Modeling multilingual unrestricted coreference in OntoNotes. In *Joint Conference on EMNLP and CoNLL - Shared Task*, pages 1–40, Jeju Island, Korea. Association for Computational Linguistics.

Patti J Price. 1990. Evaluation of Spoken Language Systems: The ATIS Domain. In *Speech and Natural Language: Proceedings of a Workshop Held at Hidden Valley, Pennsylvania, June 24-27, 1990*.

Nils Reimers and Iryna Gurevych. 2017. Reporting Score Distributions Makes a Difference: Performance Study of LSTM-networks for Sequence Tagging. In *Proceedings of the 2017 Conference on*

Empirical Methods in Natural Language Processing (EMNLP), pages 338–348, Copenhagen, Denmark.

Nils Reimers and Iryna Gurevych. 2018. Why Comparing Single Performance Scores Does Not Allow to Draw Conclusions About Machine Learning Approaches. *CoRR*, abs/1803.09578.

Robert Remus. 2012. Domain adaptation using domain similarity-and domain complexity-based instance selection for cross-domain sentiment analysis. In *2012 IEEE 12th international conference on data mining workshops*, pages 717–723. IEEE.

Michael T. Rosenstein, Zvika Marx, Leslie Pack Kaelbling, and Thomas G. Dieterich. 2005. To transfer or not to transfer. In *In NIPS'05 Workshop, Inductive Transfer: 10 Years Later*.

Sebastian Ruder and Barbara Plank. 2017. Learning to select data for transfer learning with Bayesian optimization. In *Proceedings of the 2017 Conference on Empirical Methods in Natural Language Processing*, pages 372–382, Copenhagen, Denmark. Association for Computational Linguistics.

Fynn Schröder and Chris Biemann. 2020. Estimating the influence of auxiliary tasks for multi-task learning of sequence tagging tasks. In *Proceedings of the 58th Annual Meeting of the Association for Computational Linguistics*, pages 2971–2985, Online. Association for Computational Linguistics.

Claudia Schulz, Steffen Eger, Johannes Daxenberger, Tobias Kahse, and Iryna Gurevych. 2018. Multi-task learning for argumentation mining in low-resource settings. In *Proceedings of the 2018 Conference of the North American Chapter of the Association for Computational Linguistics: Human Language Technologies, Volume 2 (Short Papers)*, pages 35–41.

Anders Søgaard. 2011. Data point selection for cross-language adaptation of dependency parsers. In *Proceedings of the 49th Annual Meeting of the Association for Computational Linguistics: Human Language Technologies*, pages 682–686, Portland, Oregon, USA. Association for Computational Linguistics.

Anders Søgaard and Yoav Goldberg. 2016. Deep multi-task learning with low level tasks supervised at lower layers. In *Proceedings of the 54th Annual Meeting of the Association for Computational Linguistics (Volume 2: Short Papers)*, pages 231–235, Berlin, Germany. Association for Computational Linguistics.

Huasha Zhao, Yi Yang, Qiong Zhang, and Luo Si. 2018. Improve neural entity recognition via multi-task data selection and constrained decoding. In *Proceedings of the 2018 Conference of the North American Chapter of the Association for Computational Linguistics: Human Language Technologies, Volume 2 (Short Papers)*, pages 346–351, New Orleans, Louisiana. Association for Computational Linguistics.

A Label Mapping

ATIS Slot	OntoNotes Label
AIRLINE_NAME	ORG
AIRPORT_NAME	FAC
ARRIVE_DATE, DAY_NAME, DAY_NUMBER, DEPART_DATE, DEPART_TIME, FLIGHT_DAYS, TIME_RELATIVE, TODAY_RELATIVE	DATE
ARRIVE_TIME, MONTH_NAME, PERIOD_OF_DAY, RETURN_TIME, TIME	TIME
CITY_NAME, FROM_LOC, STATE_CODE, STATE_NAME, STOP_LOC, TO_LOC	GPE
COST_RELATIVE, FARE_AMOUNT	MONEY
DAYS_CODE, ECONOMY, FARE_BASIS_CODE, FLIGHT_MOD, MEAL, MEAL_CODE, MEAL_DESCRIPTION, MOD, FLIGHT_STOP, FLIGHT_MOD, OR, RESTRICTION_CODE, ROUNDTRIP, TRANSPORT_TYPE	O
FLIGHT_NUMBER	CARDINAL

Table 3: Label Mapping from ATIS to OntoNotes.

MIT Movie Slot	OntoNotes Label
CHARACTER, ACTOR, DIRECTOR	PER
YEAR	DATE
PLOT, RATING, TITLE, REVIEW, SONG, RATINGS_AVERAGE, GENRE, TRAILER	O

Table 4: Label Mapping from MIT Movie to OntoNotes.

B Domain Similarity

$\mathcal{D}_\mathcal{T}$	$\mathcal{D}_\mathcal{S}$						Avg	Δ
	TC	NW	BC	BN	WB	MZ		
TC	-	0.74	0.84	0.80	0.83	0.77	0.80	1.7
NW	0.74	-	0.85	0.91	0.91	0.90	0.86	0.7
BC	0.84	0.85	-	0.90	0.90	0.86	0.87	0.02

Table 5: Domain Similarity (JSD) for each $\mathcal{D}_\mathcal{T}$ and $\mathcal{D}_\mathcal{S}$

C Hyperparameters

Hyperparameter	Value
LSTM cell size	100
Dropout	0.5
Word embedding dimension	300
Character embedding dimension	100
Mini-batch size	128
Clip norm	1
Optimizer	Adam
Number of epoch	20
Early stopping	10

Table 6: Neural model hyperparameters

Parameter	Adopted value
Surrogate model	Gaussian Processes with MCMC sampling
Acquisition function	Expected Logarithmic Improvement
Number of initial evaluation points	3
Search space upper bound	1
Search space lower bound	-1
Number of iterations	50

Table 7: Parameters used by the Bayesian Optimizer.

Evaluating the Effectiveness of Efficient Neural Architecture Search for Sentence-Pair Tasks

Ansel MacLaughlin[1][*], Jwala Dhamala[2], Anoop Kumar[2], Sriram Venkatapathy[2],
Ragav Venkatesan[3], Rahul Gupta[2]
[1] Khoury College of Computer Sciences, Northeastern University, Boston, MA
[2] Amazon Alexa, Cambridge, MA
[3] Amazon Alexa, Seattle, WA
ansel@ccs.neu.edu   {jddhamal, anooamzn, vesriram, ragavven, gupra}@amazon.com

Abstract

Neural Architecture Search (NAS) methods, which automatically learn entire neural model or individual neural cell architectures, have recently achieved competitive or state-of-the-art (SOTA) performance on variety of natural language processing and computer vision tasks, including language modeling, natural language inference, and image classification. In this work, we explore the applicability of a SOTA NAS algorithm, Efficient Neural Architecture Search (ENAS) (Pham et al., 2018) to two sentence pair tasks, paraphrase detection and semantic textual similarity. We use ENAS to perform a micro-level search and learn a task-optimized RNN cell architecture as a drop-in replacement for an LSTM. We explore the effectiveness of ENAS through experiments on three datasets (MRPC, SICK, STS-B), with two different models (ESIM, BiLSTM-Max), and two sets of embeddings (Glove, BERT). In contrast to prior work applying ENAS to NLP tasks, our results are mixed – we find that ENAS architectures sometimes, but not always, outperform LSTMs and perform similarly to random architecture search.

1 Introduction

Neural Architecture Search (NAS) methods aim to automatically discover neural architectures that perform well on a given task and dataset. These methods search over a space of possible model architectures, looking for ones that perform well on the task and will generalize to unseen data. There has been substantial prior work on how to define the architecture search space, search over that space, and estimate model performance (Elsken et al., 2019).

Recent works, however, cast doubt on the quality and performance of NAS-optimized architectures (Sciuto et al., 2020; Li and Talwalkar, 2019), showing that current methods fail to find the best performing architectures for a given task and perform similarly to random architecture search.

In this work, we explore applications of a SOTA NAS algorithm, ENAS (Pham et al., 2018), to two sentence-pair tasks, paraphrase detection (PD) and semantic textual similarity (STS). We conduct a large set of experiments testing the effectiveness of ENAS-optimized RNN architectures across multiple models (ESIM, BiLSTM-Max), embeddings (BERT, Glove) and datasets (MRPC, SICK, STS-B). We are the first, to our knowledge, to apply ENAS to PD and STS, to explore applications across multiple embeddings and traditionally LSTM-based NLP models, and to conduct extensive SOTA HPT across multiple ENAS-RNN architecture candidates.

Our experiments suggest that baseline LSTM models, with appropriate hyperparameter tuning (HPT), can sometimes match or exceed the performance of models with ENAS-RNNs. We also observe that random architectures sampled from the ENAS search space offer a strong baseline, and can sometimes outperform ENAS-RNNs. Given these observations, we recommend that researchers (i) conduct extensive HPT (preferably using automated methods) across various candidate architectures for the fairest comparisons; (ii) compare the performances of ENAS-RNNs against both standard architectures like LSTMs and RNN cells randomly sampled from the ENAS search space; (iii) examine the computational (memory and runtime) requirements of ENAS methods alongside the gains observed.

2 Related Work

NAS methods have shown strong performance on many NLP and CV tasks, such as language model-

---

Work completed while interning at Amazon.

Proceedings of the First Workshop on Insights from Negative Results in NLP, pages 22–31
Online, November 19, 2020. ©2020 Association for Computational Linguistics

ing and image classification (Zoph and Le, 2017; Pham et al., 2018; Luo et al., 2018; Liu et al., 2019). Applications in NLP, such as NER (Jiang et al., 2019; Li et al., 2020), translation (So et al., 2019), text classification (Wang et al., 2020), and natural language inference (NLI) (Pasunuru and Bansal, 2019; Wang et al., 2020) have also been explored.

Current SOTA approaches focus on learning new cell architectures as replacements for LSTM or convolutional cells (Zoph and Le, 2017; Pham et al., 2018; Liu et al., 2019; Jiang et al., 2019; Li et al., 2020) or entire model architectures to replace hand-designed models such as the transformer or DenseNet (So et al., 2019; Pham et al., 2018).

Recently, the superiority of NAS to random architecture search and traditional architectures with SOTA HPT methods has been called into question. Li and Talwalkar (2019) discuss reproducibility issues with current NAS methods and find that, on language modeling and image classification tasks, NAS algorithms perform similarly to random architecture search. Similarly, Sciuto et al. (2020) find minimal differences in performance between NAS and random search and that the popular weight-sharing strategy (Pham et al., 2018) decreases performance. With this in perspective, we conduct a study to investigate the value added by ENAS to two NLP tasks, PD and STS, which, to our knowledge, have not been been explored in previous NAS literature.

3 Neural Architecture Search for Sentence-Pair Tasks

In this work, we explore applications of ENAS to two sentence-pair tasks, PD and STS. We select ENAS because prior work (Pasunuru and Bansal, 2019; Wang et al., 2020) has shown promising results applying it to a closely-related task, NLI, with gains of up to 1.3% absolute over LSTMs and 1.6% over an RNN with a random architecture. Through our evaluations on PD and STS, we aim to study whether the ENAS methods used in prior work for NLI are generalizable and whether the results hold when applied to related tasks and datasets.

ENAS models consist of two parts: 1) a search space over model architectures, i.e. child models, and 2) a controller that samples architectures from that search space. The primary contribution of ENAS is that all child models in the search space share their weights, so each child model does not have to be trained from scratch to evaluate it. Train-ing the child models and controller proceeds as follows – first, the controller is fixed, and the child models are trained together for one epoch on the dataset, sampling a new architecture from the controller to use for each minibatch. Then, the child model shared parameters are fixed, and the controller is updated – we sample child architectures from its policy and update the controller to maximize the expected reward on the dev set (e.g. dev set accuracy). This two-step process then repeats for a specified number of epochs. After training is complete, a number of child models are sampled from the controller and the best one is trained from scratch and evaluated on the test set. We refer the reader to Pham et al. (2018) for further details on ENAS.

In this work, we follow the setup of Pasunuru and Bansal (2019), using standard LSTM-based NLP models and replacing the LSTMs with RNN cells sampled from the ENAS controller. We leave the rest of the model architecture (e.g. attention, pooling, output layers) the same, so the child model search space consists of every possible ENAS-RNN architecture with the standard model architecture around it. As with standard ENAS training, the parameters of the ENAS-RNNs and standard model architecture (e.g. final output layer) are shared across all child models.

3.1 Experiments

We evaluate ENAS on three sentence-pair datasets using two models and two sets of embeddings:

3.1.1 Sentence-Pair Datasets

- **Microsoft Research Paraphrase Corpus** (MRPC; Dolan and Brockett (2005)): binary label (sentences are paraphrases or not).

- **Semantic Textual Similarity Benchmark** (STS-B; Cer et al. (2017)): similarity score for each sentence-pair in 0 - 5.

- **SICK-R** (Marelli et al., 2014): similarity score for each sentence-pair in 1 - 5.

3.1.2 Models

- **BiLSTM-Max** (BLM, Conneau et al. (2017)): uses a BiLSTM + max-pooling to form a representation of each sentence (s_1, s_2) and forms a joint representation $h = [s_1; s_2; |s_1 - s_2|; s_1 \odot s_2]$. h is then fed through a feedforward layer and a projection to single predicted value. Pasunuru and Bansal (2019) use BLM in their work applying ENAS to NLI.

- **ESIM** (Chen et al., 2017): uses 2 BiL-STMs, with a cross-sentence attention module in between, then mean and max pooling get representations of each sentence. It then forms a joint representation $h = [s_{1,avg}; s_{1,max}; s_{2,avg}; s_{2,max}]$ which is fed through a feedforward layer and a final projection to single predicted value.

3.1.3 Embeddings

- **Feature-based BERT-base** (Devlin et al., 2019): Following Peters et al. (2019), we jointly encode the sentence pair (rather than encoding each separately). and learn a linear weighted combination of BERT's layers. BERT is frozen during training.

- **Glove** (Pennington et al., 2014): 300 dimensional vectors trained on Wikipedia and Gigaword. Embeddings are frozen during training.[1]

3.2 LSTM Baselines

We first benchmark LSTM implementations of both models. We adapt the BLM implementation from Pasunuru and Bansal (2019) and use the AllenNLP implementation of ESIM (Gardner et al., 2018). To have the most competitive baselines possible, we perform extensive HPT, running 500 trials using a Tree-structured Parzen Estimator (TPE; Bergstra et al. (2011)). We tune the hidden dimension sizes, dropout rates, batch size, loss function (only for regression tasks: mean squared error or mean absolute error), learning rate, weight decay, grad norm, and random seed. See Appendix A.2 for full HPT experiment details. Note that we put emphasis on extensive, automated HPT and conduct hundreds of HPT trials (as opposed to only tens of trials typically used in prior work, e.g. Yogatama et al. (2015)).

Given that we train BLM and ESIM on top of frozen embeddings, we use the ESIM + BERT results from Peters et al. (2019) as a baseline. Our reproduced results are in the same ballpark (Table 1, rows 2-3), albeit with small deviations.

3.3 ENAS Training

After finding the best hyperparameters for each ⟨dataset, embedding, model⟩ LSTM configuration, we run ENAS to search for a new RNN for each configuration. Following Pasunuru and Bansal (2019), we use 6 node ENAS-RNNs. We use Microsoft NNI's (Microsoft, 2020) ENAS implementation. We replace the BiLSTM in BLM and both BiLSTMs in ESIM with the ENAS BiRNNs (we use same architecture in both ESIM layers). We train ENAS for 150 epochs with early-stopping. For each ⟨dataset, embedding, model⟩ configuration, we train the ENAS models with the same hyperparameters as the best corresponding LSTM model, except learning rate of 1e-4 and grad norm 0.25, which are used across all ENAS models[2]. We follow the hyperparameter configurations from Pham et al. (2018) for the ENAS controller.

3.4 Training Discovered Architectures

After training ENAS, we sample 10 architectures from the controller. Just as during ENAS training, we then use these architectures as drop-in replacements for LSTMs, replacing a model's BiLSTM layer(s) with ENAS BiRNN(s). We then train the models from scratch and repeat HPT, extending the original LSTM hyperparameter search space with a choice over the 10 sampled architectures. We run 200 trials of HPT. We note that, unlike the CUDA implementations for LSTMs, it is non-trivial to implement highly optimized arbitrary ENAS-RNN architectures. We discuss these limitations and the overall compute dedicated for HPT on LSTM and ENAS-RNN based models in Appendix A.2.

In addition to experiments replacing all BiLSTM layers with ENAS BiRNNs, we also examine mixing ENAS-RNN and LSTM layers in the multi-layer ESIM model. Specifically, we experiment with only replacing the 1st BiLSTM layer in ESIM with an ENAS BiRNN and only replacing the 2nd BiLSTM layer. These models have the same hyperparameter search space as the ESIM model with ENAS-RNNs in both layers (i.e. same possible ENAS-RNN architectures), but we tune and evaluate them separately (see Table 1, rows 5-6, 11-12).

---

[1]Our initial experiments found that static Glove embeddings outperformed non-static ones.

[2]Training is unstable with the higher learning rates found during HPT for our LSTM models and those suggested in Pasunuru and Bansal (2019); Pham et al. (2018)

	Author	Embedding	Model	RNN	Dev Performance			Test Performance		
					SICK-R	MRPC	STS-B	SICK-R	MRPC	STS-B
1.	Devlin et al. (2019)	BERT	fine-tuned	–	–	–	–	**88.7**	**84.8**	**87.1**
2.	Peters et al. (2019)	BERT	ESIM	L / L	–	–	–	86.4	78.1	82.9
3.		BERT	ESIM	L / L	88.9	**88.0**	88.0	87.0	80.2	82.0
4.	Ours	BERT	ESIM	E / E	88.6	87.0	**88.5**	86.8	80.8	82.2
5.		BERT	ESIM	E / L	**89.3**	87.5	**88.5**	**87.4**	**81.0**	**83.0**
6.		BERT	ESIM	L / E	88.0	87.0	88.2	86.5	79.8	81.8
7.	Ours	BERT	BLM	L	87.4	88.0	88.1	84.8	80.4	80.1
8.		BERT	BLM	E	**87.8**	**88.5**	**88.7**	**85.5**	**82.8**	**83.3**
9.		Glove	ESIM	L / L	88.6	**79.9**	**83.3**	**86.1**	**73.7**	75.5
10.	Ours	Glove	ESIM	E / E	88.2	76.0	**83.3**	85.1	69.0	75.3
11.		Glove	ESIM	E / L	**88.7**	77.2	83.0	85.7	71.0	72.7
12.		Glove	ESIM	L / E	88.2	78.2	83.0	85.2	72.5	**76.0**
13.	Ours	Glove	BLM	L	86.3	**78.4**	79.7	82.5	71.8	73.0
14.		Glove	BLM	E	**87.0**	**78.4**	**81.6**	**84.1**	**73.4**	**74.8**

Table 1: Dev & Test set performances for LSTM and ENAS-RNN based models. Following Peters et al. (2019), we report pearson correlation for SICK-R and STS-B and accuracy for MRPC. In the RNN collumn, "E" stands for ENAS-RNN and "L" stands for LSTM. For ESIM there can be different of cells in different layers, e.g. E / L stands for ENAS-RNN in the 1st layer and LSTM in the 2nd layer.

	Embedding	Model	RNN	RNN Optimized For	Dev Performance			Test Performance		
					SICK-R	MRPC	STS-B	SICK-R	MRPC	STS-B
1.	BERT	ESIM	E / L	SICK-R	**89.3**	87.0	–	**87.4**	**81.3**	–
2.	BERT	ESIM	E / L	MRPC	89.0	**87.5**	–	86.9	81.0	–
3.	BERT	ESIM	E / L	STS-B	–	–	**88.5**	–	–	**83.0**
4.	BERT	ESIM	RND / L	Random	88.9	87.0	88.4	87.2	79.0	81.2
5.	Glove	BLM	E	SICK-R	87.0	77.5	–	84.1	71.9	–
6.	Glove	BLM	E	MRPC	87.3	78.4	–	83.5	73.4	–
7.	Glove	BLM	E	STS-B	–	–	**81.6**	–	–	**74.8**
8.	Glove	BLM	RND	Random	**87.6**	**79.9**	81.1	**84.7**	**75.5**	**74.8**

Table 2: Evaluation of how well ENAS-RNNs transfer to other datasets and compare to random search. We report pearson correlation for SICK-R and STS-B and accuracy for MRPC. In the RNN collumn, "E" stands for ENAS-RNN, "L" stands for LSTM, and "RND" for random RNN. For ESIM we use an ENAS or random RNN in the 1st layer and an LSTM in the 2nd layer.

4 Results

Table 1 lists the dev and test results for all datasets, embeddings, and models. We focus our discussion on the test results. On the whole, the results are mixed. ⟨BLM, ENAS⟩ outperforms ⟨BLM, LSTM⟩ across all datasets and embeddings by an average of 1.9%. ⟨ESIM, ENAS⟩, on the other hand, fails to consistently outperform ⟨ESIM, LSTM⟩. ESIM models with ENAS-RNNs in both layers lag behind LSTMs by 0.9%, on average.

Focusing first on BLM, we find that ⟨BLM, ENAS⟩ outperforms ⟨BLM, LSTM⟩ by an average of 2.1% across all three datasets using BERT (row 8) and 1.7% using Glove (row 14). These results parallel those of Pasunuru and Bansal (2019), who find that ⟨BLM, ENAS⟩ with ELMO embeddings (Peters et al., 2018) outperforms ⟨BLM, LSTM⟩ on two NLI datasets and is on par on a third. However, both in our experiments and those of Pasunuru and Bansal (2019), the 6 node ENAS-RNNs have more parameters than the corresponding LSTM models[3], making it difficult to get a clear picture of the effects of just changing the RNN architecture. To

control for this, in §4.1 we conduct experiments comparing ENAS-RNNs to RNNs randomly sampled from the same search space.

Examining ESIM, the results are mixed. ESIM models with ENAS-RNNs in both layers (rows 4, 10) are worse than ⟨ESIM, LSTM⟩ on 4 of 6 ⟨dataset, embedding⟩ configurations. The best ⟨ESIM, ENAS⟩ performance is actually achieved using a mix of ENAS-RNNs and LSTMs across different layers. In fact, the only configurations in which ⟨ESIM, ENAS⟩ outperforms ⟨ESIM, LSTM⟩ across all three datasets is ⟨BERT, ENAS / LSTM⟩ (row 5), where we only replace the first LSTM layer with an ENAS-RNN. The gains, however, are modest compared to those of the BLM model, improving over ⟨ESIM, LSTM⟩ by 0.73% on average. Further, changing the embeddings to Glove ⟨Glove, ENAS / LSTM⟩ (row 11), ⟨ESIM, ENAS⟩ underperforms ⟨ESIM, LSTM⟩ across all 3 datasets by nearly 2% on average. Since we do not observe similar performance gains with ESIM as with BLM, we hypothesize that optimization of specific RNN architectures might matter less as model complexity (e.g. number of layers) increases. We suggest future work further examine the importance of ENAS as it relates to model complexity, especially

---

[3] The exact ratio in number of parameters between 6 node ENAS-RNNs and LSTMs depends on the input and hidden dimensions

on tasks where an RNN's architecture might have a higher impact on modeling performance.

4.1 Random & Transfer Architectures

In addition to comparisons to LSTMs, we evaluate two common claims about NAS methods: 1) NAS outperforms random search (Pham et al., 2018; Zoph and Le, 2017; Luo et al., 2018; Liu et al., 2019) 2) NAS architectures are transferable to related datasets and tasks (Zoph and Le, 2017; Liu et al., 2019; Luo et al., 2018). We choose two configurations to evaluate these claims: (i) ⟨Glove, BLM⟩ and (ii) ⟨BERT, ESIM, ENAS / LSTM⟩ with ENAS-RNNs only in the first layer, keeping the second BiLSTM layer. We chose these configurations since they perform well relative to LSTMs and, between them, cover all embeddings and models.

For claim #1, we first randomly sample 10 RNN architectures from the ENAS search space. Then, just as for the ENAS-RNNs, we perform 200 HPT trials, replacing the 10 ENAS-RNN candidates with the 10 randomly sampled RNN candidates. For claim #2, we test the transferability of SICK-R and MRPC cells to/from each other. We do not evaluate the transferability of STS-B cells, since STS-B contains data from SICK-R and MRPC. We again perform 200 HPT trials, but with the different dataset's ENAS-RNN cells in the search space.

Table 2 shows our results. We again focus on test results. For claim #1, we find mixed results, with ENAS outperforming random search by an average of 1.33% in the configuration ⟨BERT, ESIM, ENAS / LSTM⟩ (rows 1-4), but performing worse or on par with random on ⟨GLOVE, BLM⟩ (rows 5-8) (average 0.9% decrease). These results contrast those of Pham et al. (2018); Pasunuru and Bansal (2019), who report gains over random search on language modeling (25.4% decrease in perplexity) and NLI datasets (1.53% increase in accuracy). We hypothesize that these differences are due, in part, to our emphasis on creating strong baselines by searching over multiple architectures and performing extensive HPT for all models and settings.

For claim #2, we find that transfer architectures underperform dataset-specific ENAS architectures by 0.58% and random architectures by 0.7%, on average. Only one architecture (row 1, SICK to MRPC) outperforms either of the corresponding random or dataset-specific architectures. Together with our findings for claim #1, these results cast further doubt on the ability of ENAS to find the best architecture for a specific task, its superiority to well-tuned random architectures, and the transferability of its discovered architectures.

5 Conclusion

Unlike prior work applying ENAS to NLP, we find that ENAS-RNNs only outperform LSTMs and random search on some ⟨dataset, embedding, model⟩ configurations. Our findings parallel recent work (Li and Talwalkar, 2019; Sciuto et al., 2020) which question the effectiveness of current NAS methods and their superiority to random architecture search and SOTA HPT methods. Given our mixed results, we recommend researchers: (i) extensively tune hyperparameters for standard (e.g. LSTM) and randomly sampled architectures to create strong baselines; (ii) benchmark ENAS performance across multiple simple and complex model architectures (e.g. BLM & ESIM); (iii) present computational requirements alongside gains observed with ENAS methods.

References

James Bergstra, Rémi Bardenet, Yoshua Bengio, and Balázs Kégl. 2011. Algorithms for hyper-parameter optimization. In *NIPS*.

Daniel Cer, Mona Diab, Eneko Agirre, Iñigo Lopez-Gazpio, and Lucia Specia. 2017. SemEval-2017 task 1: Semantic textual similarity multilingual and crosslingual focused evaluation. In *Proceedings of the 11th International Workshop on Semantic Evaluation (SemEval-2017)*, pages 1–14, Vancouver, Canada. Association for Computational Linguistics.

Qian Chen, Xiaodan Zhu, Zhen-Hua Ling, Si Wei, Hui Jiang, and Diana Inkpen. 2017. Enhanced LSTM for natural language inference. In *Proceedings of the 55th Annual Meeting of the Association for Computational Linguistics (Volume 1: Long Papers)*, pages 1657–1668, Vancouver, Canada. Association for Computational Linguistics.

Alexis Conneau, Douwe Kiela, Holger Schwenk, Loïc Barrault, and Antoine Bordes. 2017. Supervised learning of universal sentence representations from natural language inference data. In *Proceedings of the 2017 Conference on Empirical Methods in Natural Language Processing*, pages 670–680, Copenhagen, Denmark. Association for Computational Linguistics.

Jacob Devlin, Ming-Wei Chang, Kenton Lee, and Kristina Toutanova. 2019. BERT: Pre-training of deep bidirectional transformers for language understanding. In *Proceedings of the 2019 Conference of the North American Chapter of the Association for Computational Linguistics: Human Language Technologies, Volume 1 (Long and Short Papers)*, pages 4171–4186, Minneapolis, Minnesota. Association for Computational Linguistics.

William B. Dolan and Chris Brockett. 2005. Automatically constructing a corpus of sentential paraphrases. In *IWP@IJCNLP*.

Thomas Elsken, Jan Hendrik Metzen, and Frank Hutter. 2019. Neural architecture search: A survey. *JMLR*.

Matt Gardner, Joel Grus, Mark Neumann, Oyvind Tafjord, Pradeep Dasigi, Nelson F. Liu, Matthew E. Peters, Michael Schmitz, and Luke Zettlemoyer. 2018. Allennlp: A deep semantic natural language processing platform. *ArXiv*, abs/1803.07640. ESIM implementation `https://github.com/matt-peters/allennlp/blob/mp/esim/allennlp/models/esim.py`.

Matthew Honnibal and Ines Montani. 2017. spaCy 2: Natural language understanding with Bloom embeddings, convolutional neural networks and incremental parsing. To appear.

Yufan Jiang, Chi Hu, Tong Xiao, Chunliang Zhang, and Jingbo Zhu. 2019. Improved differentiable architecture search for language modeling and named entity recognition. In *Proceedings of the 2019 Conference on Empirical Methods in Natural Language Processing and the 9th International Joint Conference on Natural Language Processing (EMNLP-IJCNLP)*, pages 3585–3590, Hong Kong, China. Association for Computational Linguistics.

Liam Li and Ameet Talwalkar. 2019. Random search and reproducibility for neural architecture search. In *UAI*.

Yinqiao Li, Chi Hu, Yuhao Zhang, Nuo Xu, Yufan Jiang, Tong Xiao, Jingbo Zhu, Tongran Liu, and changliang li. 2020. Learning architectures from an extended search space for language modeling. In *Proceedings of the 58th Annual Meeting of the Association for Computational Linguistics*, pages 6629–6639, Online. Association for Computational Linguistics.

Hanxiao Liu, Karen Simonyan, and Yiming Yang. 2019. Darts: Differentiable architecture search. In *ICLR*.

Renqian Luo, Fei Tian, Tao Qin, and Tie-Yan Liu. 2018. Neural architecture optimization. In *NeurIPS*.

Marco Marelli, Stefano Menini, Marco Baroni, Luisa Bentivogli, Raffaella Bernardi, and Roberto Zamparelli. 2014. A SICK cure for the evaluation of compositional distributional semantic models. In *Proceedings of the Ninth International Conference on Language Resources and Evaluation (LREC-2014)*, pages 216–223, Reykjavik, Iceland. European Languages Resources Association (ELRA).

Microsoft. 2020. Neural network intelligence. `https://github.com/microsoft/nni`.

Ramakanth Pasunuru and Mohit Bansal. 2019. Continual and multi-task architecture search. In *Proceedings of the 57th Annual Meeting of the Association for Computational Linguistics*, pages 1911–1922, Florence, Italy. Association for Computational Linguistics. Github Repository: `https://github.com/ramakanth-pasunuru/CAS-MAS`.

Jeffrey Pennington, Richard Socher, and Christopher Manning. 2014. Glove: Global vectors for word representation. In *Proceedings of the 2014 Conference on Empirical Methods in Natural Language Processing (EMNLP)*, pages 1532–1543, Doha, Qatar. Association for Computational Linguistics.

Matthew Peters, Mark Neumann, Mohit Iyyer, Matt Gardner, Christopher Clark, Kenton Lee, and Luke Zettlemoyer. 2018. Deep contextualized word representations. In *Proceedings of the 2018 Conference of the North American Chapter of the Association for Computational Linguistics: Human Language Technologies, Volume 1 (Long Papers)*, pages 2227–2237, New Orleans, Louisiana. Association for Computational Linguistics.

Matthew E. Peters, Sebastian Ruder, and Noah A. Smith. 2019. To tune or not to tune? adapting pretrained representations to diverse tasks. In *Proceedings of the 4th Workshop on Representation Learning for NLP (RepL4NLP-2019)*, pages 7–14, Florence, Italy. Association for Computational Linguistics.

Hieu Pham, Melody Y. Guan, Barret Zoph, Quoc V. Le, and Jeff Dean. 2018. Efficient neural architecture search via parameter sharing. In *ICML*.

Christian Sciuto, Kaicheng Yu, Martin Jaggi, Claudiu Musat, and Mathieu Salzmann. 2020. Evaluating the search phase of neural architecture search. In *ICLR*.

David R. So, Chen Liang, and Quoc V. Le. 2019. The evolved transformer. In *ICML*.

Yujing Wang, Yaming Yang, Yi-Ren Chen, Jing Bai, Ce Zhang, Guinan Su, Xiaoyu Kou, Yunhai Tong, Mao Yang, and Lidong Zhou. 2020. Textnas: A neural architecture search space tailored for text representation. In *AAAI*.

Thomas Wolf, Lysandre Debut, Victor Sanh, Julien Chaumond, Clement Delangue, Anthony Moi, Pierric Cistac, Tim Rault, Rémi Louf, Morgan Funtowicz, Joe Davison, Sam Shleifer, Patrick von Platen, Clara Ma, Yacine Jernite, Julien Plu, Canwen Xu, Teven Le Scao, Sylvain Gugger, Mariama Drame, Quentin Lhoest, and Alexander M. Rush. 2019. Huggingface's transformers: State-of-the-art natural language processing. *ArXiv*, abs/1910.03771.

Hyperparameter	Search Space
batch size	[16, 32, 64]
learning rate	0.0001 - 0.01
loss function	classification: cross entropy regression: [mae, mse]
weight decay	0.001 - 0.1
grad norm	0.25 - 20.0
hidden dimensions	w/ bert: [384, 512, 768, 1152, 1536] w/ glove: [150, 200, 300, 450, 600]
dropouts	0.25 - 0.75
random seed	[0, 1, 2, 3, 4, 5]
epochs	75 (with early stopping)
RNN Architecture	Choice of 10 unique architectures (only for models with ENAS-RNNs)

Table 3: Hyperparameter search space for all experiments.

Dani Yogatama, Lingpeng Kong, and Noah A. Smith. 2015. Bayesian optimization of text representations. In *Proceedings of the 2015 Conference on Empirical Methods in Natural Language Processing*, pages 2100–2105, Lisbon, Portugal. Association for Computational Linguistics.

Barret Zoph and Quoc V. Le. 2017. Neural architecture search with reinforcement learning. In *NeurIPS*.

A Implementation Details

All models were implemented with Pytorch and run on Amazon p3 instances (16GB Nvidia V100).

A.1 Embeddings

Experiments with BERT used the Huggingface Transformers library (Wolf et al., 2019). Experiments with Glove vectors used 300 dimensional vectors trained on Wikipedia 2014 + Gigaword 5[4]. Glove vectors weren't updated training, and out-of-vocabulary tokens were replaced with the token "[UNK]" with an embedding of all 0s ($\approx$ 6% of tokens are OOV). In initial experiments, we found no differences between our all-0 embeddings and embeddings randomly initialized according to a Gaussian distribution.

A.2 Hyperparameter Tuning

All HPT was run using Microsoft NNI's parallel implementation of TPE[5] with concurrency 8. Table 3 contains the search space for our experiments. Table 5 contains the best hyperparameter settings for all of our experiments.

---

[4] http://nlp.stanford.edu/data/glove.6B.zip

[5] https://nni.readthedocs.io/en/latest/CommunitySharings/ParallelizingTpeSearch.html

A.2.1 Memory Limitations for HPT with ENAS-RNNs

In order for a model to fit on a single GPU (16GB Nvidia V100), we had to limit the search space slightly for models using both ENAS-RNNs and BERT embeddings. This is because the ENAS-RNN search space contains weight matrices $W_{\ell,j}^{h}$ between each pair of nodes ℓ, j in the RNN search space DAG, which greatly expands memory usage (see Pham et al. (2018), sections 2.1 and Appendix A). For both BLM and ESIM models, hidden dimensions were limited to [384, 512, 768]. Further, for ESIM models with ENAS-RNNs in both layers, the batch size was also limited to [16, 32].

A.2.2 Timing limitations for HPT with ENAS-RNNs

Since our ENAS-RNNs are, similar to prior NAS research code, implemented using a Python for-loop over time steps, the implementation is significantly slower ($\approx$ 25x) than the cuda-optimized LSTM equivalent. Thus, due to computational limits, we only perform 200 trials of HPT for the models with ENAS-RNNs (vs. 500 for models with LSTMs). Though the number of HPT trials is lower than for LSTMs, due to their slow speed, the total compute time devoted to tuning the ENAS-RNN models is roughly 10x+ higher. As an example, Table 4 shows the total compute time dedicated to HPT for BLM models (both LSTM-based models and ENAS-RNN based models), measured as the total number of hours spent on a single p3.16xlarge instance[6] to finish all HPT trials. Note, the models with ENAS-RNNs are not always exactly 10x slower than the LSTM equivalent – since we are also searching over batch size during HPT, runtimes can vary significantly.

A.3 Memory Limitations for Training ENAS

As noted in §3.3, we train the ENAS child models ⟨BLM, ESIM⟩ using the same parameters as the corresponding best LSTM model for the given configuration ⟨dataset, embeddings, model⟩. For the configuration ⟨STS-B, BERT, ESIM⟩, the corresponding ENAS child models would not fit on a single GPU (16GB Nvidia V100). This is due to the large memory footprint of ENAS as discussed in A.2. Thus, for ⟨STS-B, BERT, ESIM⟩ we decrease the batch size from 64 to 32 and the hidden dimensions from 1152 to 768.

---

[6] https://aws.amazon.com/ec2/instance-types/p3/

Configuration	# HPT Trials	Runtime (hours)
(BLM, BERT, LSTM, SICK)	500	19.14
(BLM, BERT, LSTM, MRPC)	500	23.99
(BLM, BERT, LSTM, STS-B)	500	47.30
(BLM, BERT, ENAS, SICK)	200	79.21
(BLM, BERT, ENAS, MRPC)	200	67.29
(BLM, BERT, ENAS, STS-B)	200	141.09
(BLM, Glove, LSTM, SICK)	500	5.35
(BLM, Glove, LSTM, MRPC)	500	4.90
(BLM, Glove, LSTM, STS-B)	500	9.36
(BLM, Glove, ENAS, SICK)	200	78.65
(BLM, Glove, ENAS, MRPC)	200	113.33
(BLM, Glove, ENAS, STS-B)	200	193.93

Table 4: Compute time spent on HPT for BLM models (both LSTM-based models and ENAS-RNN based models). Compute time measured as total number of hours on a single p3.16xlarge instance. All HPT was run using Microsoft NNI's parallel implementation of TPE[7] with concurrency 8 (one trial running on each of the 8 GPUs in the p3.16xlarge instance).

A.4 ESIM: Differences Between Training Child Models with ENAS and Training Models from Scratch

As described in §3.3, when training the ESIM child models jointly with the ENAS controller, we replace both of ESIM's BiLSTMs with the sampled ENAS-RNN architectures. We do this for each ⟨dataset, embedding⟩ configuration, thus running 6 total instances of ENAS (3 datasets * 2 embeddings). After the ENAS training is complete, we sample 10 ENAS-RNN architectures from the trained controller.

However, when training ESIM models from scratch, as described in §3.4, we experiment with 1) replacing both LSTM layers with the ENAS-RNN architecture (same as during ENAS training) 2) only replacing the 1st layer 3) only replacing the 2nd layer. We treat each ESIM layer configuration as its own model and tune its hyperparameters separately. Thus, for example, for the configuration (SICK-R, BERT, ESIM) we perform 200 trails of HPT for the configuration with ENAS-RNNs in both layers, 200 trials of HPT for the configuration with an ENAS-RNN in layer 1 and an LSTM in layer 2, and finally 200 trials of HPT for the configuration with an LSTM in layer 1 and an ENAS-RNN in layer 2. Note, however, that these three separate instances of HPT share the same search space over ENAS-RNN architectures – all three are searching over the same 10 ENAS-RNNs sampled from the same controller. In total, we run 18 different instances of HPT (3 datasets * 2 embeddings * 3 layer configs). The results from each configuration are presented separately in Table 1 (in the main portion of the paper).

A.5 RNN Architectures Sampled from ENAS Search Space

Table 6 shows the architectures of all RNNs used in our experiments (ENAS-RNNs, transferred ENAS-RNNs, random RNNs). Each architecture is numbered 1-26. Table 5, which displays the hyperparameter settings for each model and configuration, lists which RNN architecture each configuration uses.

Note, some of the architectures are the same across different model configurations. This is due to two reasons:

- As discussed in §3.4 and §A.4, we experiment with mixing ENAS-RNN and LSTM layers in the multi-layer ESIM model. The ESIM models with ENAS RNNs in both layers share the same possible ENAS-RNN architectures as the corresponding ESIM models with an ENAS-RNN only in the 1st layer or 2nd layer.

- We sampled 10 total random architectures from the ENAS-RNN search space then used those same 10 architectures in the search spaces for all ⟨dataset, model, embedding⟩ configurations. Thus, some configurations might use the same architecture.

A.6 Datasets

For MRPC and STS-B, we use the data provided by Glue[8]. For SICK-R, we use the data provided by SemEval-2014 Task 1[9]. We use scikit-learn[10] to split the provided SICK-R training data into train and dev splits.

For our experiments with BERT, we use the Bert-Tokenizer from the Huggingface Transformers library (Wolf et al., 2019). We cap each sentence-pair at a certain number of total wordpiece tokens (SICK: 64, MRPC: 128, STS-B: 128). For our experiments with Glove, we use spacy[11] (Honnibal and Montani, 2017) to tokenize each sentence. We cap each sentence at a certain number of tokens (SICK: 30, MRPC: 46, STS-B: 39).

---

[8]`https://gluebenchmark.com/faq`
[9]`http://alt.qcri.org/semeval2014/task1/`
[10]`https://scikit-learn.org/stable/modules/generated/sklearn.model_selection.train_test_split.html`, dev size: 0.1, random state: 0
[11]`https://spacy.io/models/en#en_core_web_md`

Model	Embedding	RNN	Dataset	Batch Size	Learning Rate	Loss	Weight Decay	Grad Norm	Hidden Dim	Dropout	Variational Dropout	Rnd Seed	Architecture #
BLM	BERT	L	SICK	32	0.0046	mse	0.0514	12.3656	512	(0.3782, 0.3474)	0.4088	3	–
BLM	BERT	L	MRPC	64	0.0021	cross entropy	0.0637	12.8279	384	(0.6355, 0.4388)	0.6804	2	–
BLM	BERT	L	STS-B	32	0.0075	mse	0.0407	16.8742	512	(0.2702, 0.4525)	0.6783	2	–
BLM	Glove	L	SICK	64	0.0007	mse	0.0040	10.2636	300	(0.3555, 0.2937)	0.2774	1	–
BLM	Glove	L	MRPC	32	0.0017	cross entropy	0.0301	8.1649	450	(0.3346, 0.3751)	0.2986	5	–
BLM	Glove	L	STS-B	32	0.0004	mse	0.0201	4.9461	200	(0.2597, 0.5924)	0.4516	0	–
BLM	BERT	E	SICK	32	0.0074	mse	0.0226	11.2817	384	(0.3372, 0.5304)	0.3009	5	17
BLM	BERT	E	MRPC	32	0.0031	cross entropy	0.0670	9.4340	384	(0.5310, 0.6235)	0.4676	1	15
BLM	BERT	E	STS-B	32	0.0019	mae	0.0382	6.7670	512	(0.2507, 0.4492)	0.6193	1	19
BLM	Glove	E	SICK	64	0.0007	mse	0.0729	11.7080	450	(0.3199, 0.2711)	0.3911	5	18
BLM	Glove	E	MRPC	64	0.0001	cross entropy	0.0637	15.5210	450	(0.3352, 0.3993)	0.2948	4	16
BLM	Glove	E	STS-B	16	0.0007	mae	0.0258	2.9847	450	(0.2584, 0.6419)	0.2508	4	20
BLM	Glove	R	SICK	64	0.0016	mse	0.0647	15.0969	450	(0.2505, 0.3945)	0.2589	0	24
BLM	Glove	R	MRPC	64	0.0015	cross entropy	0.0956	12.2487	300	(0.2956, 0.3971)	0.3304	0	22
BLM	Glove	R	STS-B	64	0.0004	mse	0.0257	1.2826	600	(0.3355, 0.4312)	0.3392	3	24
BLM	Glove	T	SICK	32	0.0003	mse	0.0058	6.1308	300	(0.3809, 0.3487)	0.3273	2	25
BLM	Glove	T	MRPC	32	0.0005	cross entropy	0.0341	14.0270	200	(0.4586, 0.6012)	0.4123	0	26
ESIM	BERT	L/L	SICK	32	0.0011	mae	0.0299	12.9599	(512 1152)	(0.3171, 0.6050)	(0.6962, 0.4123)	4	–
ESIM	BERT	L/L	MRPC	64	0.0048	cross entropy	0.0448	16.0686	(384 512)	(0.2806, 0.4960)	(0.5453, 0.3357)	1	–
ESIM	BERT	L/L	STS-B	64	0.0011	mae	0.0855	18.4787	(1152 1152)	(0.4213, 0.4769)	(0.5011, 0.5806)	3	–
ESIM	Glove	L/L	SICK	32	0.0018	mse	0.0804	12.3511	(200 300)	(0.4369, 0.5705)	(0.4491, 0.3239)	1	–
ESIM	Glove	L/L	MRPC	64	0.0006	cross entropy	0.0415	16.6595	(600 200)	(0.4089, 0.7434)	(0.2795, 0.4438)	3	–
ESIM	Glove	L/L	STS-B	64	0.0027	mse	0.0741	12.3487	(300 600)	(0.2822, 0.4862)	(0.2867, 0.5283)	1	–
ESIM	BERT	E/E	SICK	16	0.0002	mae	0.0572	4.5861	(512 768)	(0.3362, 0.6338)	(0.6415, 0.3806)	1	7
ESIM	BERT	E/E	MRPC	32	0.0005	cross entropy	0.0808	15.6688	(384 768)	(0.7098, 0.6014)	(0.6504, 0.3573)	2	5
ESIM	BERT	E/E	STS-B	32	0.0024	mse	0.0684	17.1467	(384 512)	(0.4992, 0.6578)	(0.7135, 0.4686)	5	12
ESIM	Glove	E/E	SICK	64	0.0005	mse	0.0673	11.2588	(450 200)	(0.5421, 0.6383)	(0.4262, 0.4960)	1	11
ESIM	Glove	E/E	MRPC	64	0.0019	cross entropy	0.0544	16.2351	(150 600)	(0.4805, 0.6752)	(0.4711, 0.5483)	3	6
ESIM	Glove	E/E	STS-B	64	0.0005	mae	0.0579	11.3040	(450 200)	(0.3348, 0.5270)	(0.2846, 0.4997)	0	13
ESIM	BERT	E/L	SICK	16	0.0008	mse	0.0835	14.1718	(512 768)	(0.3996, 0.4231)	(0.3149, 0.3665)	0	9
ESIM	BERT	E/L	MRPC	32	0.0005	cross entropy	0.0525	13.0402	(768 512)	(0.5491, 0.2819)	(0.4482, 0.3430)	5	3
ESIM	BERT	E/L	STS-B	32	0.0008	mae	0.0995	5.6442	(384 384)	(0.6291, 0.6221)	(0.3899, 0.6917)	5	14
ESIM	Glove	E/L	SICK	32	0.0004	mse	0.0337	0.7994	(600 600)	(0.4193, 0.6904)	(0.4331, 0.6221)	2	10
ESIM	Glove	E/L	MRPC	64	0.0011	cross entropy	0.0549	5.7392	(200 150)	(0.5909, 0.4142)	(0.4288, 0.2503)	4	4
ESIM	Glove	E/L	STS-B	64	0.0003	mse	0.0302	13.5390	(450 600)	(0.4538, 0.2828)	(0.4641, 0.6847)	0	13
ESIM	BERT	R/L	SICK	64	0.0007	mse	0.0135	3.3407	(384 512)	(0.3738, 0.4779)	(0.6879, 0.3507)	2	23
ESIM	BERT	R/L	MRPC	64	0.0007	cross entropy	0.0747	12.8833	(384 768)	(0.3532, 0.6506)	(0.6440, 0.6599)	0	21
ESIM	BERT	R/L	STS-B	32	0.0014	mse	0.0240	0.3344	(512 384)	(0.6102, 0.2993)	(0.5616, 0.3264)	4	24
ESIM	BERT	T/L	SICK	64	0.0025	mse	0.0623	6.0643	(384 384)	(0.4455, 0.3305)	(0.6036, 0.4636)	3	5
ESIM	BERT	T/L	MRPC	32	0.0003	cross entropy	0.0989	19.2888	(512 768)	(0.3023, 0.2515)	(0.6723, 0.4313)	3	7
ESIM	BERT	L/E	SICK	32	0.0024	mse	0.0690	6.5209	(384 384)	(0.2935, 0.3905)	(0.5975, 0.3623)	2	7
ESIM	BERT	L/E	MRPC	32	0.0020	cross entropy	0.0637	12.9123	(768 768)	(0.3302, 0.5489)	(0.7050, 0.5593)	0	1
ESIM	BERT	L/E	STS-B	16	0.0014	mae	0.0294	19.7594	(384 384)	(0.3857, 0.5279)	(0.5551, 0.3715)	3	12
ESIM	Glove	L/E	SICK	32	0.0028	mse	0.0360	16.7776	(150 200)	(0.3367, 0.7101)	(0.3469, 0.3811)	3	8
ESIM	Glove	L/E	MRPC	64	0.0013	cross entropy	0.0151	3.7091	(300 300)	(0.4849, 0.6060)	(0.5526, 0.4104)	0	2
ESIM	Glove	L/E	STS-B	32	0.0017	mse	0.0814	0.2999	(150 200)	(0.2829, 0.3279)	(0.2622, 0.2951)	5	13

Table 5: Hyperparameter values used for all experiments. In the RNN collumn, "E" stands for ENAS-RNN, "L" stands for LSTM, "R" for random RNN, and "T" for transfer. All floating point values have been rounded to 4 significant figures after the decimal point. Variational dropout is applied before each RNN layer. For models with RNNs from the ENAS search space (all models except those with LSTMs), the column 'Architecture #' displays which RNN architecture it uses. The number corresponds to the row number in Table 6. For ESIM models, the two hidden dimension values refer to (RNN layer 1, RNN layer 2) and the two dropout numbers refer to standard dropout (applied after the 'enhancement' layer, in the final MLP layer). For BLM models, the two dropout numbers refer to standard dropout applied (after the RNN layer, before the final projection)

	Node 0 Op	Node 1 Input	Node 1 Op	Node 2 Input	Node 2 Op	Node 3 Input	Node 3 Op	Node 4 Input	Node 4 Op	Node 5 Input	Node 5 Op
1.	Tanh	0	Relu	0	Relu	0	Relu	0	Relu	0	Relu
2.	Tanh	0	Relu	1	Relu	2	Relu	0	Relu	2	Relu
3.	Tanh	0	Relu	1	Relu	0	Identity	0	Identity	0	Identity
4.	Identity	0	Relu	0	Sigmoid	0	Relu	2	Relu	1	Relu
5.	Tanh	0	Relu	0	Relu	0	Identity	0	Identity	4	Relu
6.	Identity	0	Sigmoid	0	Relu	0	Relu	2	Relu	3	Relu
7.	Tanh	0	Tanh	0	Relu	0	Tanh	3	Tanh	0	Tanh
8.	Tanh	0	Identity	0	Tanh	0	Identity	0	Identity	0	Tanh
9.	Tanh	0	Tanh	0	Relu	0	Tanh	0	Tanh	0	Tanh
10.	Tanh	0	Identity	0	Tanh	0	Identity	0	Tanh	0	Identity
11.	Tanh	0	Tanh	0	Identity	0	Tanh	0	Identity	0	Identity
12.	Relu	0	Tanh	1	Sigmoid	0	Relu	0	Sigmoid	0	Relu
13.	Identity	0	Identity	1	Identity	0	Sigmoid	3	Identity	0	Sigmoid
14.	Sigmoid	0	Relu	0	Sigmoid	0	Relu	0	Relu	0	Sigmoid
15.	Sigmoid	0	Identity	0	Tanh	0	Tanh	0	Tanh	0	Tanh
16.	Sigmoid	0	Tanh	0	Tanh	0	Identity	0	Identity	0	Identity
17.	Tanh	0	Sigmoid	1	Sigmoid	2	Relu	3	Sigmoid	1	Sigmoid
18.	Tanh	0	Sigmoid	1	Sigmoid	0	Sigmoid	1	Sigmoid	2	Sigmoid
19.	Sigmoid	0	Sigmoid	0	Sigmoid	0	Relu	0	Relu	0	Sigmoid
20.	Relu	0	Sigmoid	1	Sigmoid	0	Sigmoid	0	Sigmoid	0	Sigmoid
21.	Tanh	0	Identity	0	Sigmoid	1	Tanh	2	Sigmoid	0	Tanh
22.	Sigmoid	0	Relu	0	Sigmoid	0	Sigmoid	2	Identity	0	Identity
23.	Tanh	0	Sigmoid	0	Relu	0	Relu	2	Tanh	1	Identity
24.	Sigmoid	0	Sigmoid	1	Tanh	1	Sigmoid	1	Sigmoid	1	Relu
25.	Sigmoid	0	Tanh	0	Tanh	0	Identity	0	Tanh	1	Identity
26.	Identity	0	Sigmoid	0	Identity	0	Sigmoid	0	Sigmoid	4	Sigmoid

Table 6: RNN Architectures (from the ENAS RNN search space) used across all experiments (including ENAS-RNNs, random RNNs and transfer architectures). These architectures are matched with their corresponding model configuration in Table 5 by the column 'Architecture #'. Node_#_Input refers to the index of the previous node used as input to the current node. Node_#_Op refers to the elementwise operation applied at each node (Relu, Tanh, Sigmoid, Identity). Please see Pham et al. (2018) for more details on the ENAS RNN search space.

Which Matters Most? Comparing the Impact of Concept and Document Relationships in Topic Models

Silvia Terragni♣, Debora Nozza♠, Elisabetta Fersini♣, Enza Messina♣

♣University of Milano-Bicocca, Milan,

♠Bocconi University, Milan

♣ s.terragni4@campus.unimib.it, ♠debora.nozza@unibocconi.it,
♣{elisabetta.fersini, enza.messina}@unimib.it

Abstract

Topic models have been widely used to discover hidden topics in a collection of documents. In this paper, we propose to investigate the role of two different types of relational information, i.e. document relationships and concept relationships. While exploiting the document network significantly improves topic coherence, the introduction of concepts and their relationships does not influence the results both quantitatively and qualitatively.

1 Introduction

Topic models are a suite of generative probabilistic models aimed at discovering thematic information (or topics) of an unstructured collection of documents. These models, including the well-known Latent Dirichlet Allocation (LDA) (Blei et al., 2003), usually consider texts as the unique source of information and are based on the assumption that texts are independent and identically distributed (i.i.d. assumption). However, in several real-world cases, documents are often characterized by an underlying relational structure: scientific papers can be related through citations, web pages can present hyperlinks between each other, and users in social networks can be friends. One of the first approaches that explicitly models the relationships between documents is Relational Topic Model (RTM) (Chang and Blei, 2009), based on the intuition that connected documents likely discuss the same topics.

Traditional topic models also assume that the topic assignment of a word is independent of other hidden topics, given the document's topic distribution. However, previous work proved that the introduction of additional knowledge about the relationships between words improves the coherence of the discovered topics (Yang et al., 2015b; Chen et al., 2013b,c). This type of relationship is commonly viewed as related to the concept of synonym, but this is not always the case in a real-world scenario because of word ambiguity. Following this intuition, it is thus important to take into consideration the concept behind the word alongside the word itself for understanding its relationship with other words, because it would permit to associate the same topic to words that are actually related and not only synonyms. For example, it would be possible to grasp that the word "engine", when associated with the concept of "search engine", is distant from "motor", but similar to "information retrieval". Few works investigate the use of named entities in topic models (Kim et al., 2012; Wang et al., 2017; Allahyari and Kochut, 2016), but none of them addresses the problem in relational settings.

Contribution In this paper, we investigate the role of two different types of relational information: (1) concept relationships between words and named entities obtained by Word Embeddings and (2) document-level relationships extracted by a document network. The impact of these two types of relational information is evaluated by considering traditional topic models and by introducing two novel Entity Constrained Topic Models. The source code has been made available at the following link: `https://github.com/MIND-Lab/EC-RTM`.

2 Related Work

Latent Dirichlet Allocation (LDA) (Blei et al., 2003) is a generative probabilistic model that describes a document corpus through a set of topics K, seen as distributions of words over a fixed vocabulary. A document is assumed as composed of a mixture of the topics, following a Dirichlet distribution. Words are generated according to the topics drawn from this mixture. LDA can be extended by considering different types of relational information.

Proceedings of the First Workshop on Insights from Negative Results in NLP, pages 32–40
Online, November 19, 2020. ©2020 Association for Computational Linguistics

Word-level Relational Topic Models relax the independence assumption of words in a document or in a topic. They can be roughly divided into models that encode word-order (Wang et al., 2007; Gruber et al., 2007; Lindsey et al., 2012; Fei et al., 2014; Wallach, 2006) and syntactic dependencies (Griffiths et al., 2004; Boyd-Graber and Blei, 2008), and models that incorporate semantic or domain knowledge relationships (Andrzejewski et al., 2009, 2011; Chen et al., 2013b; Yang et al., 2015b). Lately, the growing interest in word embeddings has led to the incorporation of the relationships deriving from word embeddings (Petterson et al., 2010; Zhao et al., 2017; Das et al., 2015; Nguyen et al., 2015; Li et al., 2016; Batmanghelich et al., 2016; Nozza et al., 2016).

Document-level Relational Topic Models assume that two linked documents are more likely to have similar topic distributions. Relational Topic Model (RTM) and its extensions (Chen et al., 2013a; Terragni et al., 2020; Zhang et al., 2013; Yang et al., 2015a, 2016), ground on LDA and model each link as a binary variable considering the existence of a link between pairs of documents. Other approaches include the regularized topic models (He et al., 2017; Mei et al., 2008), which augment the model's objective function with a network regularization penalty, and the Dirichlet Multinomial Regression (Mimno and McCallum, 2008) and its extensions (Hefny et al., 2013; Wahabzada et al., 2010), incorporating links by viewing them as per-document attributes. A promising paradigm uses neural variational inference to infer topics (Miao et al., 2016; Bianchi et al., 2020a,b). Neural Relational Topic Model (NRTM) (Bai et al., 2018), is based on Stacked Variational AutoEncoder (SVAE) to infer topics and predict links using a multilayer perceptron.

3   Entity Constrained Topic Models

We propose **Entity Constrained Latent Dirichlet Allocation (EC-LDA)** and **Entity Constrained Relational Topic Models (EC-RTM)**, two classes of models aimed at incorporating entity-entity and entity-word relationships in traditional topic models. Following (Yang et al., 2015b; Terragni et al., 2020), we constrain the joint distribution of LDA and RTM through the use of potential functions that model entity-entity and/or entity-word relationships. The potential can be factored out of the joint distribution and the posterior can be derived using a collapsed Gibbs sampling for inference. In addition to EC-LDA, EC-RTM also assumes that two linked documents are likely to discuss the same topics. We report the joint distributions of the proposed models in the Appendix A. For further details on Constrained Topic Models, we refer the reader to (Yang et al., 2015b; Terragni et al., 2020).

We define the vocabulary E containing the unique named entities of the corpus, and the vocabulary W containing the unique words. We derive the vocabulary Γ as the union of the word and named entity vocabularies. Relationships are denoted by the set of knowledge L and each piece of knowledge $l \in L$ is incorporated by a potential function $f_l(z, u)$, which represents a real-valued score for the hidden topic assignment z of the word or named entity token u.

We derive the knowledge L using Skip-Gram (Mikolov et al., 2013). Given a word embeddings training set composed of a large but finite set Λ, the word embeddings model can be expressed as a mapping function $C' : \Gamma \mapsto \mathbb{R}^t$. For each token $u \in \Gamma$, we define a *must-constraint* set L_u^m, containing words and named entities that are likely to share the same themes of u. L_u^m is defined as:

$$L_u^m = \{v \in \Gamma | sim(C'(u), C'(v)) > \epsilon_m\} \quad (1)$$

where sim is the cosine similarity between two vectors, and ϵ_m is a given threshold. We also define a *cannot-constraint* set L_u^c, that contains the words and named entities that are not likely to share the same themes of u. L_u^c is defined as:

$$L_u^c = \{v \in \Gamma | sim(C'(u), C'(v)) < \epsilon_c\} \quad (2)$$

where ϵ_c is a given threshold.

An example of a must-constraint set for the named entity "*Artificial neural network*" may be { *Artificial neuron, ANN, perceptron*} which contains named entities that are likely to be assigned to the same topic. Analogously, an example of cannot-constraint set for the named entity "*Artificial neural network*" may be {*Olympic games, Athlete*} which denotes named entities related to sports and not to Machine Learning.

3.1   Entity-Entity Potential Function

We specify an entity-entity potential function that models the relationships between named entities. Let $N_{ze'}$ be the maximum between 1 and the topic-entities counts, i.e. the number of occurrences of e'

assigned to topic z. The function $f_l(z, u)$ is as follows:

$$f_l(z, u) = \begin{cases} \displaystyle\sum_{\substack{e' \in L_u^m \\ e' \in E}} \log N_{ze'} + \sum_{\substack{e' \in L_u^c \\ e' \in E}} \log \frac{1}{N_{ze'}} & \text{if } u \in E \\ 0 & \text{otherwise} \end{cases}$$

$$(3)$$

The function increases the probability that the entity u will be assigned to the same topics as those of the entities belonging to L_u^m. Similarly, the potential function decreases the probability that a named entity u will be drawn from the same topics as those of entities contained in the L_u^c.

The models that can encode the Entity-Entity (EE) potential function will be referred to EC-LDA-EE and EC-RTM-EE.

3.2 Entity-Word Potential Function

Let $N_{zw'}$ be the maximum between 1 and the topic-word counts, i.e. the counts of word w' assigned to topic z. The following potential function deals with relationships between entities and word tokens:

$$f_l(z, u) = \begin{cases} \displaystyle\sum_{\substack{w' \in L_u^m \\ w' \in W}} \log N_{zw'} + \sum_{\substack{w' \in L_W^c \\ w' \in W}} \log \frac{1}{N_{zw'}} & \text{if } u \in E \\ \displaystyle\sum_{\substack{e' \in L_u^m \\ e' \in E}} \log N_{ze'} + \sum_{\substack{e' \in L_u^c \\ e' \in E}} \log \frac{1}{N_{ze'}} & \text{if } u \in W \end{cases}$$

$$(4)$$

The potential function models the following cases:
- if u is a named entity, then we consider only the words that are contained in u's must- and cannot-constraint sets, i.e. L_u^m and L_u^c;
- if u is a word, then we consider only the named entities that are contained in u's must- and cannot-constraint sets, i.e. L_u^m and L_u^c.

The models encoding Entity-Word (EW) relationships are named EC-LDA-EW and EC-RTM-EW.

4 Experimental setting

Datasets The experimental investigation has been performed on two relational benchmark datasets: (1) *Cora-ML* (McCallum et al., 2005), a citation network on the set of Machine Learning papers (Sen et al., 2008) and (2) *WebKB*[1], a website dataset collected from 4 different universities, where links are hyperlinks. Table 1 reports the basic statistics of the datasets.

Datasets	#Docs	#Links	Document Type	Link Type
Cora-ML	2,708	5,278	Title+Abstract	Citation
WebKB	877	1,608	Webpage	Hyperlink

Table 1: Statistics of benchmark datasets.

Preprocessing The identification of named entities in text is typically performed through a series of techniques that refer to the task of Named Entity Recognition (NER) (Fersini et al., 2014; Ritter et al., 2011; Li et al., 2020). Once the named entities are recognized, the next step is to associate them to unambigous concepts, as for example resources in a Knowledge Base. This process is known as the task of Named Entity Linking (NEL) (Cucerzan, 2007; Dredze et al., 2010; Basile et al., 2015; Cecchini et al., 2016; Nozza et al., 2019).

In this paper, we used the DBPedia Spotlight tool (Mendes et al., 2011) (confidence = 0.5 and support = 0.0) to identify named entities in the text and associate them to DBPedia units. We added the prefix "NE/" to each identified entity to discriminate it from words. We applied a common preprocessing technique on the text. We considered only must-constraints, that have been extracted from Wikipedia2Vec (Yamada et al., 2018). For details on the hyperparameters and preprocessing, see the Appendix A.

Compared Models We compared the proposed models (i.e., EC-LDA-EE, EC-LDA-EW and EC-RTM-EE, EC-RTM-EW) with the significant state-of-the-art approaches, i.e. Latent Dirichlet Allocation (LDA) (Blei et al., 2003), Relational Topic Model (RTM) (Chang and Blei, 2009), Stacked Variational Auto-Encoder (SVAE) and Neural Relational Topic Model (NRTM) (Bai et al., 2018).

Metrics We use *KL-U*, *KL-V*, and *KL-B* to measure semantic importance and identify junk and insignificant topics (AlSumait et al., 2009). We also measure how different are the topics from each other by computing Topic Diversity (*TD*) (Dieng et al., 2019). Finally, we consider two metrics of topic coherence, i.e. *NPMI* (Aletras and Stevenson, 2013) and C_V (Röder et al., 2015) that measure how much the 10-top words of a topic are related to each other. The scores are computed using the Palmetto toolkit[2] and Wikipedia[3] as reference corpus.

---

[1] www.cs.cmu.edu/~WebKB/ILP-data.html

[2] http://github.com/dice-group/Palmetto
[3] English Wikipedia dump of the 23rd of May, 2019.

	KL–U			KL–V			KL–B			TD			NPMI			C_V		
	10	30	50	10	30	50	10	30	50	10	30	50	10	30	50	10	30	50
LDA	1.855	1.572	1.259	1.226	1.231	1.059	0.052	0.119	0.168	0.816	0.736	0.654	0.098	0.080	0.071	0.399	0.389	0.386
RTM	2.001	2.046	1.820	1.357	1.563	1.460	0.095	**0.207**	**0.283**	0.814	**0.747**	0.666	0.099	0.082	0.071	0.348	0.391	0.392
EC-LDA-EE	1.845	1.520	1.375	1.225	1.238	1.066	0.052	0.119	0.167	0.814	0.742	0.659	0.098	0.079	0.069	0.397	0.390	0.389
EC-LDA-EW	1.800	1.518	1.381	1.230	1.236	1.065	0.052	0.119	0.168	0.817	0.740	0.660	0.094	0.079	0.070	0.395	0.389	0.387
EC-RTM-EE	2.033	**2.082**	**1.849**	**1.362**	1.564	**1.472**	0.095	0.205	0.280	0.817	0.747	**0.675**	**0.099**	0.081	0.071	0.402	0.394	0.392
EC-RTM-EW	**2.079**	1.990	1.643	1.361	**1.565**	1.470	**0.096**	0.206	0.282	0.820	0.746	0.671	0.098	**0.082**	**0.072**	0.340	0.392	0.392
SVAE	-	-	-	-	-	-	-	-	-	**0.893**	0.694	0.577	-0.099	-0.095	-0.096	**0.456**	**0.456**	**0.453**
NRTM	-	-	-	-	-	-	-	-	-	0.857	0.525	0.381	-0.083	-0.082	-0.082	0.442	0.447	0.446

Table 2: Performance on the *Cora-ML* dataset with the number of topics equal to 10, 30, 50.

	KL–U			KL–V			KL–B			TD			NPMI			C_V		
	10	30	50	10	30	50	10	30	50	10	30	50	10	30	50	10	30	50
LDA	1.695	1.256	1.130	1.054	0.943	0.775	0.069	0.142	0.199	0.761	0.617	0.538	0.039	0.040	0.030	0.378	0.379	0.379
RTM	**1.986**	1.795	1.430	**1.202**	1.239	1.109	**0.119**	0.225	**0.303**	0.760	0.608	0.532	0.043	0.043	0.036	0.377	0.380	0.380
EC-LDA-EE	1.643	1.289	1.061	1.055	0.948	0.780	0.069	0.143	0.200	0.769	0.623	0.542	0.043	0.041	0.033	0.379	0.380	0.381
EC-LDA-EW	1.736	1.345	1.075	1.062	0.981	0.784	0.069	0.138	0.198	0.764	**0.651**	**0.547**	0.042	0.038	0.033	0.376	0.381	0.382
EC-RTM-EE	1.867	**1.944**	1.468	1.199	1.246	1.119	0.118	**0.226**	0.303	0.760	0.612	0.536	**0.048**	**0.043**	**0.039**	0.377	0.382	0.381
EC-RTM-EW	1.979	1.786	**1.646**	1.199	**1.294**	**1.127**	0.117	0.217	0.302	0.759	0.639	0.543	0.045	0.042	0.036	0.377	0.382	0.384
SVAE	-	-	-	-	-	-	-	-	-	**0.829**	0.563	0.454	-0.116	-0.110	-0.112	**0.460**	0.450	0.452
NRTM	-	-	-	-	-	-	-	-	-	0.734	0.360	0.283	-0.114	-0.117	-0.119	0.454	**0.455**	**0.458**

Table 3: Performance on the *WebKB* dataset with the number of topics equal to 10, 30, 50.

5 Experimental Results

Quantitative Results Tables 2 and 3 show the performance of the models in terms of all the considered scores over an increasing number of topics on the datasets.[4] Results show that models that consider relational information generally obtain higher performance than their non-relational counterpart. Differently, the introduction of the concept constraints in EC-RTM-EE and EC-RTM-EW models does not seem to provide significant improvements with respect to RTM. This can be motivated by the fact that the constraint sets additionally included in the EC-RTM models are already captured in the word-topic distribution obtained by RTM.

Different behaviors can be observed for the C_V scores, for which NRTM and SVAE obtain significantly higher performance. This opposite trend with respect to the other topic scores can be explained by the fact that C_V rewards the presence of rare words even if they are contained in junk topics as stated by the author of (Röder et al., 2015)[5].

Qualitative Results In Table 4, we show the top-10 words for Cora-ML concerning an example topic "Genetic Programming" for EC-RTM-EE, EC-RTM-EW, LDA, RTM, SVAE, and NRTM. To analyze if the named entity annotation can contribute to topic interpretability, we report the words

Models	Top-10 words
LDA*	problem genetic algorithms problems programming search optimization fitness population space
RTM*	genetic control programming fitness reinforcement population algorithms paper environment behavior
EC-RTM-EE	NE/Genetic_programming programs NE/Genetic_algorithm population fitness genetic evolutionary program NE/Evolution strategies
EC-RTM-EW	NE/Genetic_programming NE/Genetic_algorithm population fitness genetic evolutionary NE/Evolution encoding operator operators
SVAE	koza NE/Multidisciplinary_design_optimization splice bitsback NE/Genetic_programming fitness orientation NE/Ploidy NE/Exon coded
NRTM	genetic reactive NE/Genetic_programming NE/Case casebased neuroevolution ssa NE/Genetic_algorithm coevolutionary problemsolving

Table 4: "Genetic Programming" topic in *Cora-ML*.

of LDA and RTM (referred as LDA* and RTM*) run on Cora-ML composed of words only. As expected from the quantitative results, the topics extracted by the proposed models do not significantly differ from RTM*, further demonstrating the hypothesis that the imposed constraints were already captured by the original model.

Qualitative considerations can be made regarding the exploitation of the novel entity-level modeling of the documents. While this representation leads to topics containing explicit concepts (e.g., "NE/Genetic_programming"), topics obtained by RTM* seem to be equally interpretable because they can identify named entities in the form of

---

[4]Computing the KL- metrics is impractical for SVAE and NRTM since they do not model word- and document-topic distributions.

[5]https://bit.ly/3jApSAC

distinct words (e.g., "genetic, programming, algorithm"). Moreover, the difference in representation is only evident when named entities are composed of two or more words (e.g., "NE/Evolution" and "evolution" are equivalent). The benefit of applying NEEL techniques for recognizing named entities in topics may come in handy for automatically providing links to KB (such as Wikipedia), at the computational cost of discovering named entities. Moreover, the proposed novel potential function would allow users to artificially manipulate the model to derive explanations for the topic assignments or force entities in the same topic based on human domain knowledge.

Regarding SVAE and NRTM, their topics seem hard to interpret from a qualitative perspective, confirming the results of the quantitative evaluation.

6 Conclusion

We propose two classes of Entity Constrained Topic Models for incorporating different types of relational information. Results demonstrated that models exploiting document-level relationships achieve improvements with respect to their non-relational counterparts. Differently, concept relationships do not significantly improve either topic coherence or interpretability. As future work, we plan to investigate multi-relational topic models extracting other relationships from the data and to exploit contextual encoding method for entity representation also in multilingual settings (Devlin et al., 2019; Nozza et al., 2020).

References

Nikolaos Aletras and Mark Stevenson. 2013. Evaluating topic coherence using distributional semantics. In *Proceedings of the 10th International Conference on Computational Semantics, IWCS 2013, March 19-22, 2013, University of Potsdam, Potsdam, Germany*, pages 13–22. The Association for Computer Linguistics.

Mehdi Allahyari and Krys Kochut. 2016. Discovering coherent topics with entity topic models. In *Proceedings of the 2016 IEEE/WIC/ACM International Conference on Web Intelligence, WI 2016, Omaha, NE, USA, October 13-16, 2016*, pages 26–33.

Loulwah AlSumait, Daniel Barbará, James Gentle, and Carlotta Domeniconi. 2009. Topic significance ranking of LDA generative models. In *Machine Learning and Knowledge Discovery in Databases, European Conference, ECML PKDD 2009*, pages 67–82.

David Andrzejewski, Xiaojin Zhu, and Mark Craven. 2009. Incorporating domain knowledge into topic modeling via dirichlet forest priors. In *Proceedings of the 26th Annual International Conference on Machine Learning, ICML 2009, Montreal, Quebec, Canada, June 14-18, 2009*, pages 25–32.

David Andrzejewski, Xiaojin Zhu, Mark Craven, and Benjamin Recht. 2011. A framework for incorporating general domain knowledge into latent dirichlet allocation using first-order logic. In *IJCAI 2011, Proceedings of the 22nd International Joint Conference on Artificial Intelligence, Barcelona, Catalonia, Spain, July 16-22, 2011*, pages 1171–1177.

Haoli Bai, Zhuangbin Chen, Michael R. Lyu, Irwin King, and Zenglin Xu. 2018. Neural relational topic models for scientific article analysis. In *Proceedings of the 27th ACM International Conference on Information and Knowledge Management, CIKM 2018, Torino, Italy, October 22-26, 2018*, pages 27–36.

Pierpaolo Basile, Annalina Caputo, Giovanni Semeraro, and Fedelucio Narducci. 2015. UNIBA: Exploiting a Distributional Semantic Model for Disambiguating and Linking Entities in Tweets. In *Proc. of the 5th Workshop on Making Sense of Microposts co-located with the 24th International World Wide Web Conference*, volume 1395, page 62.

Kayhan Batmanghelich, Ardavan Saeedi, Karthik Narasimhan, and Samuel Gershman. 2016. Nonparametric spherical topic modeling with word embeddings. In *Proceedings of the 54th Annual Meeting of the Association for Computational Linguistics, ACL 2016, August 7-12, 2016, Berlin, Germany, Volume 2: Short Papers*.

Federico Bianchi, Silvia Terragni, and Dirk Hovy. 2020a. Pre-training is a hot topic: Contextualized document embeddings improve topic coherence. *arXiv preprint arXiv:2004.03974*.

Federico Bianchi, Silvia Terragni, Dirk Hovy, Debora Nozza, and Elisabetta Fersini. 2020b. Cross-lingual contextualized topic models with zero-shot learning. *arXiv preprint arXiv:2004.07737*.

David M. Blei, Andrew Y. Ng, and Michael I. Jordan. 2003. Latent dirichlet allocation. *Journal of Machine Learning Research*, 3:993–1022.

Jordan L. Boyd-Graber and David M. Blei. 2008. Syntactic topic models. In *Advances in Neural Information Processing Systems 21, Proceedings of the 22nd Annual Conference on Neural Information Processing Systems, Vancouver, British Columbia, Canada, December 8-11, 2008*, pages 185–192.

Flavio Massimiliano Cecchini, Elisabetta Fersini, Pikakshi Manchanda, Enza Messina, Debora Nozza, Matteo Palmonari, and Cezar Sas. 2016. UNIMIB@NEEL-IT: Named Entity Recognition and Linking of Italian Tweets. In *Proc. of 3rd Italian Conference on Computational Linguistics & 5th*

Evaluation Campaign of Natural Language Processing and Speech Tools for Italian, volume 1749.

Jonathan Chang and David M. Blei. 2009. Relational topic models for document networks. In *Proceedings of the 12th International Conference on Artificial Intelligence and Statistics, AISTATS 2009, Clearwater Beach, Florida, USA, April 16-18, 2009*, pages 81–88.

Ning Chen, Jun Zhu, Fei Xia, and Bo Zhang. 2013a. Generalized relational topic models with data augmentation. In *Proceedings of the 23rd International Joint Conference on Artificial Intelligence, IJCAI 2013, Beijing, China, August 3-9, 2013*, pages 1273–1279.

Zhiyuan Chen, Arjun Mukherjee, Bing Liu, Meichun Hsu, Malú Castellanos, and Riddhiman Ghosh. 2013b. Discovering coherent topics using general knowledge. In *Proceedings of the 22nd ACM International Conference on Information and Knowledge Management, CIKM'13, San Francisco, CA, USA, October 27 - November 1, 2013*, pages 209–218.

Zhiyuan Chen, Arjun Mukherjee, Bing Liu, Meichun Hsu, Malú Castellanos, and Riddhiman Ghosh. 2013c. Leveraging Multi-Domain Prior Knowledge in Topic Models. In *Proceedings of the 23rd International Joint Conference on Artificial Intelligence (IJCAI)*, pages 2071–2077.

Silviu Cucerzan. 2007. Large-Scale Named Entity Disambiguation Based on Wikipedia Data. In *Proc. of the 2007 Joint Conference on Empirical Methods in Natural Language Processing and Computational Natural Language Learning*, pages 708–716.

Rajarshi Das, Manzil Zaheer, and Chris Dyer. 2015. Gaussian LDA for topic models with word embeddings. In *Proceedings of the 53rd Annual Meeting of the Association for Computational Linguistics and the 7th International Joint Conference on Natural Language Processing of the Asian Federation of Natural Language Processing, ACL 2015, July 26-31, 2015, Beijing, China, Volume 1: Long Papers*, pages 795–804.

Jacob Devlin, Ming-Wei Chang, Kenton Lee, and Kristina Toutanova. 2019. BERT: pre-training of deep bidirectional transformers for language understanding. In *Proceedings of the 2019 Conference of the North American Chapter of the Association for Computational Linguistics: Human Language Technologies, NAACL-HLT 2019, Volume 1 (Long and Short Papers)*, pages 4171–4186. Association for Computational Linguistics.

Adji B. Dieng, Francisco J. R. Ruiz, and David M. Blei. 2019. Topic modeling in embedding spaces. *CoRR*, abs/1907.04907.

Mark Dredze, Paul McNamee, Delip Rao, Adam Gerber, and Tim Finin. 2010. Entity disambiguation for knowledge base population. In *Proc. of the 23rd*

International Conference on Computational Linguistics, pages 277–285.

Geli Fei, Zhiyuan Chen, and Bing Liu. 2014. Review topic discovery with phrases using the pólya urn model. In *Proceedings of the 25th International Conference on Computational Linguistics, COLING 2014, August 23-29, 2014, Dublin, Ireland*, pages 667–676.

Elisabetta Fersini, Enza Messina, Giovanni Felici, and Dan Roth. 2014. Soft-constrained inference for Named Entity Recognition. *Information Processing & Management*, 50(5):807–819.

T. L. Griffiths and M. Steyvers. 2004. Finding Scientific Topics. *Proceedings of the National Academy of Sciences*, 101(Suppl. 1):5228–5235.

Thomas L. Griffiths, Mark Steyvers, David M. Blei, and Joshua B. Tenenbaum. 2004. Integrating topics and syntax. In *Advances in Neural Information Processing Systems 17 [Neural Information Processing Systems, NIPS 2004, December 13-18, 2004, Vancouver, British Columbia, Canada]*, pages 537–544.

Amit Gruber, Yair Weiss, and Michal Rosen-Zvi. 2007. Hidden topic markov models. In *Proceedings of the 11th International Conference on Artificial Intelligence and Statistics, AISTATS 2007, San Juan, Puerto Rico, March 21-24, 2007*, pages 163–170.

Yuan He, Cheng Wang, and Changjun Jiang. 2017. Modeling document networks with tree-averaged copula regularization. In *Proceedings of the 10th ACM International Conference on Web Search and Data Mining, WSDM 2017, Cambridge, United Kingdom, February 6-10, 2017*, pages 691–699.

Ahmed Hefny, Geoffrey Gordon, and Katia Sycara. 2013. Random walk features for network-aware topic models. In *NIPS 2013 Workshop on Frontiers of Network Analysis*, volume 6.

Hyungsul Kim, Yizhou Sun, Julia Hockenmaier, and Jiawei Han. 2012. ETM: entity topic models for mining documents associated with entities. In *Proceedings of the 12th IEEE International Conference on Data Mining, ICDM 2012*, pages 349–358.

Chenliang Li, Haoran Wang, Zhiqian Zhang, Aixin Sun, and Zongyang Ma. 2016. Topic modeling for short texts with auxiliary word embeddings. In *Proceedings of the 39th International ACM SIGIR conference on Research and Development in Information Retrieval, SIGIR 2016, Pisa, Italy, July 17-21, 2016*, pages 165–174.

Jing Li, Aixin Sun, Jianglei Han, and Chenliang Li. 2020. A survey on deep learning for named entity recognition. *IEEE Transactions on Knowledge and Data Engineering*.

Robert V. Lindsey, William Headden, and Michael Stipicevic. 2012. A phrase-discovering topic model using hierarchical pitman-yor processes. In *Proceedings of the 2012 Joint Conference on Empirical Methods in Natural Language Processing and Computational Natural Language Learning, EMNLP-CoNLL 2012, July 12-14, 2012, Jeju Island, Korea*, pages 214–222.

Andrew McCallum, Andrés Corrada-Emmanuel, and Xuerui Wang. 2005. Topic and role discovery in social networks. In *Proceedings of the 19th International Joint Conference on Artificial Intelligence, IJCAI-05, Edinburgh, Scotland, UK, July 30 - August 5, 2005*, pages 786–791.

Qiaozhu Mei, Deng Cai, Duo Zhang, and ChengXiang Zhai. 2008. Topic modeling with network regularization. In *Proceedings of the 17th International Conference on World Wide Web, WWW 2008, Beijing, China, April 21-25, 2008*, pages 101–110.

Pablo N. Mendes, Max Jakob, Andrés García-Silva, and Christian Bizer. 2011. Dbpedia spotlight: shedding light on the web of documents. In *Proceedings of the 7th International Conference on Semantic Systems, I-SEMANTICS 2011, Graz, Austria, September 7-9, 2011*, ACM International Conference Proceeding Series, pages 1–8. ACM.

Yishu Miao, Lei Yu, and Phil Blunsom. 2016. Neural variational inference for text processing. In *Proceedings of the 33nd International Conference on Machine Learning, ICML 2016, New York City, NY, USA, June 19-24, 2016*, volume 48 of *JMLR Workshop and Conference Proceedings*, pages 1727–1736. JMLR.org.

Tomas Mikolov, Ilya Sutskever, Kai Chen, Gregory S. Corrado, and Jeffrey Dean. 2013. Distributed representations of words and phrases and their compositionality. In *Advances in Neural Information Processing Systems 26: 27th Annual Conference on Neural Information Processing Systems 2013. Proceedings of a meeting held December 5-8, 2013, Lake Tahoe, Nevada, United States.*, pages 3111–3119.

David M. Mimno and Andrew McCallum. 2008. Topic models conditioned on arbitrary features with dirichlet-multinomial regression. In *UAI 2008, Proceedings of the 24th Conference in Uncertainty in Artificial Intelligence, Helsinki, Finland, July 9-12, 2008*, pages 411–418.

Dat Quoc Nguyen, Richard Billingsley, Lan Du, and Mark Johnson. 2015. Improving topic models with latent feature word representations. *Transactions of the Association for Computational Linguistics*, 3:299–313.

Debora Nozza, Federico Bianchi, and Dirk Hovy. 2020. What the [mask]? making sense of language-specific bert models. *arXiv preprint arXiv:2003.02912*.

Debora Nozza, Elisabetta Fersini, and Enza Messina. 2016. Unsupervised irony detection: a probabilistic model with word embeddings. In *International Conference on Knowledge Discovery and Information Retrieval*, volume 2, pages 68–76. SCITEPRESS.

Debora Nozza, Cezar Sas, Elisabetta Fersini, and Enza Messina. 2019. Word embeddings for unsupervised named entity linking. In *International Conference on Knowledge Science, Engineering and Management*, pages 115–132. Springer.

James Petterson, Alexander J. Smola, Tibério S. Caetano, Wray L. Buntine, and Shravan M. Narayanamurthy. 2010. Word features for latent dirichlet allocation. In *Advances in Neural Information Processing Systems 23: 24th Annual Conference on Neural Information Processing Systems 2010. Proceedings of a meeting held 6-9 December 2010, Vancouver, British Columbia, Canada.*, pages 1921–1929.

Alan Ritter, Sam Clark, Mausam, and Oren Etzioni. 2011. Named Entity Recognition in Tweets: An Experimental Study. In *Proc. of the 2011 Conference on Empirical Methods in Natural Language Processing*, pages 1524–1534.

Michael Röder, Andreas Both, and Alexander Hinneburg. 2015. Exploring the space of topic coherence measures. In *Proceedings of the 8th ACM International Conference on Web Search and Data Mining, WSDM 2015, Shanghai, China, February 2-6, 2015*, pages 399–408.

Prithviraj Sen, Galileo Namata, Mustafa Bilgic, Lise Getoor, Brian Gallagher, and Tina Eliassi-Rad. 2008. Collective classification in network data. *AI Magazine*, 29(3):93–106.

Silvia Terragni, Elisabetta Fersini, and Enza Messina. 2020. Constrained relational topic models. *Information Sciences*, 512:581 – 594.

Mirwaes Wahabzada, Zhao Xu, and Kristian Kersting. 2010. Topic models conditioned on relations. In *Machine Learning and Knowledge Discovery in Databases, European Conference, ECML PKDD 2010, Barcelona, Spain, September 20-24, 2010, Proceedings, Part III*, pages 402–417.

Hanna M. Wallach. 2006. Topic modeling: beyond bag-of-words. In *Proceedings of the 23rd International Conference on Machine Learning, (ICML 2006), Pittsburgh, Pennsylvania, USA, June 25-29, 2006*, pages 977–984.

Qilin Wang, Dandan Song, and Xiuquan Li. 2017. Incorporating entity correlation knowledge into topic modeling. In *Proceedings of the IEEE International Conference on Big Knowledge, ICBK 2017, Hefei, China, August 9-10, 2017*, pages 254–258.

Xuerui Wang, Andrew McCallum, and Xing Wei. 2007. Topical n-grams: Phrase and topic discovery, with an application to information retrieval. In *Proceedings of the 7th IEEE International Conference on Data Mining (ICDM 2007), October 28-31, 2007, Omaha, Nebraska, USA*, pages 697–702.

Ikuya Yamada, Akari Asai, Hiroyuki Shindo, Hideaki Takeda, and Yoshiyasu Takefuji. 2018. Wikipedia2vec: an optimized tool for learning embeddings of words and entities from wikipedia. *arXiv preprint arXiv:1812.06280*.

Weiwei Yang, Jordan L. Boyd-Graber, and Philip Resnik. 2015a. Birds of a feather linked together: A discriminative topic model using link-based priors. In *Proceedings of the 2015 Conference on Empirical Methods in Natural Language Processing, EMNLP 2015, Lisbon, Portugal, September 17-21, 2015*, pages 261–266.

Weiwei Yang, Jordan L. Boyd-Graber, and Philip Resnik. 2016. A discriminative topic model using document network structure. In *Proceedings of the 54th Annual Meeting of the Association for Computational Linguistics, ACL 2016, August 7-12, 2016, Berlin, Germany, Volume 1: Long Papers*.

Yi Yang, Doug Downey, and Jordan L. Boyd-Graber. 2015b. Efficient methods for incorporating knowledge into topic models. In *Proceedings of the 2015 Conference on Empirical Methods in Natural Language Processing, EMNLP 2015, Lisbon, Portugal, September 17-21, 2015*, pages 308–317.

Aonan Zhang, Jun Zhu, and Bo Zhang. 2013. Sparse relational topic models for document networks. In *Machine Learning and Knowledge Discovery in Databases - European Conference, ECML PKDD 2013, Prague, Czech Republic, September 23-27, 2013, Proceedings, Part I*, pages 670–685.

He Zhao, Lan Du, and Wray L. Buntine. 2017. A word embeddings informed focused topic model. In *Proceedings of The 9th Asian Conference on Machine Learning, ACML 2017, Seoul, Korea, November 15-17, 2017.*, pages 423–438.

A Appendix

A.1 Preprocessing

We lowercased the text, removed English stopwords and words occurring less than 10 times, and filtered out documents composed of less than 2 words. Details on the vocabulary composition are reported in Table 5.

A.2 Hyperparameters

Each experiment, with a given set of parameters, is repeated for 100 times and the performance measures are averaged by the number of the samples.

The hyperparameters α and β are set equal to $50/K$ and 0.1 respectively (as reported in (Griffiths and Steyvers, 2004)) for all the considered models. All the compared models are trained for 1,500 Gibbs iterations.

In our evaluation, we consider only must-constraint relations that can be generated by entities

and words. To select the most appropriate value for the threshold ϵ_m, we studied the performance of the topic coherence of our models by varying the value of the parameter. The values for the models with the potential functions EE and EW are, respectively, 0.8 and 0.7 for the dataset Cora, and 0.6 and 0.6 for WebKB.

A.3 Joint Distributions of the Proposed Models

For the sake of completeness, we report the joint distribution of the proposed models. Entity Constrained Latent Dirichlet Allocation (EC-LDA) defines the following joint probability distribution:

$$P(\mathbf{u}, \mathbf{z}, \boldsymbol{\theta}, \boldsymbol{\Phi} | \alpha, \beta, L) \propto \qquad (5a)$$

$$\prod_{d=1}^{D} p(\theta_d | \alpha) \prod_{n=1}^{N_d} p(u_{nd} | \Phi_{z_{nd}}) p(z_{nd} | \theta_d) \quad (5b)$$

$$\prod_{k}^{K} p(\Phi_k | \beta) \cdot \xi(\mathbf{z}, L) \qquad (5c)$$

where

- D denotes the set of documents
- N_d is the length of document d
- K denotes the fixed number of topics
- $\mathbf{u}$ denotes the set of word and named entity tokens
- $\mathbf{z}$ represents the set of topic assignments
- $\boldsymbol{\theta}$ represents the document-topic distribution
- $\boldsymbol{\Phi}$ denotes the topic-word distribution
- α and β are the Dirichlet hyperparameters related to θ and Φ
- $\xi(\mathbf{z}, L) = \prod_{z \in \mathbf{z}} \exp f_l(z, u)$.

Similarly, the joint probability distribution of Entity Constrained Relational Topic Models is defined as follows:

$$P(\mathbf{u}, \mathbf{z}, \mathbf{y}, \boldsymbol{\theta}, \boldsymbol{\Phi} | \alpha, \beta, \eta, \nu, L) \propto \qquad (6a)$$

$$\prod_{d=1}^{D} p(\theta_d | \alpha) \prod_{n=1}^{N_d} p(u_{nd} | \Phi_{z_{nd}}) p(z_{nd} | \theta_d) \qquad (6b)$$

$$\prod_{k}^{K} p(\Phi_k | \beta) \prod_{\substack{d,d' \in D \\ d' \neq d}} \psi_\sigma(y_{d,d'} | z_d, z_{d'}, \eta, \nu) \cdot \xi(\mathbf{z}, L)$$

$$(6c)$$

where ψ_σ is the link probability function defined as $\psi_\sigma(y = 1) = \sigma(\eta^T(\overline{\mathbf{z}}_d \circ \overline{\mathbf{z}}_{d'}) + \nu)$, σ is the sigmoid function and $\overline{\mathbf{z}}_d = \frac{1}{N_d} \sum_n z_{nd}$. The link

	Processed corpus			Unprocessed corpus
	# unique entities	# unique words	# unique entities and words	# unique words
Cora	384	2,675	3,059	3,012
WebKB	355	1,874	2,229	2,247

Table 5: Summary of the vocabularies for the benchmark datasets before and after the preprocessing phase.

function models each per-pair binary variable related to links as a logistic regression (with hidden covariates), parameterized by coefficients η and intercept ν.

A.4 Computing Infrastructure

Experiments were run on three common computers using CPUs. Models can be run with basic infrastructure. Two computers have 8GB of RAM and the other has 16GB of RAM.

On Task-Level Dialogue Composition of Generative Transformer Model

Prasanna Parthasarathi [*]
McGill University / Mila

Arvind Neelakantan [†]
OpenAI

Sharan Narang
Google Brain

Abstract

Task-oriented dialogue systems help users accomplish tasks such as booking a movie ticket and ordering food via conversation. Generative models parameterized by a deep neural network are widely used for next turn response generation in such systems. It is natural for users of the system to want to accomplish multiple tasks within the same conversation, but the ability of generative models to compose multiple tasks is not well studied. In this work, we begin by studying the effect of training human-human task-oriented dialogues towards improving the ability to compose multiple tasks on Transformer generative models. To that end, we propose and explore two solutions: (1) creating synthetic multiple task dialogue data for training from human-human single task dialogue and (2) forcing the encoder representation to be invariant to single and multiple task dialogues using an auxiliary loss. The results from our experiments highlight the difficulty of even the sophisticated variant of transformer model in learning to compose multiple tasks from single task dialogues.

1 Introduction

Recent years have seen a tremendous surge in the application of deep learning methods for dialogue in general (Vinyals and Le, 2015; Rojas-Barahona et al., 2017; Budzianowski et al., 2018; Lewis et al., 2017) and task-oriented dialogue (Wen et al., 2015; Einolghozati et al., 2019; Neelakantan et al., 2019) specifically. Task-oriented dialogue systems help users accomplish tasks such as booking a movie ticket and ordering food via conversation. Generative models are a popular choice for next turn response generation in such systems

(Rojas-Barahona et al., 2017; Wen et al., 2017; Eric and Manning, 2017). These models are typically learned using large amounts of dialogue data for every task (Budzianowski et al., 2018; Byrne et al., 2019). It is natural for users of the task-oriented dialogue system to want to accomplish multiple tasks within the same conversation, e.g. booking a movie ticket and ordering a taxi to the movie theater within the same conversation. The brute-force solution would require collecting dialogue data for every task combination which might be practically infeasible given the combinatorially many possibilities.

While the ability of generative dialogue models to compose multiple tasks has not yet been studied in the literature, there has been some investigation on the compositionality skills of deep neural networks. Lake and Baroni (2017) propose a suite of tasks to evaluate a method's compositionality skills and find that deep neural networks generalize to unseen compositions only in a limited way. Kottur et al. (2017) analyze whether the language emerged when multiple generative models interact with each other is compositional and conclude that compositionality arises only with strong regularization.

Motivated by the practical infeasibility of collecting data for combinatorially many task compositions, we focus on task-level compositionality of text response generation models. We begin by studying the effect of training data size of human-human multiple task dialogues on the performance of Transformer (Vaswani et al., 2017) generative models. Next, we explore two solutions to improve task-level compositionality. First, we propose a data augmentation approach (Simard et al., 2003; Schmidhuber, 2012; Krizhevsky et al., 2012; Baird, 1992; Sennrich et al., 2016) where we create synthetic multiple task dialogues for training from human-human single task dialogue; we add a portion of one dialogue as a prefix to another to

---

[*] This work was done when the author was an intern at Google Brain. `pparth2@cs.mcgill.ca`

[†] This work was done when the author was a Research Scientist at Google Brain.

Proceedings of the First Workshop on Insights from Negative Results in NLP, pages 41–47
Online, November 19, 2020. ©2020 Association for Computational Linguistics

simulate multiple task dialogues during training. As a second solution, we draw inspiration from the domain adaptation literature (Ganin and Lempitsky, 2015; Tzeng et al., 2015; Xu and Yang, 2017; Chen et al., 2016; Xu et al., 2017; Sun et al., 2018) and encourage the model to learn domain invariant representations with an auxiliary loss to learn representations that are invariant to single and multiple task dialogues.

We conduct our experiments on the Multiwoz dataset (Budzianowski et al., 2018). The dataset contains both single and multiple task dialogues for training and evaluation. In Multiwoz, the tasks in multiple task dialogues are only the combinations of tasks in single task dialogues. This allows the dataset to be an appropriate benchmark for our experiments.

To summarize, our key findings are:

- We study task-level compositionality of text response generation models and find that they are heavily reliant on multiple task conversations at train time to do well on such conversations at test time.

- We explore two novel unsupervised solutions to improve task-level compositionality: (1) creating synthetic multiple task dialogue data from human-human single task dialogue and (2) forcing the encoder representation to be invariant to single and multiple task dialogues using an auxiliary loss.

- Highlighting the difficulty of composing tasks in generative dialogues with experiments on the Multiwoz dataset, where both the methods combined result only in a 8.5% BLEU (Papineni et al., 2002) score improvement when zero-shot evaluated on multiple task dialogues.

2   Background

Let $d_1, d_2, \ldots, d_M$ be the dialogues in the training set and every dialogue $d_m = ((u_m^1, a_m^1), (u_m^2, a_m^2), \ldots, (u_m^{n_m}, a_m^{n_m})$ ($\forall m \in \{1, 2, \ldots, M\}$) consists of n_m turns each of user and assistant. Further each user and assistant turn consists of a sequence of word tokens. The individual dialogue could be either single task or multiple task depending on the number of tasks being accomplished in the dialogue.

The response generation model is trained to generate each turn of the assistant response given the conversation history. The generative model learns a probability distribution given by $P(a^i \mid (u^1, a^1), \ldots, (u^{i-1}, a^{i-1}), u^i)$. We drop the symbol m that denotes a particular training example for simplicity. The assistant turn a^i consists of a sequence of word tokens, $a^i = (w_1^i, w_2^i, \ldots, w_{l^i}^i)$. The response generation model factorizes the joint distribution left-to-right given by,

$$P(a^i \mid x^i) = \prod_{j=1}^{l^i} P(w_j \mid x^i, w_1^i, \ldots, w_{j-1}^i)$$

where $x^i = ((u^1, a^1), \ldots, (u^{i-1}, a^{i-1}), u^i)$ refers to the conversation history till the ith turn.

We use a Transformer (Vaswani et al., 2017) sequence-to-sequence model to parameterize the above distribution. Given a training set of dialogues, the parameters of the Transformer model are learned to optimize the conditional language modelling objective given by,

$$L_{LM} = \sum_{m=1}^{M} \sum_{i=1}^{n_m} \log P(a^i \mid x^i, \Theta) \qquad (1)$$

where Θ refers to the parameters of the Transformer model.

3   Data Augmentation

The first solution we explore for task compositionality generates synthetic multiple task dialogues for training from human-human single task dialogues [1]. Here, we sample two dialogues from the training set, and add a portion of one dialogue as a prefix to another. While this procedure might not create dialogues of the quality equivalent to human-human multiple task dialogue, it is an unsupervised way to create approximate multiple task dialogues that the model could theoretically benefit from.

Concretely, we randomly sample two single task dialogues d_i and d_j from the training set and create a noisy multiple task dialogue by adding a fraction of the dialogue d_j as a prefix to dialogue d_i. The fraction of dialogue taken from dialogue d_j is given by the hyperparameter $augment\_fraction$. The number of times dialogue d_i is augmented by a randomly sampled dialogue is given by the hyperparameter $augment\_fold$.

We consider two strategies for sampling the dialogue d_j. In $Random\_Augment$, the dialogue is uniformly randomly sampled from the remainder of the training set. A potential issue with the random strategy is that it might create spurious

---

[1]Code repository

task combinations and the model might fit to this noise. Motivated by the spurious task combination phenomenon, we consider another sampling strategy $Targeted\_Augment$ where we create synthetic multiple task dialogues only for task combinations that exist in the development set. Here, d_j is sampled from a set of dialogues whose task is compatible with the task of dialogue d_i. The Transformer model is now trained on the augmented training set using the objective function given in Equation 1. The effect of the sampling strategy and the hyperparameters on the model performance is discussed in the experiments section (Section 5).

4 Domain Invariant Transformer

We propose Domain Invariant Transformer model (Figure 1) to maintain a domain invariant representation of the encoder by training the encoder representation for an auxiliary task. Here, the auxiliary task for the network is to predict the label $,^i\hat{l},$ denoting the type of task (single or multi-task) in the encoded conversation history. The model takes as input the sequence of byte pair encoded tokens that are represented at the encoder hidden state as a set of attention weights from the multi-head multiple layer attention mechanism of transformer. The conditional language model (Equation 1) is learnt by a transformer decoder on top that attends over the encoder states.

The discriminator task network is trained with average pooling of the encoder summary over the attention heads (h_j)as shown in Equation 2.

$$^i e^s = \sum_{j=1}^{k} \frac{(h_j)}{k} \qquad (2)$$

The average pooled encoder summary is passed as input to a two-layer feed forward discriminator. The discriminator network has a dropout (Srivastava et al., 2014) layer in-between the two fully connected layers (f_1 and f_2) (Equation 3).

$$\hat{y}_i = f_2 \left(f_1 \left(^i e^s \right) \right) \qquad (3)$$

The binary cross-entropy loss, L_{disc}, for the predicted label, $\hat{y}_i$, an input context i is computed as in Equation 4.

$$L_{disc} = -\left(y_i \log \left(\hat{y}_i \right) + (1 - y_i) \log \left(1 - \hat{y}_i \right) \right) \qquad (4)$$

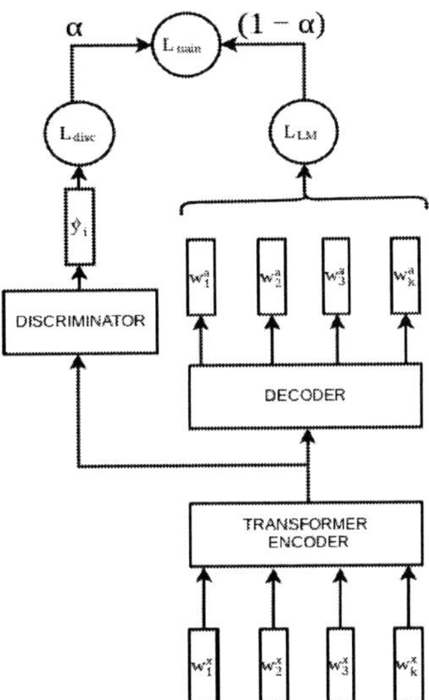

Figure 1: Domain Invariant Transformer Architecture.

The Domain Invariant Transformer model optimizes a convex combination of the two losses as shown in Equation 5.

$$L_{train} = \alpha * L_{disc} + (1 - \alpha) * L_{LM} \qquad (5)$$

The language model loss makes sure that the model learns to generate the next utterance while the discriminator loss makes sure the model is aware of the nature of task. To understand the effect of the auxiliary loss we experiment with different values for α (ref Appendix).

5 Experiments

5.1 Importance of multiple task dialogues

We measure the importance of multiple task dialogue on the overall performance of transformer by training the model with varying amount of multiple task dialogues and keeping the task distribution between multiple and single domain dialogues almost similar in the experiments. We keep increasing the number of multiple task dialogues while reducing the single task dialogues to keep the total number of dialogues constant at $2, 150$. The model should be able to learn to generalize to multiple tasks as the set of tasks are the same between the train and test sets with only the nature in which the task is posed by the user is different. We use the Tensor2Tensor (Vaswani et al., 2018) framework to run our experiments with (tiny) hyper-parameter setting in the framework.

Training Data		BLEU	
Single	Multiple	Multiple Only	Overall
2150	0	7.17	6.81
1836	314	7.25	6.87
1522	628	7.94	7.84
1208	942	8.68	8.68
894	1256	8.83	8.27
580	1570	9.33	8.84
266	1884	9.10	9.25

Table 1: Ablation study to understand the usefulness of Multiple task dialogues.

As shown in Table 1, the quality of the model improves significantly as number of multiple task dialogues increases. Interestingly, even though the total number of dialogues are kept fixed, the overall validation BLEU score also improves as the number of multiple task dialogues increase in the training set. The results show that the models may be better at decomposing than composing in the domain of goal oriented dialogues or the model at best can only mimic surface level token distribution (Appendix B). Though training with more multi-task dialogues can potentially improve the performance, it is not a scalable solution. We will test two of the out-of-the-shelf techniques to improve the task level compositionality in the following section.

5.2 Zero-shot Compositionality Experiments

We experiment on Transformer to evaluate the performance on handling zero-shot compositional tasks by training the baseline model only on single task dialogues, and with the proposed data augmentation techniques. The results, in Table 2, show that the *Targeted_Augment* technique increased the performance on multiple-task dialogues by 8.5% BLEU score while the scores of the model slightly dropped in the performance of all dialogues.

Data	BLEU	
	Multiple	Overall
SNG	7.17	6.81
SNG + RS	7.46	7.14
SNG +TS	7.78	7.09

Table 2: SNG: Single task dialogues, RS: Random_Augment Synthetic, and TS: Targeted_Augment Synthetic.

The reason for only a minor BLEU improvement could be due to the noise in generation process. Although the task distributions are matched, the token level distributions appear to be significantly differ-

ent between the single and multiple-tasks. The results suggest that the method may inject more noise in the token level distribution thereby not improving the model performance significantly.

5.3 Domain Invariant Transformer

We compared the proposed architecture and the baseline Transformer model to understand the effects of domain invariant encoder representation towards language generation in multi-task dialogues. We observed from our experiments in Table 3 that Domain Invariant Transformer or Transformer model fails to generalize with few-shot multi-task dialogues. The data augmentation techniques too appear to not contribute towards improving the performance. But, Domain Invariant Transformer model improved the performance to a BLEU score when trained only on all of training data, which, though was not the intended objective. Although that seems good, the model is still heavily reliant on human-human multiple domain dialogues and zero-shot or few-shot generalization in compositional dialogues seem quite difficult to achieve.

Model	Training Data		BLEU	
	Multiple	Synthetic	Multiple	Overall
Transformer	1.00	No	14.06	14.00
Transformer	0.50	Yes	11.4	12.43
	1.00	Yes	11.89	12.32
Transformer Discriminator	0.50	No	12.24	12.13
	1.00	No	15.06	14.81
Transformer Discriminator	0.50	Yes	11.05	11.60
	1.00	Yes	11.29	12.13

Table 3: 0.5 and 1.0 correspond to half and all of multitask samples respectively during training. Synthetic refers to *Targeted_Augment* dialogues.

The poor performance of the data augmentation techniques can be due to the overwhelming noise in token distribution of input contexts, which skews the language model that the model learns.

6 Conclusion

We studied the problem of composing multiple dialogue tasks to predict next utterance in a single multiple-task dialogue. We found that even powerful transformer models do not naturally compose multiple tasks and the performance is severely relied on multiple task dialogues. In this paper, we explored two solutions that only further showed the difficulty of composing multiple dialogue tasks.

The challenge in generalizing to zero-shot composition, as observed in the experiments, hints at the possibility of transformer model potentially mimicking only the surface level tokens without understanding the underlying task. The token overlap distribution in Appendix B supports the possibility.

References

Henry Baird. 1992. Document image defect models. *Springer.*

Paweł Budzianowski, Tsung-Hsien Wen, Bo-Hsiang Tseng, Iñigo Casanueva, Stefan Ultes, Osman Ramadan, and Milica Gasic. 2018. Multiwoz - a large-scale multi-domain wizard-of-oz dataset for task-oriented dialogue modelling. *EMNLP.*

Bill Byrne, Karthik Krishnamoorthi, Chinnadhurai Sankar, Arvind Neelakantan, Daniel Duckworth, Semih Yavuz, Ben Goodrich, Amit Dubey, Andy Cedilnik, and Kyu-Young Kim. 2019. Taskmaster-1: Toward a realistic and diverse dialog dataset. *EMNLP.*

Xilun Chen, Ben Athiwaratkun, Yu Sun, Kilian Q. Weinberger, and Claire Cardie. 2016. Adversarial deep averaging networks for cross-lingual sentiment classification. *TACL.*

Arash Einolghozati, Panupong Pasupat, Sonal Gupta, Rushin Shah, Mrinal Mohit, Mike Lewis, and Luke Zettlemoyer. 2019. Improving semantic parsing for task oriented dialog. *arXiv.*

Mihail Eric and Christopher Manning. 2017. A copy-augmented sequence-to-sequence architecture gives good performance on task-oriented dialogue. *EACL.*

Yaroslav Ganin and Victor S. Lempitsky. 2015. Unsupervised domain adaptation by backpropagation. *ICML.*

Satwik Kottur, José M. F. Moura, Stefan Lee, and Dhruv Batra. 2017. Natural language does not emerge 'naturally' in multi-agent dialog. *EMNLP.*

Alex Krizhevsky, Ilya Sutskever, and Geoffrey E Hinton. 2012. Imagenet classification with deep convolutional neural networks. *NeurIPS.*

Brenden M. Lake and Marco Baroni. 2017. Still not systematic after all these years: On the compositional skills of sequence-to-sequence recurrent networks. *Arxiv.*

Mike Lewis, Denis Yarats, Yann N. Dauphin, Devi Parikh, and Dhruv Batra. 2017. Deal or no deal? end-to-end learning for negotiation dialogues. *EMNLP.*

Arvind Neelakantan, Semih Yavuz, Sharan Narang, Vishaal Prasad, Ben Goodrich, Daniel Duckworth, Chinnadhurai Sankar, and Xifeng Yan. 2019. Neural assistant: Joint action prediction, response generation, and latent knowledge reasoning. *Arxiv.*

Kishore Papineni, Salim Roukos, Todd Ward, and Wei-Jing Zhu. 2002. Bleu: a method for automatic evaluation of machine translation. In *Proceedings of the 40th annual meeting on association for computational linguistics.* ACL.

Lina Maria Rojas-Barahona, Milica Gasic, Nikola Mrksic, Pei-Hao Su, Stefan Ultes, Tsung-Hsien Wen, Steve J. Young, and David Vandyke. 2017. A network-based end-to-end trainable task-oriented dialogue system. *EACL.*

Jurgen Schmidhuber. 2012. Multi-column deep neural networks for image classification. *CVPR.*

Rico Sennrich, Barry Haddow, and Alexandra Birch. 2016. Improving neural machine translation models with monolingual data. *ACL.*

Patrice Y. Simard, Dave Steinkraus, and John C. Platt. 2003. Best practices for convolutional neural networks applied to visual document analysis. *ICDAR.*

Nitish Srivastava, Geoffrey Hinton, Alex Krizhevsky, Ilya Sutskever, and Ruslan Salakhutdinov. 2014. Dropout: A simple way to prevent neural networks from overfitting. *JMLR.*

Sining Sun, Ching-Feng Yeh, Mei-Yuh Hwang, Mari Ostendorf, and Lei Xie. 2018. Domain adversarial training for accented speech recognition. *Arxiv.*

Eric Tzeng, Judy Hoffman, Trevor Darrell, and Kate Saenko. 2015. Simultaneous deep transfer across domains and tasks. *ICCV.*

Ashish Vaswani, Samy Bengio, Eugene Brevdo, Francois Chollet, Aidan N. Gomez, Stephan Gouws, Llion Jones, Łukasz Kaiser, Nal Kalchbrenner, Niki Parmar, Ryan Sepassi, Noam Shazeer, and Jakob Uszkoreit. 2018. Tensor2tensor for neural machine translation. *Arxiv.*

Ashish Vaswani, Noam Shazeer, Niki Parmar, Jakob Uszkoreit, Llion Jones, Aidan N Gomez, Ł ukasz Kaiser, and Illia Polosukhin. 2017. Attention is all you need. *NeurIPS.*

Oriol Vinyals and Quoc V. Le. 2015. A neural conversational model. *CoRR.*

Tsung-Hsien Wen, Milica Gasic, Nikola Mrkšić, Pei-Hao Su, David Vandyke, and Steve Young. 2015. Semantically conditioned lstm-based natural language generation for spoken dialogue systems. *EMNLP.*

Tsung-Hsien Wen, Yishu Miao, Phil Blunsom, and Steve J. Young. 2017. Latent intention dialogue models. *ICML.*

Gao Xu, Yongming Zhang, Qixing Zhang, Gaohua Lin, and Jinjun Wang. 2017. Domain adaptation from synthesis to reality in single-model detector for video smoke detection. *ArXiv.*

Ruochen Xu and Yiming Yang. 2017. Cross-lingual distillation for text classification. *ACL.*

A Preprocessing

The MultiWoZ 2.0 dataset has a JSON metadata that maintains a dictionary of slot-value pairs provided by the user to the agent in every utterance. We use this metadata to construct a local and a global knowledge of slot-value shared by the user and split to relabel the dataset for single domain and multidomain dialogues. The preprocessing step removed the noise in the labeling of dialogues. We used this approach to keep a test set of multi-domain dialogues to evaluate the model performance on compositional tasks. On the clean split of single domain dialogues we generate synthetic multidomain dialogues using two different approaches:

A.1 Random Synthetic (RS)

In this approach, we pick a single task dialogue $^iD^{SNG}$ and randomly select a set of K single task dialogues, $\left(^iD^{SNG}_{noise}\right)^K_{k=1}$, to inject noise in D^{SNG}. With an hyperparameter, *percentCopy*, we select the number of utterances to be copied from every dialogue in the set noiseDialogues and add it as a prefix to D^{SNG}. This results in K negative samples of synthetic multidomain dialogues, $\left(^iD^{MUL}_{RS}\right)^K_{k=1}$, for every single domain dialogues in the dataset.

A.2 Targetted Synthetic (TS)

We bucket the single domain dialogues based on the conversation domain (*taxi, hotel, attraction* etc.,). Similarly, we bucket the multi-task dialogues in the training set to measure the topic distributions in multi-task dialogues. Using the computed distribution of composite tasks in *true* multidomain dialogues and the domain label of every $^iD^{SNG}$, we constrain the selection of random dialogues to conform to the training distribution of *true* composite tasks in the training set. The hyperparameters and the remainder of the procedure is similar to RS except when combining the single domain dialogues from two different domains $\left(^iDom,^jDom\right)$, we inject the topic change exchanges randomly sampled from $TC^{\left(^jDom1,^iDom2\right)}$.

For training the proposed Domain Invariant Transformer model, we create the labels for the auxiliary tasks using the preprocessing steps used to split the dataset into single and multi-domain dialogues

A.3 Experiments varying α

α	BLEU (MUL)	BLEU(BOTH)
0.0	14.07	13.94
0.00001	13.74	13.31
0.0001	14.13	14.11
0.001	15.06	**14.81**
0.01	14.61	14.40
0.1	14.70	14.41

Table 4: Varying the α to understand the effect of the discriminator on decoder performance

We experimented with different values of α to understand the influence of the discriminator loss. The results in Table 4 show that Domain Invariant Transformer performed better when α is 0.001. The experiment also shows consistent performance improvement in all the experiments with different α highlighting the usefulness of training an auxiliary network to train domain invariant encoder representations.

B Token distribution

We analyze the token distribution in the dataset to understand the negative result further. We observed that despite the task distributions are matched the underlying token distribution in different set up is not (Table 5). We looked at the overlap of the distribution of 4-grams in conversations on the different splits we used for training. We observed that Multi-task dialogues (MUL) training set has as much 4-gram overlap with MUL Valid and SNG (Single task dialogues) Valid sets as the combined (SNG + MUL) training data.

The analysis raises doubts in the performance of transformer model with increased MUL train dialogues that the performance improvement cannot be only because of the model's ability to decompose multiple tasks but may be because the MUL train has higher 4-gram overlap with SNG Valid and MUL Valid. This shows that despite the dialogues carrying rich information in task oriented dialogues, the model at best only mimics the surface level token distribution. Hence, it is not clear if the Transformer model can generalize to multi-task dialogues with an understanding of the underlying task structure.

USER:I'm looking for the Lensfield Hotel. Can you help me find it ?
ASSISTANT:Yes of course, it is located in 53-57 lensfield road. Would you like me to book you a reservation ?
USER: No thank you. Could you give me the postcode and tell me if they have free parking ?
ASSISTANT: Yes, they have free parking. The postcode is cb21en. Is there anything else you'd like to know about this hotel ?
USER:No, that's all I needed. Thanks! Bye!
ASSISTANT: You are welcome. Goddbye!

USER:I'd like to find a train that leaves after 17:00 on Saturday.
ASSISTANT: Absolutely, I need departure and destination information and a time you need to arrive by.
USER: I will be departing from Broxbourne and I'd like to go to Cambridge.
ASSISTANT: I have 7 available. The first leaves at 17:32, and arrives at 18:32. Would you like me to book that for you ?
USER:I am not looking to book at the moment, can I just get the train ID? Thanks.
ASSISTANT: Of course! TR0811 leaves at 17:32, arrives at 18:32, with a duration of 60 minutes. The price is 14.32 pounds. May I assist you with anything else ?
USER: That is all I need for today. Thank you. Good bye.
ASSISTANT: Okay glad I could help you. Enjoy your trip.

USER:I'm looking for the Lensfield Hotel. Can you help me find it ?
ASSISTANT:Yes of course, it is located in 53-57 lensfield road. Would you like me to book you a reservation ?
USER: No thank you. Coul you give me the postcode and tell me if they have free parking ?
ASSISTANT: Yes, they have free parking. The postcode is cb21en. Is there anything else you'd like to know about this hotel ?
USER:I'd like to find a train that leaves after 17:00 on Saturday.
ASSISTANT: Absolutely, I need departure and destination information and a time you need to arrive by.
USER: I will be departing from Broxbourne and I'd like to go to Cambridge.
ASSISTANT: I have 7 available. The first leaves at 17:32, and arrives at 18:32. Would you like me to book that for you ?
USER:I am not looking to book at the moment, can I just get the train ID? Thanks.
ASSISTANT: Of course! TR0811 leaves at 17:32, arrives at 18:32, with a duration of 60 minutes. The price is 14.32 pounds. May I assist you with anything else ?
USER: That is all I need for today. Thank you. Good bye.
ASSISTANT: Okay glad I could help you. Enjoy your trip.

Figure 2: An example of combining two single-task dialogues in color1 and color2 together to form a single multi-task dialogue.

(a) Table 1

MUL Train	492688
SNG Valid	16907
Intersection	9238
% Unseen	45.36

(b) Table 2

MUL Train	492688
MUL Valid	104261
Intersection	48076
% Unseen	53.89%

(c) Table 3

SNG Train	124038
MUL Valid	104261
Intersection	22254
% Unseen	78.66%

(d) Table 4

SNG Train	124038
SNG Valid	16907
Intersection	6562
% Unseen	61.19%

(e) Table 5

SNG+MUL Train	568674
SNG Valid	104261
Intersection	49999
% Unseen	52.04%

(f) Table 6

SNG+MUL Train	568674
SNG Valid	16907
Intersection	9746
% Unseen	42.36%

Table 5: Analysis of 4-gram overlap across different combinations of train and validation splits that were used in the experiments. The analysis show that the %Unseen in validation set is higher when training with SNG (Single domain dialogues) but considerably lower when trained with MUL. The composition task requires models to understand the underlying task structure but the data distribution and performance of transformer strongly correlate to show that the transformer model at best mimics the surface level token distribution than understanding the nature of task.

How Effectively Can Machines Defend Against Machine-Generated Fake News? An Empirical Study

Meghana Moorthy Bhat
The Ohio State University
`bhat.89@osu.edu`

Srinivasan Parthasarathy
The Ohio State University
`srini@cse.ohio-state.edu`

Abstract

We empirically study the effectiveness of machine-generated fake news detectors by understanding the model's sensitivity to different synthetic perturbations during test time. The current machine-generated fake news detectors rely on provenance to determine the veracity of news. Our experiments find that the success of these detectors can be limited since they are rarely sensitive to semantic perturbations and are very sensitive to syntactic perturbations. Also, we would like to open-source our code and believe it could be a useful diagnostic tool for evaluating models aimed at fighting machine-generated fake news.

1 Introduction

The advancement of language models (LM) in text generation has raised concerns over misusing LM in generating fake news, misleading reviews, spreading rumor and propaganda (Vosoughi et al., 2018; Solaiman et al., 2019; Varshney et al., 2019, 2020). Fact-checking is one approach that involves studying veracity of the news using external evidence (Popat et al., 2018; Nie et al., 2018). However, it remains a challenging task since the performance of the current automatic fact-checking models are not satisfactory (Thorne et al., 2018). Rashkin et al. (2017) studied automated fact-checking by examining the role of stylistic bias to help verify the truthfulness of an article. Another approach which has recently gained traction to combat mass-scale production of fake news is detecting stylistic differences in human-written and machine-generated news[1](Radford et al., 2019). Later, Grover (Zellers et al., 2019), a transformer based model (Vaswani et al., 2017) trained on news corpora was proposed to determine machine-generated fake news.

The detection of machine-generated fake news purely based on stylistic biases can be hard because: (1) legitimate human-written articles can be easily corrupted at scale by machines, (2) an attacker can overlay the distributional features of human-written text over machine-generated text to fool the style-based classifiers and vice-versa, (3) legitimate text can be generated with LM and the current machine-generated fake news detectors rely on similar distribution for generation of legitimate and fake news (Schuster et al., 2019). However, to the best of our knowledge, there has not been a systematic empirical evaluation to validate these claims. We devise six different perturbations to study the behavior of models[2]. In this study we do not cover (3) since generative models for applications like summarization (See et al., 2017; Nallapati et al., 2016), text completion (Vaswani et al., 2017; Radford et al., 2019) can be directly tested for veracity on detector models. From our experiments, we see that models are insensitive to semantic types of perturbations considered in this work, and moreover are extremely sensitive to grammatical perturbations, that do not change the semantics.

2 Related Work

Universal Attacks in NLP: Ribeiro et al. (2018) debugged models using semantic-preserving perturbations that forced changes in predictions for downstream tasks such as sentiment analysis, visual QA and machine comprehension. Behjati et al. (2019) crafted data-independent adversarial sequences that can fool text classifier when added to any input sample. Alternatively, Wallace et al. (2019) study triggers in the form of a word or a few words to analyze models and biases in datasets for LM, text

---

[1]https://openai.com/blog/gpt-2-1-5b-release/

[2]For easy convention, we refer machine-generated fake news detectors as models in this work

Proceedings of the First Workshop on Insights from Negative Results in NLP, pages 48–53
Online, November 19, 2020. ©2020 Association for Computational Linguistics

classification.

Machine-generated text detection: Bakhtin et al. (2019) study the generalization ability of models trained to detect real text from the machine-generated text, Gehrmann et al. (2019) show statistical distributional differences between human-written and machine-generated text and provide a tool to the readers to detect machine generated text. Zellers et al. (2019) proposed defense against machine-generated fake news, Grover, by building a linear classifier on top of the last hidden state of its controlled generator model trained on a large news corpora.

Fake news detection: Shu et al. (2017) study fake news detectors in social media from a data mining perspective. Similarly, Zhou et al. (2019) study vulnerabilities of the Fakebox tool, an open-source fake news detector and emphasized the necessity of crowd-source based knowledge graphs and fact checking based solutions to combat fake news. Automatic fact checking is another approach that is being studied actively with synthetic (Thorne et al., 2018) and real datasets (Wang, 2017; Augenstein et al., 2019). In parallel work, Schuster et al. (2019) discusses the limitations of stylistic based approaches for machine-generated fake news detection. They devised two benchmarks: (1) text completion using LM and, (2) negating the meaning of human-written articles by maintaining the distribution of human-written text as learned by the model.

Our work is orthogonal to these efforts in the following ways: (1) we study (in)sensitivity of multiple models for semantic perturbations by keeping the distribution of human-written text intact, (2) we also study the sensitivity of models to semantic-preserving syntactic perturbations with the goal of overlaying distribution of human-written text over machine-generated text, (3) our experiments can be used as a diagnostic evaluation tool for future machine-generated fake news detectors and, (4) our semantic perturbations can be used to evaluate and study fact-checking based solutions as well.

3 Methodology

We measure the performance of models by looking at accuracy with respect to perturbations introduced in this work. All models are trained without any perturbations and the behavior is studied only at test time. We consider the following models in our experiments - Grover Mega discriminator[3], GPT2 output detector[4] and Fakebox[5] and use RealNews dataset[6].

3.1 Types of Perturbations

We devise perturbations across real news (human-written) articles to test the model behavior. The perturbations in this work are broadly categorized in two main streams: semantic and syntactic. The semantic perturbations are sentence-level perturbations while the syntactic are word-level perturbations. At $N\%$ perturbation level, for any type of semantic perturbation, semantics of $N\%$ of sentences are changed; whereas in a syntactic perturbation, $N\%$ of the words are modified.

3.1.1 Semantic perturbations

The semantic perturbations are intended to turn a real news (human-written text) into a fake news. Our aim is to understand to what extent the content and factuality of text influences model decisions. The psychology studies show that people try to diverge as little as possible from the truth while lying (Mazar et al., 2008). Hence, we study perturbations at various levels to understand the sensitivity of models. Understandably, models find difficulty in spotting minor perturbations (except article shuffling) and the performance improves as we add more noise to the real articles. An ideal model will flip its decision to all the semantic perturbations introduced in this work. Below is a brief description of types of semantic perturbations we consider.

varying sentiment: We change the polarity of sentences within an article, by replacing positive, or comforting words to negative words and vice-versa; thereby changing the overall sentiment of the article. In order to reverse the polarity of sentences, we replace one randomly chosen word in a sentence with its antonym from Stanford NLTK[7].

source-target exchange: The source and the target entities[8] in a sentence are interchanged that do not have coordinating or correlating conjunctions.

article shuffling: We perturb a real article by randomly adding $N\%$ of sentences from a fake article where N is the perturbation level. We also

---

[3] https://grover.allenai.org/detect
[4] https://huggingface.co/openai-detector
[5] https://machinebox.io/docs/fakebox
[6] https://rowanzellers.com/grover/
[7] https://www.nltk.org/

Perturbation type	Real article	Fake article
varying sentiment	— Google said **last** year it spent more than $100 million on Content ID. They say the **automatic** filters are blunt — **Some** consumers worry that the new rules would bring an end. The EU **denies** this.	— Google said **first** year it spent more than $100 million on Content ID. They say the **manual** filters are blunt — **No** consumers worry that the new rules would bring an end. The EU **admit** this.
source-target exchange	— **Lokuhettige** had 14 days to respond to the new charges, the **ICC** added. **Sri Lanka Cricket** has been thrown into turmoil as the **ICC** continues to investigate corruption allegations in the island nation. —	— **ICC** had 14 days to respond to the new charges, the **Lokuhettige** added. **ICC** has been thrown into turmoil as the **Sri Lanka Cricket** continues to investigate corruption allegations in the island nation. —
article shuffling	— Rose feels not enough action is being taken and the disparity in the punishment highlights its ineffectiveness. **"Obviously, it is a bit sad (to feel like this) but when countries only get fined what I'd probably spend on a night out in London, what do you expect" he added.** "You see my manager get banned for two games for just being —"	— Rose feels not enough action is being taken and the disparity in the punishment highlights its ineffectiveness. **This would pave the way for Daenerys Targaryen to bring the Wall down.** "You see my manager get banned for two games for just being —"
entity replacement	**A New Jersey** bus driver's incredible note to the parents of two children who reached out to another student with a disability went viral.—	**Pribbernow, New Kilgore** bus driver's incredible note to the parents of two children who reached out to another student with a parents went viral.—
altering numerical facts	**Mueller Report: 10 Instances of Possible Obstruction** of Justice by Trump Special counsel Robert Mueller's report on Russian interference in the 2016 presidential election included instances of potential obstruction by President Donald Trump.	**Mueller Report: 67497 Instances of Possible Obstruction** of Justice by Trump Special counsel Robert Mueller's report on Russian interference in the 2016 presidential election included instances of potential obstruction by President Donald Trump.
syntactic perturbation	**There is** no way to fully understand **what is** going on in crypto **world. I am** not even sure anyone could even if you tried to. I can tell you that recent surge in BitCoin is an opportunity to buy **long term** real assets	**There's** no way to fully understand **what's** going on in **the** crypto **world - I am** not sure anyone could even if you tried to. I can tell you that **the** recent surge in BitCoin is an opportunity to buy **long-term** real assets.

Table 1: Examples of excerpts from articles subjected to perturbations. Humans in general find difficulty in detecting fake news articles without scrutiny.

remove an equal number of sentences from the real article to maintain the total article length. The fake article chosen for shuffling will not have entities present in the title of real article.

entity replacement: We replace entities[8] with another irrelevant entity of the same type. The irrelevant entities are picked from the fake articles which are not present in real articles.

alter numerical facts: The numerical facts are distorted in a real news article. A numerical figure (digits and words) less than hundred thousand will be scaled up to a random number in the range of 1 million to 1 trillion and vice-versa.

Table 1 represents examples of articles subjected to perturbations in this work. We use spacy[8] to identify entities and entity types in our experiments.

3.1.2 Syntactic perturbations

Ippolito et al. (2019) recently studied the influence of excerpt length for classification of machine-generated and human-written text. In the training dataset of Grover, we observe that machine-generated articles have shorter length but longer sentences than human-written articles. We perturb these features by: (i) breaking longer sentences, (ii) removing definite articles if they appear among the most repeated words in an article, (iii) using semantic-preserving rules (for example converting *that's →that is*) (Ribeiro et al., 2018), (iv) reformatting paragraphs of machine-generated text. These perturbations preserve semantics of articles, hence an ideal model should *not flip* its decision.

4 Results and Analysis

Table 2 summarizes the performance of models when subjected to different types of perturbations at test time. For our experiments, we pick 2K samples for every perturbation type (real for semantic and fake for syntactic perturbations) from the RealNews dataset that are classified correctly (100% accuracy) by all the models without any perturbations introduced in this work. We start with 25% perturbation level because very small perturbation levels may not be enough to change the overall semantics of the article. However, Grover identifies its own generated text even at 1% perturbation level (18% accuracy on article shuffling perturbation). On manual examination, we found that on an average 5% of the real articles did not change semantics on perturbing for varying sentiment and source-target exchange. Fakebox performance is not reported due to very low accuracy for all the perturbations introduced in this work. Since the details of Fakebox tool is not publicly available,

<hr>

[8]https://spacy.io/

50

Perturbation levels (%)	Models	Semantic perturbations (accuracy (%))					Syntactic perturbations (accuracy (%))
		varying sentiment	source-target exchange	article shuffling	entity replacement	alter numerical facts	machine to human
25	Grover	0	$3.8_{(\pm0.28)}$	$45.2_{(\pm1.88)}$	$1.98_{(\pm0.45)}$	$0.2_{(\pm0.0)}$	$23.07_{(\pm2.21)}$
	GPT2	$3.83_{(\pm0.52)}$	0	$15.8_{(\pm0.42)}$	$8.68_{(\pm0.29)}$	$0.1_{(\pm0.0)}$	$17.7_{(\pm1.27)}$
50	Grover	0	$9.4_{(\pm0.73)}$	$72.66_{(\pm1.98)}$	$3.9_{(\pm0.32)}$	$0.2_{(\pm0.01)}$	$12.83_{(\pm0.55)}$
	GPT2	$7.37_{(\pm0.56)}$	0	$35.3_{(\pm0.42)}$	$26.9_{(\pm0.79)}$	$0.1_{(\pm0.01)}$	$13.83_{(\pm0.6)}$
75	Grover	0	$11.44_{(\pm0.29)}$	$83.14_{(\pm2.03)}$	$6.11_{(\pm0.39)}$	$0.23_{(\pm0.08)}$	$10.07_{(\pm0.68)}$
	GPT2	$8.03_{(\pm0.67)}$	0	$40.36_{(\pm0.61)}$	$48.53_{(\pm0.54)}$	$0.13_{(\pm0.02)}$	$3.83_{(\pm0.49)}$
100	Grover	0	$18.39_{(\pm0.61)}$	NA	$8.68_{(\pm0.19)}$	$0.28_{(\pm0.06)}$	$6_{(\pm1.45)}$
	GPT2	$6.11_{(\pm0.21)}$	0	NA	$67.82_{(\pm0.42)}$	$0.13_{(\pm0.02)}$	$1.1_{(\pm0.45)}$

Table 2: *Performance of detectors for perturbations measured in accuracy. The cell values contain the mean and standard deviation across 5 runs of experiments. We choose real articles for devising semantic perturbations and fake articles for devising syntactic perturbations. For semantic perturbations, we see that model performance increases with level of perturbations while for syntactic perturbation, models tend to perform bad with increase in attributes of human-written text. We mark 'NA' in article shuffling for 100% perturbation level since 100% shuffling will be a full machine-generated text which was already classified correctly by the detectors.*

we omit them from analysis. The code is publicly available[9]. From our experiments, we make the following observations:

- All the machine-generated fake news detectors considered in this work are vulnerable to semantic perturbations even under extreme perturbations indicating that actuality of the articles do not aid in model decision.
- Grover performs well on article shuffling indicating that it learns sentence structures of its own generated text pretty well.
- The machine-generated fake news detectors are also vulnerable to semantic preserving syntactic perturbations indicating they could possibly be learning sentence structures. Another reason could be due to data bias since the training dataset of machine-generated text has longer sentences, punctuation and definite articles when compared to human-written text.
- Grover fails to detect sentiment changes in articles indicating that it is insensitive to polarity between entities. From manual examination we found that 5% of real articles perturbed due to varying sentiment have uncommon phrases which would have aided the GPT2 detector. For example, *Police say Aranda told them he would **go** to the mall →Police say Aranda told them he **stay_in_place** to the mall*
- Current machine-generated fake news detectors rely on previously seen data without ex-

ternal resources for classification. This could possibly explain the performance drop of GPT2 in varying sentiment at 100% perturbation level since there will be no inconsistent polarity towards entities unlike perturbations at 50% or 75%.

- Transformers are insensitive to perturbations like word-level shuffling and possibly learn bag-of-word like distribution (Sankar et al., 2019). GPT2 fails to identify source-target exchange indicating they adhere to the above observations. The marginal gains of Grover probably indicates better understanding of linguistic cues in sentences.
- The better performance of GPT2 in entity replacement could be due to non-existence of replaced entities in articles labeled real in the training dataset of GPT2.

5   Conclusion

With the advances in language modeling for text generation, the detection of fake news becomes challenging. We find that success of style-based classifiers are limited when real articles are perturbed even under extreme modifications. We believe our experiments motivates to explore integration of multiple dimensions like examine source credibility, fact-checking via external resources, model robustness by adversarial training, common-sense reasoning to machine-generated fake news detectors. By open-sourcing our code, we believe our methodology of studying vulnerabilities in the

[9]https://github.com/meghu2791/evaluateNeuralFakenews Detectors

fake news detectors can aid in creation of robust models in the future.

Acknowledgments

We thank our reviewers for their feedback and suggestions. This work is supported by the National Science Foundation grant EAR-1520870. All content presented represents the opinion of the authors, and is not necessarily endorsed by their sponsors.

References

Isabelle Augenstein, Christina Lioma, Dongsheng Wang, Lucas Chaves Lima, Casper Hansen, Christian Hansen, and Jakob Grue Simonsen. 2019. Multifc: A real-world multi-domain dataset for evidence-based fact checking of claims. *Proceedings of the 2019 Conference on Empirical Methods in Natural Language Processing and the 9th International Joint Conference on Natural Language Processing (EMNLP-IJCNLP)*.

Anton Bakhtin, Sam Gross, Myle Ott, Yuntian Deng, Marc'Aurelio Ranzato, and Arthur Szlam. 2019. Real or fake? learning to discriminate machine from human generated text. *CoRR*, abs/1906.03351.

M. Behjati, S. Moosavi-Dezfooli, M. S. Baghshah, and P. Frossard. 2019. Universal adversarial attacks on text classifiers. In *ICASSP 2019 - 2019 IEEE International Conference on Acoustics, Speech and Signal Processing (ICASSP)*, pages 7345–7349.

Sebastian Gehrmann, Hendrik Strobelt, and Alexander Rush. 2019. GLTR: Statistical detection and visualization of generated text. In *Proceedings of the 57th Annual Meeting of the Association for Computational Linguistics: System Demonstrations*, pages 111–116, Florence, Italy. Association for Computational Linguistics.

Daphne Ippolito, Daniel Duckworth, Chris Callison-Burch, and Douglas Eck. 2019. Automatic detection of generated text is easiest when humans are fooled.

Nina Mazar, On Amir, and Dan Ariely. 2008. The dishonesty of honest people: A theory of self-concept maintenance. *Journal of Marketing Research*, 45(6):633–644.

Ramesh Nallapati, Bing Xiang, and Bowen Zhou. 2016. Sequence-to-sequence rnns for text summarization. *CoRR*, abs/1602.06023.

Yixin Nie, Haonan Chen, and Mohit Bansal. 2018. Combining fact extraction and verification with neural semantic matching networks. *CoRR*, abs/1811.07039.

Kashyap Popat, Subhabrata Mukherjee, Andrew Yates, and Gerhard Weikum. 2018. Declare: Debunking fake news and false claims using evidence-aware deep learning. *CoRR*, abs/1809.06416.

Alec Radford, Jeffrey Wu, Rewon Child, David Luan, Dario Amodei, and Ilya Sutskever. 2019. Language models are unsupervised multitask learners.

Hannah Rashkin, Eunsol Choi, Jin Yea Jang, Svitlana Volkova, and Yejin Choi. 2017. Truth of varying shades: Analyzing language in fake news and political fact-checking. In *Proceedings of the 2017 Conference on Empirical Methods in Natural Language Processing, EMNLP 2017, Copenhagen, Denmark, September 9-11, 2017*, pages 2931–2937. Association for Computational Linguistics.

Marco Tulio Ribeiro, Sameer Singh, and Carlos Guestrin. 2018. Semantically equivalent adversarial rules for debugging NLP models. In *Proceedings of the 56th Annual Meeting of the Association for Computational Linguistics (Volume 1: Long Papers)*, pages 856–865, Melbourne, Australia. Association for Computational Linguistics.

Chinnadhurai Sankar, Sandeep Subramanian, Christopher J. Pal, Sarath Chandar, and Yoshua Bengio. 2019. Do neural dialog systems use the conversation history effectively? an empirical study. *CoRR*, abs/1906.01603.

Tal Schuster, Roei Schuster, Darsh J Shah, and Regina Barzilay. 2019. Are we safe yet? the limitations of distributional features for fake news detection. *arXiv preprint arXiv:1908.09805*.

Abigail See, Peter J. Liu, and Christopher D. Manning. 2017. Get to the point: Summarization with pointer-generator networks. In *Proceedings of the 55th Annual Meeting of the Association for Computational Linguistics (Volume 1: Long Papers)*, pages 1073–1083, Vancouver, Canada. Association for Computational Linguistics.

Kai Shu, Amy Sliva, Suhang Wang, Jiliang Tang, and Huan Liu. 2017. Fake news detection on social media: A data mining perspective. *SIGKDD Explor. Newsl.*, 19(1):22–36.

Irene Solaiman, Miles Brundage, Jack Clark, Amanda Askell, Ariel Herbert-Voss, Jeff Wu, Alec Radford, Gretchen Krueger, Jong Wook Kim, Sarah Kreps, Miles McCain, Alex Newhouse, Jason Blazakis, Kris McGuffie, and Jasmine Wang. 2019. Release strategies and the social impacts of language models.

James Thorne, Andreas Vlachos, Christos Christodoulopoulos, and Arpit Mittal. 2018. FEVER: a large-scale dataset for fact extraction and VERification. In *NAACL-HLT*.

Lav R. Varshney, Nitish Shirish Keskar, and Richard Socher. 2019. Pretrained ai models: Performativity, mobility, and change.

Lav R. Varshney, Nitish Shirish Keskar, and Richard Socher. 2020. Limits of detecting text generated by large-scale language models.

Ashish Vaswani, Noam Shazeer, Niki Parmar, Jakob Uszkoreit, Llion Jones, Aidan N. Gomez, Lukasz Kaiser, and Illia Polosukhin. 2017. Attention is all you need. In *NIPS*.

Soroush Vosoughi, Deb Roy, and Sinan Aral. 2018. The spread of true and false news online. *Science*, 359(6380):1146–1151.

Eric Wallace, Shi Feng, Nikhil Kandpal, Matt Gardner, and Sameer Singh. 2019. Universal adversarial triggers for attacking and analyzing NLP. In *Empirical Methods in Natural Language Processing*.

William Yang Wang. 2017. "liar, liar pants on fire": A new benchmark dataset for fake news detection. *ArXiv*, abs/1705.00648.

Rowan Zellers, Ari Holtzman, Hannah Rashkin, Yonatan Bisk, Ali Farhadi, Franziska Roesner, and Yejin Choi. 2019. Defending against neural fake news. In *Advances in Neural Information Processing Systems 32: Annual Conference on Neural Information Processing Systems 2019, NeurIPS 2019, 8-14 December 2019, Vancouver, BC, Canada*, pages 9051–9062.

Zhixuan Zhou, Huankang Guan, Meghana Moorthy Bhat, and Justin Hsu. 2019. Fake news detection via NLP is vulnerable to adversarial attacks. *CoRR*, abs/1901.09657.

Label Propagation-Based Semi-Supervised Learning
for Hate Speech Classification

Ashwin Geet D'Sa[1], **Irina Illina**[1], **Dominique Fohr**[1], **Dietrich Klakow**[2], **Dana Ruiter**[2]
[1]Université de Lorraine, CNRS, Inria, LORIA
[2]Spoken Language System Group, Saarland University

Abstract

Research on hate speech classification has received increased attention. In real-life scenarios, a small amount of labeled hate speech data is available to train a reliable classifier. Semi-supervised learning takes advantage of a small amount of labeled data and a large amount of unlabeled data. In this paper, label propagation-based semi-supervised learning is explored for the task of hate speech classification. The quality of labeling the unlabeled set depends on the input representations. In this work, we show that pre-trained representations are label agnostic, and when used with label propagation yield poor results. Neural network-based fine-tuning can be adopted to learn task-specific representations using a small amount of labeled data. We show that fully fine-tuned representations may not always be the best representations for the label propagation and intermediate representations may perform better in a semi-supervised setup.

1 Introduction

Online hate speech is anti-social communicative behavior and targets minority sections of the society based on religion, ethnicity, gender, etc. (Delgado and Stefancic, 2014). It leads to threat, fear, and violence to an individual or a group. As monitoring these contents by humans is expensive and time-consuming, machine learning-based classification techniques can be used. The last few years have seen a tremendous increase in research towards hate speech classification (Badjatiya et al., 2017; Nobata et al., 2016; Del Vigna et al., 2017; Malmasi and Zampieri, 2018). The performance of these classifiers depends on the amount of available labeled data. However, in many real life scenarios there is a limited amount of labeled data and abundant unlabeled data. In need of data, different data augmentation techniques based on synonym replacement (Rizos et al., 2019), text generation

(Rizos et al., 2019; Wullach et al., 2020), back translation (Aroyehun and Gelbukh, 2018), knowledge graphs (Sharifirad et al., 2018), etc, have been employed for up-sampling the training data in the field of hate speech classification. The performance gain by these techniques is small, and they fail to take advantage of the available unlabeled data.

Semi-supervised learning is a technique to combine a small amount of labeled data with a large amount of unlabeled data during training (Abney, 2007), intending to improve the performance of the classifiers. Label propagation (Xiaojin and Zoubin, 2002) is a graph-based semi-supervision technique analogous to the k-Nearest-Neighbours algorithm. It assumes that data points close to each other tend to have a similar label. These algorithms rely on the representation of data points to create a distance graph which captures their proximity.

Recently, pre-trained word embeddings such as Word2Vec, fastText, Global Vectors for Word Representation (GloVe) have been used for representing words for hate speech classification (Waseem et al., 2017; Badjatiya et al., 2017). Furthermore, pre-trained sentence embeddings such as InferSent, Universal Sentence Encoder, Embeddings from Language Models (ELMo) have been used for the task of hate speech classification (Indurthi et al., 2019; Bojkovskỳ and Pikuliak, 2019). These pre-trained sentence embeddings are generic representations and are unaware of task-specific classes. Transforming the pre-trained sentence embeddings to task-specific representations can be helpful for label propagation, and our work explores this direction. The contributions of this article are:

- evaluation of label propagation based semi-supervised learning for hate speech classification;
- comparison of label propagation on pre-trained and task-specific representations learned from a small labeled corpus.

54

Proceedings of the First Workshop on Insights from Negative Results in NLP, pages 54–59
Online, November 19, 2020. ©2020 Association for Computational Linguistics

The rest of the paper is organized as follows: Section 2 describes label-propagation based semi-supervised learning for hate speech classification. Section 3 describes the experimental setup. Results and discussions are presented in Section 4.

2 Semi-supervised Learning

In this section, we briefly describe sentence embeddings and the label propagation algorithm. This is followed by our methodology for semi-supervised training for hate speech classification.

2.1 Sentence Embeddings

Sentence embeddings are fixed-length vector representations that capture the semantics of the sentence. These embeddings are learned from large unlabeled corpora. Similar sentences are close to each other in this vector space and hence they are used as an input representation for various downstream tasks. We use the pre-trained Universal Sentence Encoder (USE) (Cer et al., 2018) to represent the tweets.

2.2 Label Propagation

Label propagation is a graph-based semi-supervised learning technique that uses the labels from the labeled data to transduce the labels to unlabeled data. Label propagation considers two sets: $(x_1, y_1) \ldots (x_l, y_l) \in L$ as labeled set and $(x_{l+1}, y_{l+1}) \ldots (x_n, y_n) \in U$ as unlabeled set, where $y_1 \ldots y_l \in \{1 \ldots C\}$, $\{x_1 \ldots x_n\} \in \mathbb{R}^D$. Here, C is the number of classes, and the labeled set L consists of all the classes. The algorithm constructs a graph $G = (V, E)$, where V is the set of vertices representing set L and U, and the edges in set E represents the similarity between two nodes i and j with weight w_{ij}. The weight w_{ij} is computed such that nodes with smaller distances (similar nodes) will have larger weights. The algorithm uses a probabilistic transition matrix T:

$$T_{ij} = P(i \to j) = \frac{w_{ij}}{\sum_{k=1}^{n} w_{kj}}$$

The algorithm iteratively updates the labels $Y \leftarrow TY$, by clamping the labels of the labeled set, and until Y converges.

2.3 Proposed Methodology

Figure 1 outlines the semi-supervised learning setup adopted in our study. We use a Multilayer Perceptron (MLP) for two purposes: (a) to learn task-specific representations; (b) to perform multiclass classification.

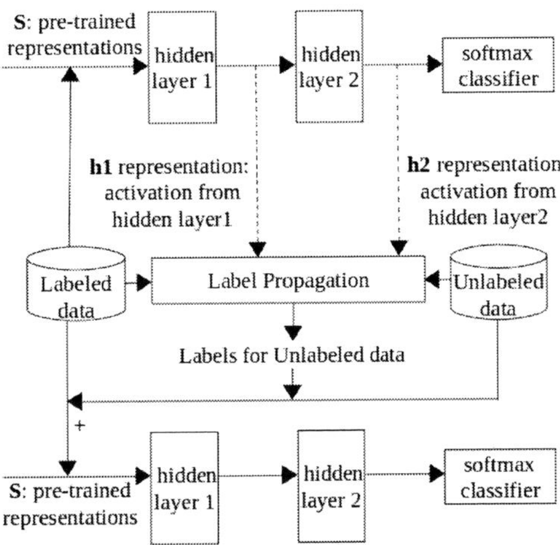

Figure 1: Block diagram for semi-supervised learning.

Task-specific representations: First, the pre-trained representation $S \in \mathbb{R}^D$ are transformed to task-specific representation $\hat{S} \in \mathbb{R}^{\hat{D}}$ with the MLP classifier trained using a small amount of available labeled set L. After training the MLP classifier, we pass the label agnostic pre-trained representation S of a given sample from the labeled set L and unlabeled set U as input to the MLP. We consider the activation from outputs of the hidden layers (h1 and h2) as two different task-specific transformed representations $\hat{S}$. Since the MLP classifier is trained with labeled data, we expect the representations h1 and h2 to capture task-specific label information.

Semi-supervised training: The pre-trained representations S or task-specific representations $\hat{S}$ will be used to represent data points in label propagation. We perform label propagation using the labeled set L and unlabeled set U, to obtain the labels for the samples in U. Finally, the pre-trained embeddings of set L and set U, along with original labels for L and labels obtained from label propagation for U will be used to train an MLP for hate speech classification.

3 Experimental Setup

3.1 Data Description

We consider two datasets, by Founta et al. (2018) and Davidson et al. (2017), containing tweets sampled from Twitter. Table 1 shows the statistics of these datasets. Both datasets have an imbalanced class distribution with 'hateful' as a minority class.

Dataset	#Samples	Normal	Abusive	Hateful
Founta	86.9K	63%	31%	6%
Davidson	24.7K	17%	77%	6%

Table 1: Dataset statistics for Founta et al. (2018) and Davidson et al. (2017)

Twitter data by Founta et al. (2018): A large part of this dataset is collected using random sampling. Since hate and abusive speech occurs in a very small percentage, the authors chose to perform boosted sampling. The dataset has four classes, namely 'normal', 'spam', 'abusive', and 'hateful'. We exclude the samples from the 'spam' class. This brings down the total number of samples in the dataset from 100K to 86.9K.

Twitter data by Davidson et al. (2017): It is collected based on the keywords from the hatebase[1] lexicon. The dataset is annotated into three classes, namely 'hate speech', 'offensive language' and 'neither'. Further in this paper, to map the class labels to Founta et al. (2018) dataset, we consider 'neither' class as 'normal' and 'offensive language' as 'abusive'. Since 'abusive speech' and 'offensive language' are strongly correlated (Founta et al., 2018), we use the terms interchangeably.

3.2 Data Processing

3.2.1 Text Preprocessing

We remove all the numbers and punctuations except '.', ',', '!', '-', and apostrophe. The repeated occurrence of the same punctuation is changed to a single one. Hashtags are preprocessed by removing the '#' symbol and those with multiple words are split based on uppercase letters. For example, "#getBackHome" is processed into "get Back Home". This is done to ensure that the text tokenizer treats multiple words as a sequence of distinct words. However, the hashtags with multiple words without any uppercase is left as it is. Twitter user handles and the symbol 'RT' which indicates re-tweet are removed.

3.2.2 Data Split

We split the datasets randomly into three portions 'training', 'validation', and 'test' sets, each containing 60%, 20%, and 20% respectively. To simulate the semi-supervised learning setup, we partition the training set into labeled and unlabeled set with a ratio of 1:4. The final labeled set consists of 12% of the entire dataset.

[1] https://www.hatebase.org

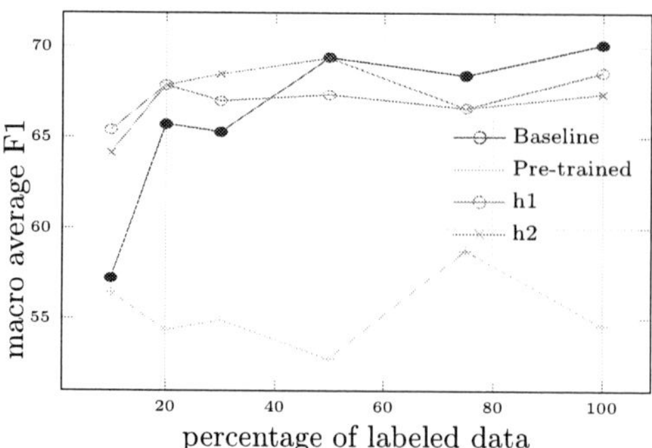

Figure 2: Performance on Founta et al. (2018) dataset.

3.3 Sentence Embeddings

We obtain pre-trained sentence embeddings from the transformer-based model of USE[2]. This model is trained on data from Wikipedia, web news, web question-answer pages, and discussion forums. Each sentence embedding is of 512 dimension.

3.4 Label Propagation

The label propagation API provided by scikit-learn library[3] is used. Euclidean distance is used to compute the distances between two data points. Based on the validation set, we have chosen 80 nearest neighbors and a maximum of 4 iterations.

3.5 Model and Representation Setup

We use an MLP with two hidden layers to perform classification and derive transformed representations. As shown in the Figure 1, the MLP model always has pre-trained representations S as its input. The hidden layers have ReLU activation. The transformed representation $\hat{S}$ are taken from the 1st or 2nd hidden layers, referred as 'h1-representation' and 'h2-representation' in our experiments, respectively. We use Adam optimizer, early-stopping based on validation set, and maximum of 10 epochs. Both the hidden layers have 50 units. The model weights learnt while training the system with only the labeled data is used to initialize the classifier before training with labeled and unlabeled data.

4 Results and Discussion

Figures 2 and 3 show percentage macro-average F1 of classification on the test set in the semi-supervised approach. The amount of unlabeled

[2] https://tfhub.dev/google/
universal-sentence-encoder-large/3
[3] https://scikit-learn.org/stable/
modules/label_propagation.html

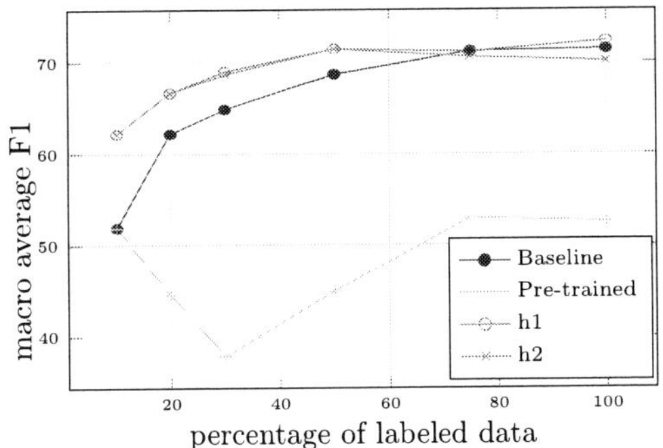

Figure 3: Performance on Davidson et al. (2017) dataset.

data is fixed, but the amount of labeled data is varied to 10%, 20%, 30%, 50% and 100% of the available labeled set. The 'Baseline' is obtained by training the MLP classifier with only the labeled set, and without using label propagation. The 'Pre-trained', 'h1', and 'h2' show the results of the classifier trained using labeled and unlabeled set, the respective representation was used to label the unlabeled set using label propagation. In all the four cases, pre-trained embeddings were used as input to the MLP classifier.

Results in Figure 2 and Figure 3 show that semi-supervised training using label propagation on pre-trained representations performs worse than the 'Baseline' classifier. This implies that label propagation to the unlabeled sets using pre-trained representations introduces significant noise in the classifier. To support this hypothesis, we analyse the intra-class and inter-class separations.

	pre-trained	h1	h2
intra-class distance			
'normal'	1.33	0.89	1.48
'abusive'	1.26	0.81	1.43
'hate'	1.25	0.87	1.63
inter-class distance			
'normal'-'abusive'	1.33	1.17	2.72
'normal'-'hate'	1.33	1.14	2.39
'abusive'-'hate'	1.33	1.14	2.99

Table 2: Average inter-class and intra-class euclidean distance across different representations for the train set of Founta et al. (2018) dataset.

Table 2 shows the average intra-class and inter-class euclidean distance across different representations on the training set, containing the labeled and unlabeled set. Ground truth labels are used for this analysis. From Table 2, we observe that

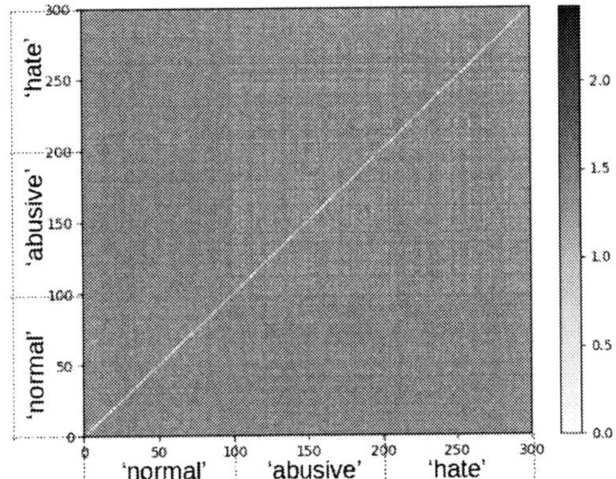

Figure 4: Color plot for distances between samples using the pre-trained representations.

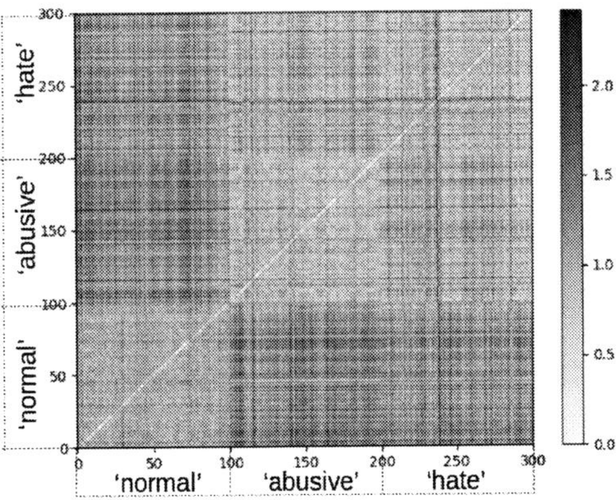

Figure 5: Color plot for distances between samples using the h1 representations.

the intra-class and inter-class distance are similar for pre-trained embeddings. This implies that the representations belonging to the samples from the same class were not close to each other and those from different classes were not far from each other. As hypothesised, h1 and h2 capture class information and hence have lower intra-class and higher inter-class distances.

Further, we qualitatively analyze the euclidean distances across pre-trained representation and h1 representation using color maps, shown in Figure 4 and Figure 5 respectively. We randomly consider 300 samples from Founta et al. (2018) dataset, of which the 1st set of 100 samples belongs to the labeled set of 'normal' class, the 2nd and the 3rd set of 100 samples belong to the labeled sets of 'abusive', and 'hate' classes respectively. From Figure 4, we observe that the pre-trained representation has similar distance across all the samples, thus appearing in a similar color. This infers that pre-trained representation does not contain any task-specific label information, and are generic. However, as shown in Figure 5, the intra-class distance of the samples within 'normal' and 'abusive' classes is smaller than their inter-class distance of h1 representation, hence appearing as lighter-colored squares. From these figures, we observe that h1 representation captures task-specific label information.

Figure 2 and Figure 3 further show that semi-supervised training using label propagation on transformed representations ('h1' and 'h2') performs better than the 'Baseline' when amount of labeled data is small. The performance is comparable for larger labeled data. Thus, semi-supervised learning with label propagation using task-specific representations can have significant advantages when the available labeled samples are very few.

Furthermore, in a few cases, label propagation using the representations from the intermediate hidden layer 'h1' performed slightly better than label propagation using the representations from the final hidden layer 'h2'. This hints that fully fine-tuned representation may not always be the best performing representations in the k-Nearest Neighbors space.

5 Conclusion

In this article, we have explored label propagation-based semi-supervised learning for hate speech classification. We evaluated our approach on two datasets of hate speech on the multi-class classification task. We showed that label propagation using the pre-trained sentence embeddings reduces the performance achieved with only the labeled data. This is because pre-trained embeddings do not contain any task-specific information. We validated this by comparing the average intra-class and inter-class distances. Further, training an MLP classifier with a small amount of labeled data and using the activations of its hidden layers as task aware representations improved the performance of the label propagation and semi-supervised training. It also appears that the fully fine-tuned representations from the MLP may not be the best representations for the label propagation. We can conclude that semi-supervised learning based on label propagation helps to improve hate speech classification in very low resource scenarios and that the performance gain reduces with more amount of labeled data.

Acknowledgments

This work was funded by the M-PHASIS project supported by the French National Research Agency (ANR) and German National Research Agency (DFG) under contract ANR-18-FRAL-0005.

References

Steven Abney. 2007. *Semi-supervised learning for computational linguistics*. CRC Press.

Segun Taofeek Aroyehun and Alexander Gelbukh. 2018. Aggression detection in social media: Using deep neural networks, data augmentation, and pseudo labeling. In *Proceedings of the First Workshop on Trolling, Aggression and Cyberbullying (TRAC-2018)*, pages 90–97.

Pinkesh Badjatiya, Shashank Gupta, Manish Gupta, and Vasudeva Varma. 2017. Deep learning for hate speech detection in tweets. In *Proceedings of the 26th International Conference on World Wide Web Companion*, pages 759–760.

Michal Bojkovský and Matúš Pikuliak. 2019. Stufiit at semeval-2019 task 5: Multilingual hate speech detection on twitter with muse and elmo embeddings. In *Proceedings of the 13th International Workshop on Semantic Evaluation*, pages 464–468.

Daniel Cer, Yinfei Yang, Sheng-yi Kong, Nan Hua, Nicole Limtiaco, Rhomni St John, Noah Constant, Mario Guajardo-Cespedes, Steve Yuan, Chris Tar, et al. 2018. Universal sentence encoder for english. In *Proceedings of the 2018 Conference on Empirical Methods in Natural Language Processing: System Demonstrations*, pages 169–174.

Thomas Davidson, Dana Warmsley, Michael Macy, and Ingmar Weber. 2017. Automated hate speech detection and the problem of offensive language. In *Eleventh international aaai conference on web and social media*.

Fabio Del Vigna, Andrea Cimino, Felice Dell'Orletta, Marinella Petrocchi, and Maurizio Tesconi. 2017. Hate me, hate me not: Hate speech detection on facebook. In *Proceedings of the First Italian Conference on Cybersecurity*, pages 86–95.

Richard Delgado and Jean Stefancic. 2014. Hate speech in cyberspace. *Wake Forest L. Rev.*, 49:319.

Antigoni Maria Founta, Constantinos Djouvas, Despoina Chatzakou, Ilias Leontiadis, Jeremy Blackburn, Gianluca Stringhini, Athena Vakali, Michael Sirivianos, and Nicolas Kourtellis. 2018. Large scale crowdsourcing and characterization of twitter abusive behavior. In *Twelfth International AAAI Conference on Web and Social Media*.

Vijayasaradhi Indurthi, Bakhtiyar Syed, Manish Shrivastava, Nikhil Chakravartula, Manish Gupta, and Vasudeva Varma. 2019. Fermi at semeval-2019 task 5: Using sentence embeddings to identify hate speech against immigrants and women in twitter. In *Proceedings of the 13th International Workshop on Semantic Evaluation*, pages 70–74.

Shervin Malmasi and Marcos Zampieri. 2018. Challenges in discriminating profanity from hate speech. *Journal of Experimental & Theoretical Artificial Intelligence*, 30(2):187–202.

Chikashi Nobata, Joel Tetreault, Achint Thomas, Yashar Mehdad, and Yi Chang. 2016. Abusive language detection in online user content. In *Proceedings of the 25th international conference on world wide web*, pages 145–153.

Georgios Rizos, Konstantin Hemker, and Björn Schuller. 2019. Augment to prevent: short-text data augmentation in deep learning for hate-speech classification. In *Proceedings of the 28th ACM International Conference on Information and Knowledge Management*, pages 991–1000.

Sima Sharifirad, Borna Jafarpour, and Stan Matwin. 2018. Boosting text classification performance on sexist tweets by text augmentation and text generation using a combination of knowledge graphs. In *Proceedings of the 2nd workshop on abusive language online (ALW2)*, pages 107–114.

Zeerak Waseem, Wendy Hui Kyong Chung, Dirk Hovy, and Joel Tetreault. 2017. Proceedings of the first workshop on abusive language online. In *Proceedings of the First Workshop on Abusive Language Online*.

Tomer Wullach, Amir Adler, and Einat Minkov. 2020. Towards hate speech detection at large via deep generative modeling. *arXiv preprint arXiv:2005.06370*.

Zhu Xiaojin and Ghahramani Zoubin. 2002. Learning from labeled and unlabeled data with label propagation. *Tech. Rep., Technical Report CMU-CALD-02–107, Carnegie Mellon University*.

Layout-Aware Text Representations Harm Clustering Documents by Type

Catherine Finegan-Dollak and **Ashish Verma**
IBM Research
1101 Kitchawan Rd, Yorktown Heights, NY 10598, USA
cfd@ibm.com, Ashish.Verma1@ibm.com

Abstract

Clustering documents by type—grouping invoices with invoices and articles with articles—is a desirable first step for organizing large collections of document scans. Humans approaching this task use both the semantics of the text and the document layout to assist in grouping like documents. LayoutLM (Xu et al., 2019), a layout-aware transformer built on top of BERT with state-of-the-art performance on document-type *classification*, could reasonably be expected to outperform regular BERT (Devlin et al., 2018) for document-type *clustering*. However, we find experimentally that BERT significantly outperforms LayoutLM on this task ($p < 0.001$). We analyze clusters to show where layout awareness is an asset and where it is a liability.

1 Introduction

Organizations are inundated by paperwork, often in the form of PDFs. Automated processing can help to organize and extract information from these documents, but the right process for a given document depends on its type: invoices are handled differently than contracts, for example. Document classification by type enables such a system; however, it requires training data for all of the desired classes, and finding such data to fit a given business's needs is difficult. There is no one-size-fits-all ontology of document types. While some types, such as invoices, may be common across industries, others, such as loan applications or home-inspection reports, are domain-specific. Users wishing to define their own classes will benefit from a system that enables them to group their own documents. To help with this, the present work addresses the task of clustering documents by type.

Humans grouping documents by type can use both the text and the appearance of documents. For example, we can distinguish a gas bill from an article at a glance, but we need to read at least a few words to determine whether a dense, two-column document is an article or a warranty. We therefore expect that a hybrid document representation that combines layout and text information should outperform a text-only representation when clustering documents by type. LayoutLM (Xu et al., 2019) is such a hybrid system and achieves state-of-the-art performance for document type *classification*, outperforming text-only baselines. We therefore hypothesized that LayoutLM would also outperform these baselines for document-type *clustering*.

Sections 3 and 4 describe the systems we compared and the experiments we used to try to confirm this hypothesis. However, the main contribution of this work is experimental evidence of the opposite: LayoutLM performed significantly worse than a simple BERT baseline on this task (Section 5). Analysis of output clusters (Section 5.1) helps to explain this unexpected result.

2 Related Work

Hybrid layout/text representations Recent work combines layout with text for information extraction. Chargrid (Katti et al., 2018) assigns each pixel on a page a vector. For pixels inside the bounding box of a character, the vector is a one-hot encoding for that character; otherwise, it is a vector of zeros. This generates a $vocabsize \times height \times width$ tensor representation of the page for input to a CNN encoder-decoder model. BERTgrid (Denk and Reisswig, 2019) is nearly identical, but it replaces the one-hot character encoding with the word's BERT encoding. Liu et al. (2019) represent a document as a fully-connected graph where text boxes are nodes. The edge embedding between two nodes incorporates the distance between them, the text boxes' aspect ratios, and their relative sizes. Similarly, ZeroShotCeres (Lockard et al., 2020) represents semi-structured web pages as

Proceedings of the First Workshop on Insights from Negative Results in NLP, pages 60–65
Online, November 19, 2020. ©2020 Association for Computational Linguistics

graphs, with text-field nodes connected by edges for vertically or horizontally adjacent text fields and siblings or cousins in the DOM tree. Both systems then use graph neural networks over the document graphs.

Document-type classification Classification of documents by type has frequently been treated as an image classification problem. Many works have used varying CNN architectures (Kang et al., 2014; Afzal et al., 2015; Harley et al., 2015; Afzal et al., 2017; Tensmeyer and Martinez, 2017; Das et al., 2018) or other vision-based techniques (Kumar et al., 2014; Sarkhel and Nandi, 2019).

Some works have combined vision and NLP for document-type classification, using OCR for text extraction. Noce et al. (2016) assigned the most relevant words unique colors, then filled the bounding boxes of those words with the corresponding color, enabling the CNN processing the image to "see" the word. Asim et al. (2019) provided the most important words as features to a CNN, later combining the output with an image stream that used an InceptionV3 CNN architecture. Dauphinee et al. (2019) concatenated the output of a CNN image classifier with a multilayer perceptron bag-of-words classifier, then fed the concatenation to a meta-classifier. Ferrando et al. (2020) used an ensemble of a BERT classifier and EfficientNets CNNs. Audebert et al. (2020) concatenated image features (from a MobileNet v2 CNN) with text features (generated by passing FastText embeddings for the text through a 1D CNN) to form the input to a multilayer perceptron. Cosma et al. (2020) used text to help pretrain part of their classifier: they performed LDA to determine documents' topics, then trained their CNN to try to predict those topics using only the document image. They ultimately used the CNN as part of a model to predict document type using the image only. All of these systems are supervised, whereas this work addresses unsupervised clustering.

Document-type clustering Csurka et al. (2016) trained models on RVL-CDIP, then used those models to generate representations for clustering other document-type datasets. Abuelwafa et al. (2019) used unsupervised feature learning to improve their representations of document images for clustering. They applied transformations to document images to generate surrogate classes, then trained a CNN to classify them. They used that trained CNN to generate representations of document images for

clustering. There is, to our knowledge, no previous work clustering RVL-CDIP.

3 Systems

We compare LayoutLM and BERT, as well as a TF-IDF baseline (sklearn's[1] (Pedregosa et al., 2011) implementation with default hyperparameters). In each case, we use the specified system to generate one vector representation for each document image, then cluster using sklearn's k-means, with k set to the number of gold classes plus one.

BERT (Devlin et al., 2018) is a transformer-based bidirectional model that generates contextualized word embeddings for a sequence of words. The input to a BERT model for the i-th token in the sequence is a sum of (a) its token embedding; (b) a position embedding for position i; and (c) a segment embedding indicating whether the token is in the first or second segment of the input sequence.

LayoutLM (Xu et al., 2019) is a BERT-like transformer model modified to generate layout-aware contextualized word embeddings. In place of BERT's single positional embedding, LayoutLM adds positional embeddings for the x- and y-coordinates of a bounding box around the token. The token's embedding thus incorporates its two-dimensional location on the page and its size. This architecture achieves state-of-the-art performance for supervised classification by document type.

Both BERT and LayoutLM output a vector for each token in the input sequence plus the special `[CLS]` token. However, k-means, like most clustering algorithms, requires a single vector representation of each example. Classifiers use the `[CLS]` embedding as a single-vector representation for the entire sequence. However, prior work (Reimers and Gurevych, 2019; Wang and Kuo, 2020) has shown that, for BERT without fine-tuning, this is not a good representation of the semantics of the entire sequence. Other options include combining all of the vectors in the output sequence by either averaging or max pooling—set the i-th value in the output vector equal to the max i-th value over all of the sequence vectors. For BERT, we use the average as our representation, since Reimers and Gurevych (2019) showed it captured semantic similarity better than the `[CLS]` token. For LayoutLM, we try all three methods.

---

[1]`https://scikit-learn.org/`

	F_1	ARI
BERT (average)	$\mathbf{0.23}_{0.002}$	$\mathbf{0.17}_{0.002}$
TF-IDF	$0.21_{0.014}$	$0.13_{0.020}$
LayoutLM (average)	$0.16*_{0.002}$	$0.09*_{0.001}$
LayoutLM ([CLS])	$0.20*_{0.003}$	$0.14*_{0.003}$
LayoutLM (max pooled)	$0.19*_{0.001}$	$0.13*_{0.000}$

Table 1: Mean F_1 and ARI over five runs, with standard error of the mean (subscript). Items marked with * are significantly different from BERT average, $p < 0.001$ based on a two-tailed t-test.

4 Experiments

We evaluate on RVL-CDIP[2] (Harley et al., 2015), scanned tobacco-litigation documents from the Illinois Institute of Technology Complex Document Information Processing (IIT-CDIP) collection, labeled with type, such as letter or invoice. The complete class list appears in Table 3. We clustered the validation set (40K pages). Like LayoutLM, we used Tesseract[3] for OCR.

We use LayoutLM's publicly-released code and base model for experiments.[4] This model was pretrained on IIT-CDIP, excluding documents in RVL-CDIP. For BERT, we use the Transformers package[5] with the bert-base-uncased model, pretrained on books and Wikipedia. Because LayoutLM's masked language model pretrained on documents from the same domain, while BERT's did not, the dataset could favor LayoutLM.

We calculate F_1 and adjusted Rand index (ARI) for each system, using Manning et al. (2008)'s definitions of true and false positives and negatives. We use sklearn (Pedregosa et al., 2011)'s implementation of ARI. We report the mean over 5 runs and use a two-tailed t-test to determine whether systems differ significantly from the BERT baseline.

5 Results

Results are shown in Table 1 and Figure 1. Our experiments show that the performance of a system using LayoutLM vectors is significantly worse ($p < 0.001$) at clustering RVL-CDIP documents by type than a simple BERT baseline. There was no significant difference between the TF-IDF and

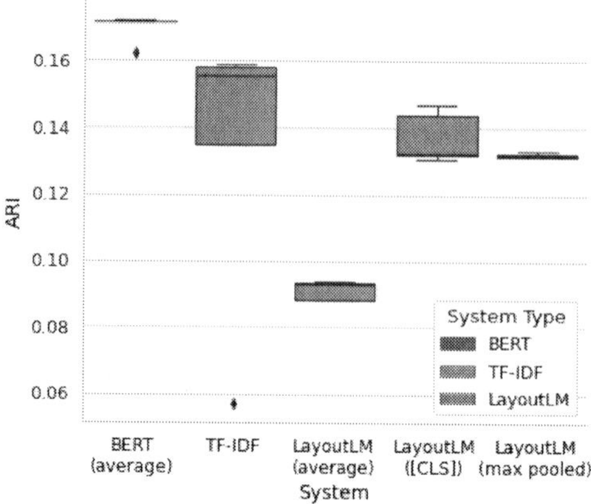

(a) Boxplot of ARI

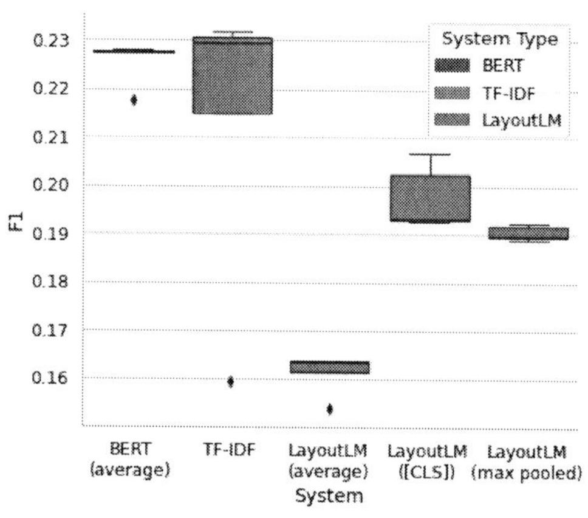

(b) Boxplot of F_1

Figure 1: Boxplots of F_1 and ARI over five runs.

BERT systems.

In contrast to prior work on BERT, where the [CLS] token was a worse representation than averaging (Reimers and Gurevych, 2019; Wang and Kuo, 2020), the best-performing LayoutLM system used the [CLS] token embedding. We suspect this is because averaging or max-pooling LayoutLM vectors blends together bounding box information for all tokens, erasing the benefits of a layout-sensitive transformer. In light of these results, we also tested [CLS] token and max-pooling for BERT on this task. Consistent with prior work, averaging outperformed both; see Table 2.

All of these scores are low, especially in comparison to classification results. The comparison is misleading, of course, since classification requires training data, and clustering addresses the case where such data is not available. Neverthe-

---

[2] https://www.cs.cmu.edu/~aharley/rvl-cdip/

[3] https://github.com/tesseract-ocr/tesseract; we used version 4.1.1.

[4] https://github.com/microsoft/unilm/tree/master/layoutlm. The version as of this writing does not include the optional image embeddings.

[5] https://github.com/huggingface/transformers

	F_1	ARI
Average	**0.23**	**0.17**
[CLS]	0.21	0.16
Max-pooled	0.20	0.15

Table 2: Comparison of different techniques of combining BERT vectors (mean F_1 and ARI over five runs)

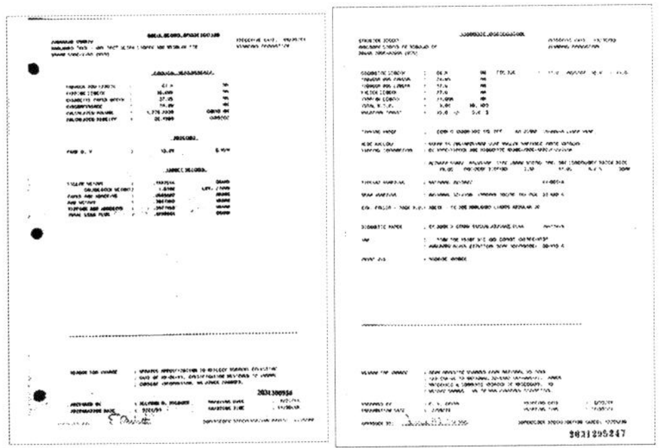

Figure 2: Specifications from a cluster with 0.97 purity.

less, much improvement will be required before document-type clustering is useful for practical applications.

5.1 Analysis

To understand this unexpected result, we reviewed example clusters from one run of the BERT system and one of LayoutLM([CLS]).

Documents in LayoutLM's best clusters had consistent layouts, illustrated in Figure 2. Specifications in the highest-purity cluster seem to have been generated from a few templates. For such documents, the layouts are so consistent that no learning is required to identify which aspects of layout to emphasize in grouping the documents. Not all specifications conform to these templates, though. Figure 3 shows some with different formats, which LayoutLM placed in a different cluster. Document layouts that are common across multiple document types also caused problems for LayoutLM. Figure 4 shows an invoice and resume with similar formats from the cluster with the lowest purity.

Table 3 lists class precision[6] for the sample clustering runs. From this, we see that LayoutLM performed well on scientific publications. A substantial fraction of this class contains two-column documents, like those in Figure 6, which LayoutLM can recognize. In contrast, BERT far outperformed LayoutLM for resumes, where page layout may

---

[6]Precision of pairs of examples where at least one has the specified gold label.

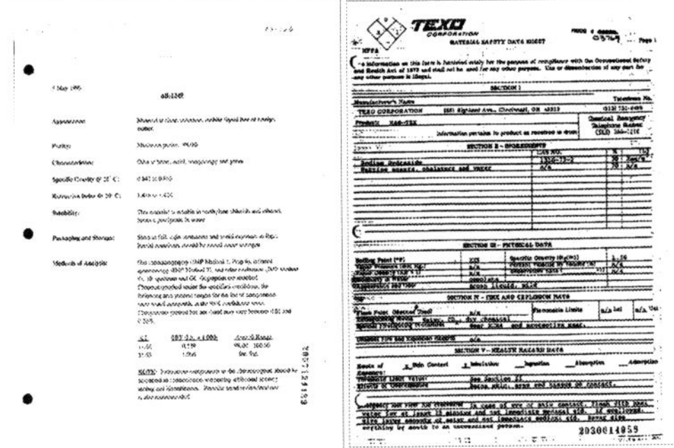

Figure 3: Specifications with different formats, which did not appear in the high-purity specification cluster.

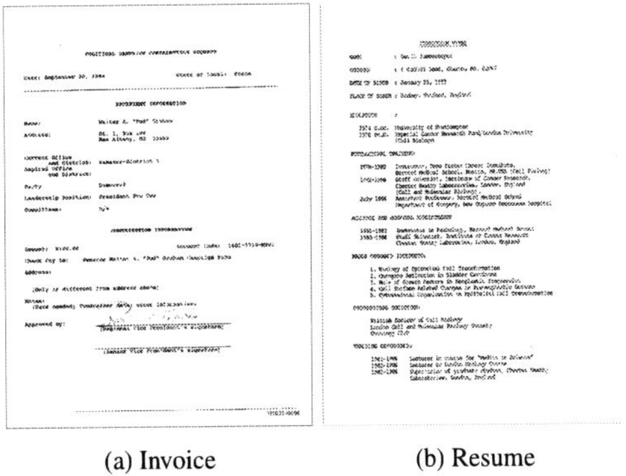

(a) Invoice	(b) Resume

Figure 4: Samples from the lowest-purity cluster.

be misleading. BERT correctly clustered the two resume images in Figure 5 together, despite their obvious layout differences. LayoutLM understandably placed them in different clusters.

6 Conclusion

LayoutLM captures textual and layout information about documents. When training data is available,

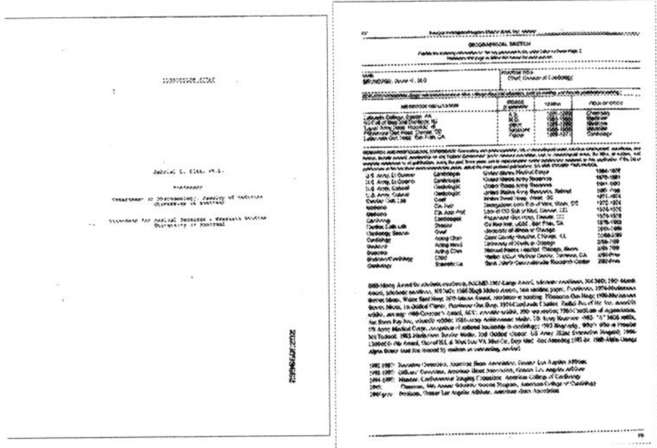

Figure 5: BERT correctly clustered these two resume pages together despite their very different layouts; LayoutLM put them in different clusters.

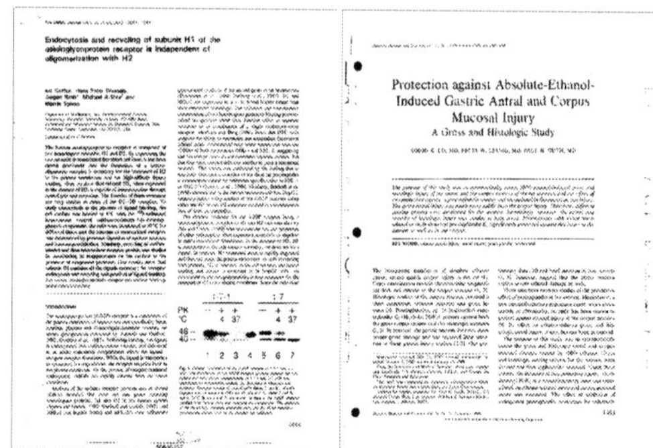

Figure 6: LayoutLM correctly clustered these two scientific documents together.

Class	BERT	LayoutLM
scientific publication	0.29	**0.37**
file folder	**0.32**	0.30
email	**0.39**	0.29
questionnaire	0.11	**0.21**
handwritten	**0.24**	0.19
specification	**0.27**	0.19
resume	**0.60**	0.16
news article	**0.15**	**0.15**
advertisement	0.09	**0.14**
memo	0.13	**0.14**
letter	**0.15**	0.12
budget	**0.13**	0.11
invoice	**0.18**	0.10
presentation	**0.16**	0.10
scientific report	**0.12**	0.09
form	**0.12**	0.09

Table 3: Class precisions for the sample clustering.

a model can learn when to leverage each. Thus, LayoutLM performed quite well at classifying documents by type. But when clustering, there is no model to indicate how to weight features in determining document similarities. In this context, layout information significantly harms performance. Future work should explore ways to incorporate benefits of layout information into a representation while limiting its harm, as well as how layout information affects tasks that fall between classification and clustering, such as semi-supervised learning. Such questions must be answered for document-type clustering to become practical.

Acknowledgments

We would like to thank the anonymous reviewers for their helpful comments, as well as Anik Saha for many discussions on LayoutLM's strengths and weaknesses for supervised tasks.

References

Sherif Abuelwafa, Marco Pedersoli, and Mohamed Cheriet. 2019. Unsupervised Exemplar-Based Learning for Improved Document Image Classification. *IEEE Access*, 7:133738–133748.

Muhammad Zeshan Afzal, Samuele Capobianco, Muhammad Imran Malik, Simone Marinai, Thomas M. Breuel, Andreas Dengel, and Marcus Liwicki. 2015. DeepDocClassifier: Document classification with deep convolutional neural network. In *2015 13th International Conference on Document Analysis and Recognition (ICDAR)*, pages 1111–1115.

Muhammad Zeshan Afzal, Andreas Kolsch, Sheraz Ahmed, and Marcus Liwicki. 2017. Cutting the error by half: Investigation of very deep cnn and advanced training strategies for document image classification. In *2017 14th IAPR International Conference on Document Analysis and Recognition (ICDAR)*, pages 883–888.

Muhammad Nabeel Asim, Muhammad Usman Ghani Khan, Muhammad Imran Malik, Khizar Razzaque, Andreas Dengel, and Sheraz Ahmed. 2019. Two Stream Deep Network for Document Image Classification. In *2019 International Conference on Document Analysis and Recognition (ICDAR)*, pages 1410–1416.

Nicolas Audebert, Catherine Herold, Kuider Slimani, and Cédric Vidal. 2020. Multimodal Deep Networks for Text and Image-based Document Classification. *Communications in Computer and Information Science*, 1167:427–443.

Adrian Cosma, Mihai Ghidoveanu, Michael Panaitescu-Liess, and Marius Popescu. 2020. Self-Supervised Representation Learning on Document Images.

Gabriela Csurka, Diane Larlus, Albert Gordo, and Jon Almazán. 2016. What is the right way to represent document images?

Arindam Das, Saikat Roy, and Ujjwal Bhattacharya. 2018. Document Image Classification with Intra-Domain Transfer Learning and Stacked Generalization of Deep Convolutional Neural Networks.

Tyler Dauphinee, Nikunj Patel, and Mohammad Rashidi. 2019. Modular Multimodal Architecture for Document Classification.

Timo I. Denk and Christian Reisswig. 2019. BERT-grid: Contextualized Embedding for 2D Document Representation and Understanding. In *Workshop on Document Intelligence at NeurIPS 2019*.

Jacob Devlin, Ming-Wei Chang, Kenton Lee, and Kristina Toutanova. 2018. BERT: Pre-training of

Deep Bidirectional Transformers for Language Understanding. *arXiv preprint arXiv:1810.04805.*

Javier Ferrando, Juan Luis Domínguez, Jordi Torres, Raúl García, David García, Daniel Garrido, Jordi Cortada, and Mateo Valero. 2020. Improving Accuracy and Speeding Up Document Image Classification Through Parallel Systems. In *Computational Science – ICCS 2020*, pages 387–400, Cham. Springer International Publishing.

Adam W. Harley, Alex Ufkes, and Konstantinos G. Derpanis. 2015. Evaluation of deep convolutional nets for document image classification and retrieval. In *Proceedings of the International Conference on Document Analysis and Recognition, ICDAR*, pages 991–995.

Le Kang, Jayant Kumar, Peng Ye, Yi Li, and David Doermann. 2014. Convolutional Neural Networks for Document Image Classification. In *2014 22nd International Conference on Pattern Recognition*, pages 3168–3172.

Anoop R. Katti, Christian Reisswig, Cordula Guder, Sebastian Brarda, Steffen Bickel, Johannes Höhne, and Jean Baptiste Faddoul. 2018. Chargrid: Towards Understanding 2D Documents. In *Proceedings of the 2018 Conference on Empirical Methods in Natural Language Processing*, pages 4459–4469, Brussels, Belgium. Association for Computational Linguistics.

Jayant Kumar, Peng Ye, and David Doermann. 2014. Structural similarity for document image classification and retrieval. *Pattern Recognition Letters*, 43:119–126.

Xiaojing Liu, Feiyu Gao, Qiong Zhang, and Huasha Zhao. 2019. Graph Convolution for Multimodal Information Extraction from Visually Rich Documents. In *Proceedings of the 2019 Conference of the North American Chapter of the Association for Computational Linguistics: Human Language Technologies, Volume 2 (Industry Papers)*, pages 32–39, Minneapolis, Minnesota. Association for Computational Linguistics.

Colin Lockard, Prashant Shiralkar, Xin Luna Dong, and Hannaneh Hajishirzi. 2020. ZeroShotCeres: Zero-Shot Relation Extraction from Semi-Structured Webpages. In *Proceedings of the 58th Annual Meeting of the Association for Computational Linguistics*, pages 8105–8117, Online. Association for Computational Linguistics.

Christopher D. Manning, Prabhakar Raghavan, and Hinrich Schütze. 2008. *Introduction to Information Retrieval.* Cambridge University Press, USA.

Lucia Noce, Ignazio Gallo, Alessandro Zamberletti, and Alessandro Calefati. 2016. Embedded Textual Content for Document Image Classification with Convolutional Neural Networks. In *Proceedings of*

the 2016 ACM Symposium on Document Engineering, DocEng '16, pages 165–173, New York, NY, USA. Association for Computing Machinery.

Fabian Pedregosa, Gaël Varoquaux, Alexandre Gramfort, Vincent Michel, Bertrand Thirion, Olivier Grisel, Mathieu Blondel, Peter Prettenhofer, Ron Weiss, Vincent Dubourg, Jake Vanderplas, Alexandre Passos, David Cournapeau, Matthieu Brucher, Matthieu Perrot, and Édouard Duchesnay. 2011. Scikit-learn: Machine Learning in Python. *Journal of Machine Learning Research*, 12:2825–2830.

Nils Reimers and Iryna Gurevych. 2019. Sentence-BERT: Sentence embeddings using Siamese BERT-networks. In *Proceedings of the 2019 Conference on Empirical Methods in Natural Language Processing and the 9th International Joint Conference on Natural Language Processing (EMNLP-IJCNLP)*, pages 3982–3992, Hong Kong, China. Association for Computational Linguistics.

Ritesh Sarkhel and Arnab Nandi. 2019. Deterministic routing between layout abstractions for multi-scale classification of visually rich documents. In *IJCAI International Joint Conference on Artificial Intelligence*, pages 3360–3366.

Chris Tensmeyer and Tony Martinez. 2017. Analysis of Convolutional Neural Networks for Document Image Classification. In *Proceedings of the International Conference on Document Analysis and Recognition, ICDAR*, volume 1, pages 388–393.

Bin Wang and C.-C. Jay Kuo. 2020. SBERT-WK: A Sentence Embedding Method by Dissecting BERT-based Word Models.

Yiheng Xu, Minghao Li, Lei Cui, Shaohan Huang, Furu Wei, and Ming Zhou. 2019. LayoutLM: Pretraining of Text and Layout for Document Image Understanding.

An Analysis of Capsule Networks for Part of Speech Tagging in High- and Low-resource Scenarios[*]

Andrew Zupon[*], Faiz Rafique[†], and Mihai Surdeanu[†]
*Department of Linguistics, †Department of Computer Science
University of Arizona
{zupon, faizr, msurdeanu}@email.arizona.edu

Abstract

Neural networks are a common tool in NLP, but it is not always clear which architecture to use for a given task. Different tasks, different languages, and different training conditions can all affect how a neural network will perform. Capsule Networks (CapsNets) are a relatively new architecture in NLP. Due to their novelty, CapsNets are being used more and more in NLP tasks. However, their usefulness is still mostly untested. In this paper, we compare three neural network architectures—LSTM, CNN, and CapsNet—on a part of speech tagging task. We compare these architectures in both high- and low-resource training conditions and find that no architecture consistently performs the best. Our analysis shows that our CapsNet performs nearly as well as a more complex LSTM under certain training conditions, but not others, and that our CapsNet almost always outperforms our CNN. We also find that our CapsNet implementation shows faster prediction times than the LSTM for Scottish Gaelic but not for Spanish, highlighting the effect that the choice of languages can have on the models.

1 Introduction

Neural networks have become a common tool in natural language processing (NLP) for many tasks, but are different architectures better suited for different tasks, languages, and/or resources? To try to answer this question, we examine the performance of two common neural network architectures, long short-term memory networks (LSTM) (Greff et al., 2017) and convolutional neural networks (CNN) (LeCun et al., 1989), against the newer capsule networks (CapsNets), another neural network architecture based on CNNs (Hinton et al., 2011).

While LSTMs and CNNs are common in NLP, capsule networks are relatively new to the field. Due to their recency, it's not always clear if or when they are better than other widely used sequence models. This paper investigates the CapsNet architecture in comparison with LSTMs and CNNs. For our analysis, we apply these three architectures to a part of speech (POS) tagging task, on two languages, and using both low- and high-resource scenarios.

Much of the focus of NLP research is on resource-rich languages like English. However, the performance of different models can depend on the linguistic properties of the language under study (Bender, 2009) and the amount of training data available. To compare the performance of these architectures under different training conditions, we look at Spanish—another resource-rich language—and Scottish Gaelic—a low-resource language using different amounts of training data. This comparison is a step in the right direction, but it does have the limitations of comparing neural network architectures implemented in different frameworks and only comparing two languages.

The main contribution of this paper is comparing the LSTM, CNN, and CapsNet architectures across different training conditions. Our analysis finds that none of the architectures consistently performs best across training conditions. This illustrates how different languages and training conditions can inform which architecture is best suited for a given NLP task, and that there is no obviously correct answer.

2 Related Work

CapsNets are a relatively new type of neural network. Hinton et al. (2011) introduces the architecture, with modifications by Sabour et al. (2017) (dynamic routing) and Hinton et al. (2018) (EM routing). A CapsNet is essentially a modified ver-

---

[*]The code and data for this paper can be found at
`https://github.com/clulab/releases/tree/`
`master/emnlp2020-capsnet`.

66

sion of a CNN that trades max pooling for a more data-retentive process called routing by agreement. Instead of the prediction with the highest score getting chosen, the weighted sum of all predictions are considered for classification. Essentially, a CapsNet uses convolution to create first round predictions for objects—primary capsules—and then utilizes routing by agreement to predict the presence of higher level objects—secondary capsules.

Many implementations of CapsNets are designed for image recognition (Hinton et al., 2011; Sabour et al., 2017; Hinton et al., 2018). However, the CapsNet architecture is being applied more and more to NLP tasks, including Chinese word segmentation (Li et al., 2018), and multi-label text classification and question answering (Zhao et al., 2019). This paper continues this path by investigating how CapsNets compare to other neural network architectures for the task of part of speech tagging.

3 Data

Our comparison considers two languages: Spanish[1] and Scottish Gaelic[2]. Spanish is a resource-rich language, being the second most spoken language by number native speakers, fourth most spoken language by total number of speakers, and the third or fourth most widely used language on the internet[3]. Scottish Gaelic is a low-resource language, with 57,375 fluent speakers in Scotland per the 2011 census[4]. The Spanish data come from the UD Spanish AnCora treebank[5]. The Scottish Gaelic data come from the UD ARCOSG treebank[6]. Both corpora use 17 part of speech tag classes.

To study how different low-resource conditions affect training, we artificially create training partitions of different sizes. From the original training data (train100), we create partitions consisting of 50% (train50), 10% (train10), and 1% (train1) of the training sentences. The amount of data for each partition is shown in Table 1 for Spanish and Table 2 for Scottish Gaelic. We use FastText word embeddings (Grave et al., 2018) for both Spanish (2,000,000 words) and Scottish Gaelic (14,318 words). The embedding dimension is 300.

Partition	Sentences	Tokens	Avg. Sent. Length
train100	14,305	446,144	31.2
train50	7,152	255,213	35.7
train10	1,430	43,480	30.4
train1	143	5,912	41.3
dev	1,654	52,511	31.7
test	1,721	52,801	30.7

Table 1: Number of sentences, tokens, and average sentence length for each partition of Spanish. The n in the train partitions corresponds to the amount (percent) of the original data used for training.

Partition	Sentences	Tokens	Avg. Sent. Length
train100	1,015	22,963	22.6
train50	507	10,870	21.4
train10	101	1,543	15.3
train1	10	67	6.7
dev	642	9,949	15.5
test	536	9,946	18.6

Table 2: Number of sentences, tokens, and average sentence length for each partition of Scottish Gaelic. The n in the train partitions corresponds to the amount (percent) of the original data used for training.

4 Approach

In this section, we describe the implementation details of our CapsNet, CNN, and LSTM methods. Our CapsNet and CNN implementations build on top of Yeung et al.'s implementation[7], which was kept as close as possible to the architectures described by Sabour et al. (2017). Importantly, we tried to keep all three models as close to each other as possible in order to make our comparison as faithful as possible. However, certain differences persist for this project—for example, the CapsNet and CNN are implemented in Python using Tensorflow[8] and Keras[9], whereas the LSTM is implemented in Scala using DyNet.[10] The hyperparameters for our CapsNet and CNN implementations were chosen to be as close as possible to the original implementation. The hyperparameters of the LSTM were chosen to be a reasonable approximation to the CapsNet and CNN models. It is important to note that our comparison does not attempt to compare the best of the best of each architecture.

---

[1] Indo-European, Romance

[2] Indo-European, Celtic

[3] Third by number internet users by language, fourth by number of websites by language

[4] Only 1.1% of Scotland's population over 3 years old

[5] UD Ancora

[6] UD Scottish Gaelic ARCOSG

[7] https://github.com/Chucooleg/CapsNet_for_NER

[8] https://www.tensorflow.org/

[9] https://keras.io/

[10] We used the implementation from the processors library (https://github.com/clulab/processors), which relies on DyNet (https://dynet.readthedocs.

Model	P	R	F1	Train t	Predict t
100% of train, caps, no learn	93.85 (0.35)	94.47 (0.24)	94.16 (0.23)	9,032 s	218 s
100% of train, cnn, no learn	93.76 (0.40)	94.20 (0.11)	93.98 (0.22)	4,802 s	200 s
100% of train, lstm, no learn	**98.54** (0.03)	**98.54** (0.03)	**98.54** (0.03)	3,222 s	165 s
50% of train, caps, no learn	92.78 (0.45)	93.58 (0.20)	93.18 (0.31)	5,386 s	223
50% of train, cnn, no learn	92.36 (0.59)	93.54 (0.12)	92.95 (0.29)	3,392 s	206 s
50% of train, lstm, no learn	**98.31** (0.03)	**98.31** (0.03)	**98.31** (0.03)	1,566 s	175 s
10% of train, caps, no learn	88.37 (0.73)	89.48 (0.67)	88.92 (0.56)	3,186 s	208 s
10% of train, cnn, no learn	88.23 (0.60)	89.17 (0.45)	88.70 (0.33)	3,373 s	191 s
10% of train, lstm, no learn	**96.89** (0.14)	**96.89** (0.14)	**96.89** (0.14)	613 s	170 s
1% of train, caps, no learn	76.63 (1.11)	80.62 (0.74)	78.56 (0.30)	3,370 s	205 s
1% of train, cnn, no learn	73.96 (2.66)	74.78 (0.68)	74.34 (1.44)	2,898 s	187 s
1% of train, lstm, no learn	**91.79** (0.24)	**91.79** (0.24)	**91.79** (0.24)	375 s	162 s
100% of train, caps, learn	96.30 (0.35)	95.61 (0.19)	96.00 (0.08)	14,223 s	219 s
100% of train, cnn, learn	96.01 (0.34)	95.43 (0.15)	95.72 (0.16)	12,794 s	211 s
100% of train, lstm, learn	**98.43** (0.04)	**98.43** (0.04)	**98.43** (0.04)	4,280 s	172 s
50% of train, caps, learn	95.59 (0.27)	94.68 (0.16)	95.13 (0.09)	11,571 s	225 s
50% of train, cnn, learn	95.36 (0.10)	94.61 (0.08)	94.98 (0.06)	11,318 s	206 s
50% of train, lstm, learn	**98.17** (0.06)	**98.17** (0.06)	**98.17** (0.06)	1,333 s	171 s
10% of train, caps, learn	92.45 (0.26)	90.18 (0.32)	91.30 (0.08)	3,767 s	209 s
10% of train, cnn, learn	91.41 (0.42)	89.49 (0.25)	90.44 (0.20)	3,832 s	191 s
10% of train, lstm, learn	**96.84** (0.07)	**96.84** (0.07)	**96.84** (0.07)	1,157 s	172 s
1% of train, caps, learn	84.12 (0.66)	82.65 (0.46)	83.38 (0.24)	3,452 s	205 s
1% of train, cnn, learn	79.71 (0.91)	75.87 (1.01)	77.73 (0.35)	2,979 s	188 s
1% of train, lstm, learn	**91.80** (0.21)	**91.80** (0.21)	**91.80** (0.21)	440 s	178 s

Table 3: Spanish Precision, Recall, and F1 scores. The scores are an average of 5 different random seeds and their standard deviation, along with the average training/prediction times of each model.

4.1 CapsNet Implementation

Our CapsNet model has two 1D convolutional layers, two routing by agreement capsule layers and one fully connected layer. Both convolutional layers have 256 channels, a kernel size of 3, and a stride of 1. The primary capsule layer has 160 capsules with 8 dimensions, a kernel size of 3 and stride of 1. There are 17 secondary capsules with dimensions of 16 and 3 dynamic routing passes.

4.2 CNN Implementation

Our CNN model has three 1D convolutional layers, a max pooling layer, and two fully connected layers. The first two convolutional layers are identical to the first two layers of the CapsNet. The third convolutional layer has 128 channels, size of 3 and stride 1. The two feed-forward layers have a size fo 328 and 192. These settings were chosen to make the CNN implementation as comparable as possible to the CapsNet implementation.

4.3 LSTM Implementation

The LSTM code we used is a reimplementation of the LSTM-CRF approach of Lample et al. (2016). To make this implementation as similar as possible with the previous two approaches, we: (a) removed the CRF layer,[11] and (b) removed the character-level biLSTM encoder from the word embeddings.

Thus, the actual LSTM architecture used consists of three layers: (i) an input layer with 300-dimensional FastText word embeddings; (ii) one biLSTM intermediate layer, where each LSTM has a hidden state of dimension 128 neurons, and (iii) a linear output layer coupled with a softmax function to output the POS tags.

5 Results

In addition to our four training data conditions per language, we evaluate the use of learning the word embeddings during training for all models ("learn" vs. "no learn"), yielding 24 training conditions per language. We trained all models five times with

io).

---

[11] In initial experiments we observed that the CRF layer had a major contribution to other sequence models such as named entity recognition, but no impact on POS tagging.

Model	P	R	F1	Train t	Predict t
100% of train, caps, no learn	**82.34** (0.82)	80.58 (0.22)	81.45 (0.32)	1,020 s	19 s
100% of train, cnn, no learn	79.40 (1.12)	77.19 (0.96)	78.27 (0.53)	651 s	16 s
100% of train, lstm, no learn	81.86 (0.30)	**81.86** (0.30)	**81.86** (0.30)	256 s	38 s
50% of train, caps, no learn	**75.90** (1.02)	73.98 (0.47)	74.92 (0.54)	809 s	18 s
50% of train, cnn, no learn	71.97 (1.62)	69.33 (0.80)	70.61 (0.47)	616 s	15 s
50% of train, lstm, no learn	75.36 (0.27)	**75.36** (0.27)	**75.36** (0.27)	119 s	37 s
10% of train, caps, no learn	49.24 (2.78)	37.36 (1.43)	42.44 (1.35)	641 s	19 s
10% of train, cnn, no learn	**54.64** (2.16)	50.04 (1.69)	52.18 (0.64)	555 s	15 s
10% of train, lstm, no learn	53.31 (8.11)	**53.31** (8.11)	**53.31** (8.11)	86 s	40 s
1% of train, caps, no learn	7.94 (1.40)	7.82 (1.28)	7.86 (1.26)	486 s	18 s
1% of train, cnn, no learn	16.87 (3.86)	8.42 (3.52)	10.58 (3.09)	546 s	16 s
1% of train, lstm, no learn	**21.37** (3.17)	**21.37** (3.17)	**21.37** (3.17)	44 s	35 s
100% of train, caps, learn	**90.81** (0.35)	87.91 (0.25)	89.34 (0.25)	1,907 s	19 s
100% of train, cnn, learn	88.82 (0.80)	85.57 (0.50)	87.17 (0.32)	1,742 s	16 s
100% of train, lstm, learn	89.84 (0.15)	**89.84** (0.15)	**89.84** (0.15)	317 s	39 s
50% of train, caps, learn	**85.38** (0.62)	81.63 (0.22)	83.46 (0.32)	1,285 s	18 s
50% of train, cnn, learn	82.26 (0.63)	77.95 (0.48)	80.05 (0.54)	1,075 s	16 s
50% of train, lstm, learn	83.66 (0.57)	**83.66** (0.57)	**83.66** (0.57)	155 s	39 s
10% of train, caps, learn	55.16 (1.55)	46.21 (2.04)	50.26 (1.45)	717 s	19 s
10% of train, cnn, learn	57.84 (3.16)	55.13 (1.53)	56.37 (1.26)	629 s	15 s
10% of train, lstm, learn	**65.49** (0.67)	**65.49** (0.67)	**65.49** (0.67)	101 s	40 s
1% of train, caps, learn	8.31 (1.99)	8.55 (2.25)	8.42 (2.10)	509 s	19 s
1% of train, cnn, learn	18.23 (3.47)	11.63 (5.57)	13.63 (5.31)	544 s	16 s
1% of train, lstm, learn	**21.37** (3.17)	**21.37** (3.17)	**21.37** (3.17)	52 s	36 s

Table 4: Scottish Gaelic Precision, Recall, and F1 scores. The scores are an average of 5 different random seeds and their standard deviation, along with the average training/prediction times of each model.

LSTM Hidden State Size	Spanish-100	Spanish-1	Scottish Gaelic-100	Scottish Gaelic-1
64	98.40	91.76	89.46	18.55
128	**98.43**	**91.80**	**89.84**	**21.37**
256	98.42	91.44	89.25	15.02
Capsule Layer Kernel Size	**Spanish-100**	**Spanish-1**	**Scottish Gaelic-100**	**Scottish Gaelic-1**
3	**96.00**	**83.38**	**89.34**	8.42
5	**96.00**	82.69	89.21	**9.92**
7	95.99	82.59	88.62	6.06

Table 5: F1 scores for different hyperparameter choices for LSTM hidden state size and CapsNet capsule layer kernel size on the Spanish and Scottish Gaelic 100% and 1% learned embeddings training conditions. The hyperparameter values in italics (hidden state size 128 and kernel size 3) are the values chosen for our bigger comparison.

a different random seed and averaged the results. Each condition trained for 10 epochs, with early stopping after 2 epochs if the loss did not improve.

The results are given in Table 3 (Spanish) and Table 4 (Scottish Gaelic). We report Precision, Recall, F1, training time, and prediction time. These results show a few trends:

1. The LSTM always outperforms the CapsNet and CNN for Spanish, but the CapsNet and CNN occasionally outperform the LSTM for Scottish Gaelic, whose training dataset is an order of magnitude smaller than the Spanish one.

2. The difference in F1 on the no learn train condition between the Spanish 10% and Scottish Gaelic 100% partitions, which have a comparable number of sentences, is greater for the LSTM (down 9.93%) than the Capsnet (down 2.98%) or CNN (up 3.93%). This suggests that properties of the language, not just the amount of data, play a role in performance.

3. The LSTM benefits only slightly from using learned embeddings, while both the CapsNet and CNN get a much larger performance boost. We see this in the Spanish 1% condition, where the LSTM

F1 improves by 0.01%, but the CapsNet and CNN models improve by 4.82% and 3.39%, respectively.

4. Another obvious difference is in the model training and prediction times. The training time for the CapsNet and CNN is much slower than the LSTM. However, for the Scottish Gaelic case CapsNets are much faster than the LSTM at prediction time. This is an encouraging result, considering that our CapsNet implementation is in Python, whereas the LSTM is implemented in a faster Scala framework.

Overall, the LSTM performs best in most conditions, but the CapsNet often comes close. The CapsNet also usually outperforms the CNN. These performance differences are potentially offset by faster prediction time, depending on the language. The balance between predictive accuracy, training time, and prediction time can be delicate, especially when looking at low-resource languages. These results suggest that depending on the use case, a CapsNet architecture may be preferable to an LSTM, despite the fact that when more resources are available, the LSTM tends to perform the best under the common hyperparameters investigated here.

We also compared different hyperparameters for the LSTM and CapsNet, which is shown in Table 5. The values we chose for the LSTM hidden state size and the CapsNet capsule layer kernel size perform the best in nearly all conditions.

6 Conclusion

In this paper, we compare the performance of three neural network architectures—LSTM, CNN, and CapsNet—on part of speech tagging and find that LSTMs are not always better under the common hyperparameters investigated. We examine how the best performing model changes under different high- and low-resource training conditions using Spanish and Scottish Gaelic. We show that the relatively new CapsNet architecture performs nearly as well as the more complex LSTM under certain conditions and outperforms the CNN under most conditions we examined. These results suggest that there is no one obviously clear choice for a model architecture, and that the properties of a language and the amount of training data can affect which architecture performs best. Future work should address the limitations of this paper. Specifically, future effort should consider more training conditions, including other languages; the consistency of these results within groups of similar languages;

and making the implementation of these architectures closer, to guarantee the performance differences are due to the architecture and not an artifact of how they were implemented.

References

Emily M. Bender. 2009. Linguistically naïve != language independent: Why NLP needs linguistic typology. In *Proceedings of the EACL 2009 Workshop on the Interaction between Linguistics and Computational Linguistics: Virtuous, Vicious or Vacuous?*, pages 26–32, Athens, Greece. Association for Computational Linguistics.

Edouard Grave, Piotr Bojanowski, Prakhar Gupta, Armand Joulin, and Tomas Mikolov. 2018. Learning word vectors for 157 languages. In *Proceedings of the International Conference on Language Resources and Evaluation (LREC 2018)*.

Klaus Greff, Rupesh K. Srivastava, Jan Koutník, Bas R. Steunebrink, and Jürgen Schmidhuber. 2017. LSTM: A search space odyssey. *IEEE Transactions on Neural Networks and Learning Systems*, 28(10):2222–2232.

Geoffrey E. Hinton, Alex Krizhevsky, and Sida D. Wang. 2011. Transforming auto-encoders. In *Artificial Neural Networks and Machine Learning*, pages 44–51. Springer.

Geoffrey E. Hinton, Sara Sabour, and Nicholas Frosst. 2018. Matrix capsules with EM routing. In *International Conference on Learning Representations*.

Guillaume Lample, Miguel Ballesteros, Sandeep Subramanian, Kazuya Kawakami, and Chris Dyer. 2016. Neural architectures for named entity recognition. *arXiv preprint arXiv:1603.01360*.

Y. LeCun, B. Boser, J. S. Denker, D. Henderson, R. E. Howard, W. Hubbard, and L. D. Jackel. 1989. Backpropagation applied to handwritten zip code recognition. *Neural Computation*, 1(4):541–551.

Si Li, Mingzheng Li, Yajing Xu, Zuyi Bao, Lu Fu, and Yan Zhu. 2018. Capsules based chinese word segmentation for ancient chinese medical books. *IEEE Access*, 6:70874–70883.

Sara Sabour, Nicholas Frosst, and Geoffrey E. Hinton. 2017. Dynamic routing between capsules. In Isabelle Guyon, Ulrike. Von Luxburg, Samy Bengio, Hanna Wallach, Rob Fergus, S.V.N. Vishwanathan, and Roman Garnett, editors, *Advances in Neural Information Processing Systems 30*, pages 3856–3866. Curran Associates, Inc.

Wei Zhao, Haiyun Peng, Steffen Eger, Erik Cambria, and Min Yang. 2019. Towards scalable and reliable capsule networks for challenging nlp applications. *Proceedings of the 57th Annual Meeting of the Association for Computational Linguistics*.

Can Knowledge Graph Embeddings Tell Us What Fact-checked Claims Are About?

Valentina Beretta[1], Katarina Boland[3], Luke Lo Seen[2],
Sébastien Harispe[1], Konstantin Todorov[2] and Andon Tchechmedjiev[1]
[1]EuroMov Digital Health in Motion, Univ Montpellier, IMT Mines Alès, Alès, France
[2]LIRMM, University of Montpellier, CNRS, Montpellier, France
[3]GESIS, Cologne, Germany
{firstname.lastname}@mines-ales.fr
katarina.boland@gesis.org, todorov@lirmm.fr

Abstract

The web offers a wealth of discourse data that help researchers from various fields analyze debates about current societal issues and gauge the effects on society of important phenomena such as misinformation spread. Such analyses often revolve around claims made by people about a given topic of interest. Fact-checking portals offer partially structured information that can assist such analysis. However, exploiting the network structure of such online discourse data is as of yet under-explored. We study the effectiveness of using neural-graph embedding features for claim topic prediction and their complementarity with text embeddings. We show that graph embeddings are modestly complementary with text embeddings, but the low performance of graph embedding features alone indicate that the model fails to capture topological features pertinent of the topic prediction task.

1 Introduction

Analysing claims shared on social media is of growing interest, from social/political sciences to Artificial Intelligence (AI). Such analyses are often performed with respect to a specific set of topics (e.g. "immigration" or "abortion") that allow carrying out targeted studies of trends, understanding/quantifying hidden biases (Garimella et al., 2018), discovering stances towards those topics (Wang et al., 2018) or their underlying falsehood propagation patterns (Vosoughi et al., 2018). Fact-checking portals offer a wealth of information about claims, their truth values and their sources. To analyse claims about a given topic, scientists need (1) access to heterogeneous repositories of claims and (2) the prior knowledge of which entities are mentioned in claims that belong to a topic (as defined by thematic keywords in each portal).

As a (partial) response to (1), recent work has presented ClaimsKG—a large dynamic knowledge graph (KG) of fact-checked claims harvested from various fact-checking portals (like politifact.com) and their metadata (e.g. truth values, authors, sources, links to DBpedia) (Tchechmedjiev et al., 2019) (cf. Figure 1).[1] ClaimsKG includes thematic *keywords* provided by the fact-checking portals (e.g. "elections" or "taxes"). However, using them to filter claims by topic is problematic as: (1) not all claims are annotated; (2) the keywords are very heterogeneous (granularity or level of abstraction; e.g. "economy" vs. "Kim Kardashian"); (3) there is no standardization within or across portals; (4) there are no links between keywords grouping related concepts and (5) existing annotations are often incomplete. We address this need for normalization and for providing missing topic annotations of claims by investigating representation learning methods for claims.

Representation learning for text (Devlin et al., 2018; Li and Yang, 2018) and graphs (Cai et al., 2018; Goyal and Ferrara, 2018) has been successfully applied to many tasks from entity linking (Radhakrishnan et al., 2018) to link prediction in large KGs (Kazemi and Poole, 2018) allowing for KG completion/fusion. However, the ability of these methods to represent claims and to transfer to other machine learning (ML) tasks (e.g. predicting the topic(s) of a claim) has not been investigated. We evaluate the capability of link prediction graph embeddings to capture pertinent information from the graph structure in order to benefit downstream tasks. We compare the performance resulting from using (1) graph embeddings (CP/N3 model on ClaimsKG enriched with relations between mentions coming from DBPedia) (2) claim textual embeddings, or (3) different combinations thereof, as features in the task of supervised **multi-**

---

[1]https://data.gesis.org/claimskg/site/

71

Proceedings of the First Workshop on Insights from Negative Results in NLP, pages 71–75
Online, November 19, 2020. ©2020 Association for Computational Linguistics

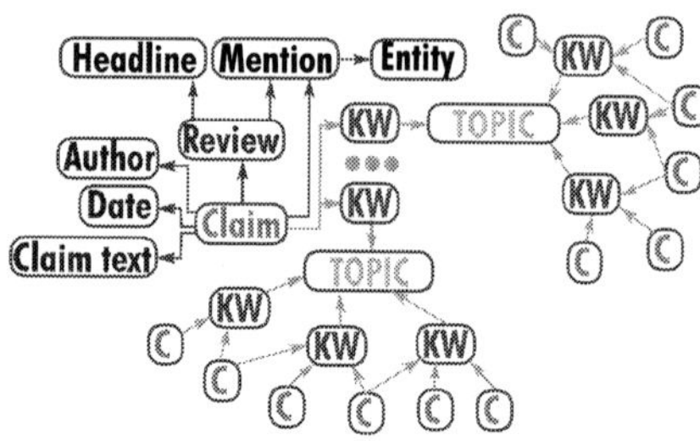

Figure 1: Simplified structure of ClaimsKG and graph baseline structures. KW=Keyword, C=Claim.

Graph	Train	Test	Dev	MRR (%)	HITS@1 (%)	HITS@3 (%)	HITS@10 (%)
CKG	9144792	190491	190403	19.45	16.79	20.86	26.36
CKG-KW	9078900	189014	189110	16.77	13.65	17.93	22.98

Table 1: Link prediction performance for ClaimsKG graph embeddings (Standard metrics: Mean Reciprocal Rank (MRR), HITS@1, HITS@3, HITS@10).

label claim topic prediction on a gold dataset. This task was chosen given that (1) it is significantly more challenging than typical topic classification tasks and (2) we can control the parameters of the evaluation by design and check for desirable properties captured by link prediction graph embeddings. We evaluate the use of claim vectors as features with or without the addition of neighbourhood vectors (outgoing relations and targets). We then perform ablation studies over different features to better characterise what is captured by the graph embeddings. Our results show that state-of-the-art link prediction models fail to capture equivalence structures and transfer poorly.

2   Claim Topic Classification Dataset

We present our semi-automatic approach to build a gold standard dataset of annotated claims for topic classification. Since ClaimsKG covers a wide range of different topics, annotating a random sample of claims would not yield a sufficient number of claims *per* topic. Thus, we identified a set of 7 topics that have a high number of claims in ClaimsKG and are relevant for claim-related studies: "healthcare " (1777), "taxes" (1519), "elections" (1074), "crime" (947), "education" (1263), "immigration" (1147) and "environment" (567). We then automatically identify claims potentially referring to these topics using the keywords assigned by the fact-checking sites. First, we mapped all keywords to common high-level concepts in two upper level taxonomies: the TheSoz thesaurus of social sciences (Zapilko et al., 2013) and the UNESCO Thesaurus[2] employing a dictionary-based entity linking approach (the concepts are noted as TOPIC in Figure 1). We then extracted a random subset of claims that are linked to at least one of the chosen topics through their keywords. Note that one claim

can correspond to several concepts thus creating a multi-label dataset. To validate and complete the semi-automatically assigned labels, we finally asked 5 annotators to re-annotate the dataset and assign the claims to all applicable topics. This gold standard, composed of 629 annotated claims, has a Krippendorff's α annotator agreement (Masi distance) (Passonneau, 2006) of 0.75 which is a reasonably high agreement but also shows that the task is not trivial. For example, consider the claim "Nobody is leaving Memphis. That's a myth." uttered by a city councilman, with the keywords "Population" and "Census" assigned by the fact-checking site.[3] At first glance, none of the selected topics seems to apply. However, the claim review explains that this claim had been uttered in context of a debate concerning the fear that a proposed one-time tax for schools might make people leave the city with this claim defending the tax. Thus, this claim may be interpreted as being about "taxes" and even "education", depending on how much of the pragmatic context is taken into account. In the final dataset[4] the topic distribution is the following: "healthcare" (25%), "taxes" (21%), "elections" (17%), "crime" (16%), "education" (13%), "immigration" (12%) and "environment" (10%).

3   Representation Learning and Evaluation Pipeline

Graph embedding models. We train[5] a CANDECOM/PARAFAC model with N3 regularization (CP-N3) (Lacroix et al., 2018).[6] We computed a model for ClaimsKG (CKG) and a variant without keywords (CKG-KW) needed in the ablation studies. The link prediction performance, reported in Table 1, is lower than for YAGO3-10, the standard dataset most similar to ClaimsKG at an equivalent

---

[2]http://vocabularies.unesco.org/thesaurus

[3]https://tinyurl.com/y6ysg4ju

[4]https://github.com/claimskg/claim_topics_dataset

[5]Code: https://github.com/twktheainur/kbc

[6]Current SOTA. Optimal parameters within hardware constraints (GeForce 2080Ti with 11GB VRAM) – CP Model, Rank 50, Adagrad optimizer, 0.1 learning rate, N3 regularizer with coefficient 0.005, 30 epochs max, batch size 150 – Approx. 3h/epoch $\times$ 3 models $\times$ 30 epochs $\times 275W \simeq 270h \times 275W \simeq 74.25 KWh@\$0.31/KWh \simeq \$23$

rank (MRR = 0.54, HITS@[1, 3, 10]=[47%, 58%, 68%]): ClaimsKG is larger and sparser (fewer triples *per* relation, more disconnected structure), which could explain this.

Feature Fusion and Evaluation Pipeline. The graph embeddings are used as features along with text embeddings in a multi-class, multi-label topic classification task. Given the small size of the dataset it was difficult to use supervised neural encoding architectures to learn intermediary representations, e.g. Bi-LSTM or Transformer, (no meaningful convergence), we rather used a classical machine learning pipeline with standard classifiers from Scikit-learn (+grid-search on held-out training data and 10-fold cross-validation).[7] Text embeddings for claims were computed through a SOTA unsupervised pooling method (Akbik et al., 2019) implemented in the `flair`[8] library on the basis of language models from the `transformers` repository. We tested most base and large models: DistilRoberta (base models) and GPT-2 (large models) consistently performed best and were retained in the evaluation.

4 Evaluation and Discussion

Comparison and combination of graph and text embeddings. We explore the performance of graph embedding vs. text embedding features and whether there is any complementarity of the two. We train and evaluate a ridge classifier (bayesian ridge regressor used as a classifier)[9] as per section 3 by using [(1) CKG] graph embedding features (claim left-hand side vector), [(2) TEDR, (3) TEGPT2] text embedding features (pooled token vectors from DistilRoberta (DR) and GPT2, [(1) & (2), (1) & (3)] the combination of both (concatenation), as reported in the first segment of Table 2. We use the topic associations extracted from the graph for the construction of the dataset (pre human-annotation) as a baseline. If graph embeddings can capture the equivalence structures that were used to create the baseline effectively, we expect that using them as features for the topic classification task will allow us to reach similar performance to that of the baseline.

Graph embeddings alone lead to poor perfor-

---

[7] Code: https://github.com/claimskg/claimskg-embeddings

[8] https://github.com/zalandoresearch/flair

[9] We evaluated several classifiers from scikit-learn, but report only RidgeClassifier as it consistently led to better average accuracy by a significant margin

Setting	Accuracy	F_1 mi.	F_1 Ma.
Complementarity of graph and text embedding features			
(1) CKG	36.40	51.77	42.84
(2) TEDR	69.60	82.80	79.38
(3) TEGPT2	74.20	86.16	84.43
(1) CKG & (2) TEDR	72.00	84.79	81.76
(1) CKG& (3) TEGPT2	68.60	81.61	79.57
Graph Baseline	81.00	89.00	88.88
Impact of neighbourhood features			
(4) CKG Flat concat	44.79	61.96	56.92
(5) CKG Triple concat	44.00	62.22	58.32
(4) CKG Flat concat & (2) TEDR	74.80	86.19	83.81
(4) CKG Flat concat & (3) TEGPT2	74.80	86.43	84.62
(5) CKG Triple concat & (2) TEDR	70.40	84.04	81.62
(5) CKG Triple concat & (3) TEGPT2	74.80	86.43	84.62
Ablation studies – Using only keywords for the text embeddings			
(6) TEDR KW Only	32.20	45.86	45.39
(7) TEGPT2 KW Only	34.00	46.40	45.35
(1) CKG & (6) TEDR KW Only	43.60	60.25	57.83
(1) CKG & (7) TEGPT2 KW Only	44.60	60.07	57.58
(4) CKG Flat concat & (6) TEDR KW Only	47.00	63.81	61.81
(4) CKG Flat concat & (7) TEGPT2 KW Only	47.60	63.23	61.24
Ablation studies – Graph embedding model without keywords			
(8) CKG No KW	0.60	1.01	0.73
(9) CKG Flat concat No KW	11.00	19.90	16.37
(8) CKG No KW & (6) TEDR KW Only	34.40	49.19	47.10
(8) CKG No KW & (7) TEGPT2 KW Only	34.40	47.08	46.33
(9) CKG Flat concat No KW & (6) TEDR KW Only	30.79	46.17	44.84
(9) CKG Flat concat No KW & (7) TEGPT2 KW Only	28.40	44.63	44.02
Ablation studies – Text embeddings of all text properties			
(10) TEDR All text	71.20	84.40	81.50
(11) TEGPT2 All text	72.80	84.61	80.19
(1) CKG& (10) TEDR All text	70.80	84.00	81.23
(1) CKG& (11) TEGPT2 All text	76.20	86.58	84.42
(4) CKG Flat concat & (10) TEDR All text	67.40	81.20	78.92
(4) CKG Flat concat & (11) TEGPT2 All text	73.20	84.65	82.37

Table 2: Results for topic classification (10-fold): avg. accuracy, F_1 micro/macro. Top – Complementarity of graph and text embedding features, Middle – Impact of different feature extraction strategies from graph embeddings, Bottom – Ablation studies.

mance, but there is a small complementarity with text embeddings. Adding graph embeddings to GPT-2 Large lowers performance: it is possible that most of the claims and associated reviews are part of GPT2's training data, thus making any information captured from the metadata superfluous. The baseline being the basis for the gold annotations prior to human annotation, it is expected to achieve a very high performance: given the poor performance of graph embedding features alone, it is likely that the model fails to capture these equivalence structures effectively.

Impact of neighbourhood features. The LHS claim embeddings did not capture much useful information for the task. Given the local nature of the link prediction training criterion, do we need to consider the embeddings of the neighbourhood to find useful features that capture the equivalence structures of the baseline? For each neighbour (author, date, sources, mentions in review and claim), we retrieve the RHS and relation vectors. We aggregate by (1) flat concatenation (Flat Concat.); (2) concat. of triple vectors (claim LHS×relation×neighbour RHS – Triple Concat.). Table 2 presents the results: using the neighbourhood brings a small improvement (+8.39/CKG, +2.80/CKG+TEDR, +0.60/CKG+GPT2), compared to CKG alone or in combination with text embeddings, particularly using concatenation, although we are far from the baseline.

Ablation studies. For the link prediction models, the most informative features arise from the claim/keyword/topic equivalence structures, as they are used to generate the graph baseline (81% accuracy). To understand if those structures are captured beyond relying on classification performance, we investigate three settings: (1) text embeddings of keywords only (KW only) (2) graph embedding without the keyword subgraph (no keywords, no topic concepts, in green in Figure 1 – CKG No KW); (3) Text embedding of all text fields (claim, review headline, author, keywords, date). Table 2 presents the results. When we remove the keyword subgraph, the graph embedding features become irrelevant for the task (0.60% for CKG No KW). Text embeddings of only keywords lead to a classification performance similar to CKG embeddings with keywords (-4.20/DR, -2.40/GPT2), but capture somewhat different information as their combination leads to an improvement over CKG alone (+10.60 with CKG+GPT2). Concatenating neighbourhood vectors for CKG without keywords leads to lower performance, meaning that the information captured that is useful for this task is captured from the keyword structures. In the last setting, we can verify if this additional information captured by claim graph embeddings is similar to what we get from augmented text embeddings that include all the text from the immediate neighbourhood: the results indicate a small complementary with GPT2 (best overall result at 76.2% accuracy), but degraded performance with DR.

Discussion. We have been able to determine, as hypothesized that most of the useful information learned by the link prediction graph embeddings comes from the subgraph pertaining to keywords (green nodes in Figure 1), however the overall resulting classification performance with only embedding features is low (with or without neighbourhood), especially compared to the baseline. One hypothesis could be that the structure of the keyword subgraph is captured to some extent in the embeddings of claims and in the neighbourhood, but since the link prediction performance itself is low compared to standard graphs, there is only some part of the structure that the graph embedding model manages to capture. Of course, the size of the topic classification dataset plays a role in the classification performance, however if the representations learned on CKG (which is in no-way a small dataset by link prediction standards) were able to capture the relevant structures, we should be able to reach results closer to the baseline and to text embedding features (on the same dataset).

In the setting of this controlled topic classification task, the structures in question are the equivalence cliques between claims, keywords and topic concepts, which are more complex than the direct links that the local link prediction objective is meant to capture. Although recent advanced in link prediction make models capable of capturing specific formal properties of a relation (transitive, reflexive, anti-symmetric, etc.) in multi-relational graphs, they do not go beyond direct links. Given that such models are increasingly used to infer new relations in complex KGs (e.g., in biomedical informatics), this is a significant limitation of using these approaches for the inference of complex relations or for a downstream classification task.

5 Conclusion and Future Work

We evaluated the effectiveness of claim embeddings as features in a topic classification dataset, produced specifically to allow probing how specific features impact classification performance. We evaluate several strategies for feature retrieval from graph embeddings and combine them with text embedding features (flair + DistilRoberta/GPT2). We found a small complimentary between the features, however, the low accuracy resulting from using graph embeddings alone (compared to the baseline) and the ablation studies show that the graph embedding model's reliance on a local link prediction objective likely limits the ability of the model to capture more complex relationships (e.g. equivalence cliques between claims, keywords and topic concepts). This echoes some of the open-problems identified in the 2019 Graph Representation Learning workshop at NeurIPS (Sumba and Ortiz, 2019). Given that link prediction models are increasingly used with complex KGs to infer new relations (KG completion), this limitation is something to keep in mind and should drive researchers working on knowledge graphs to explore more general graph representation learning approaches such as graph neural networks or random-walk approaches.

References

Alan Akbik, Tanja Bergmann, and Roland Vollgraf. 2019. Pooled contextualized embeddings for named entity recognition. In *NACACL: Human Language Technologies, Volume 1 (Long and Short Papers)*, pages 724–728, Minneapolis, Minnesota. Association for Computational Linguistics.

Hongyun Cai, Vincent W Zheng, and Kevin Chen-Chuan Chang. 2018. A comprehensive survey of graph embedding: Problems, techniques, and applications. *IEEE Transactions on Knowledge and Data Engineering*, 30(9):1616–1637.

Jacob Devlin, Ming-Wei Chang, Kenton Lee, and Kristina Toutanova. 2018. Bert: Pre-training of deep bidirectional transformers for language understanding. *arXiv preprint arXiv:1810.04805*.

Kiran Garimella, Gianmarco De Francisci Morales, Aristides Gionis, and Michael Mathioudakis. 2018. Quantifying controversy on social media. *ACM Trans. on Soc. Comp.*, 1(1):3.

Palash Goyal and Emilio Ferrara. 2018. Graph embedding techniques, applications, and performance: A survey. *Knowledge-Based Systems*, 151:78–94.

Seyed Mehran Kazemi and David Poole. 2018. Simple embedding for link prediction in knowledge graphs. In S. Bengio, H. Wallach, H. Larochelle, K. Grauman, N. Cesa-Bianchi, and R. Garnett, editors, *Advances in Neural Information Processing Systems 31*, pages 4284–4295. Curran Associates, Inc.

Timothee Lacroix, Nicolas Usunier, and Guillaume Obozinski. 2018. Canonical tensor decomposition for knowledge base completion. In *Proceedings of the 35th International Conference on Machine Learning*, volume 80 of *Proceedings of Machine Learning Research*, pages 2863–2872, Stockholmsmässan, Stockholm Sweden. PMLR.

Yang Li and Tao Yang. 2018. Word embedding for understanding natural language: a survey. In *Guide to Big Data Applications*, pages 83–104. Springer.

Rebecca Passonneau. 2006. Measuring agreement on set-valued items (MASI) for semantic and pragmatic annotation. In *Proceedings of the Fifth International Conference on Language Resources and Evaluation (LREC'06)*, Genoa, Italy. European Language Resources Association (ELRA).

Priya Radhakrishnan, Partha Talukdar, and Vasudeva Varma. 2018. Elden: Improved entity linking using densified knowledge graphs. In *NACACL: Human Language Technologies, Volume 1 (Long Papers)*, pages 1844–1853.

Xavier Sumba and José Ortiz. 2019. Between the interaction of graph neural networks and semantic web. In *Proceedings of the 2019 NeurIPS Workshop on Graph Representation Learning*.

Andon Tchechmedjiev, Pavlos Fafalios, Katarina Boland, Stefan Dietze, Benjamin Zapilko, and Konstantin Todorov. 2019. Claimskg - a knowledge graph of fact-checked claims. In *International Semantic Web Conference*. Springer.

Soroush Vosoughi, Deb Roy, and Sinan Aral. 2018. The spread of true and false news online. *Science*, 359(6380):1146–1151.

Xuezhi Wang, Cong Yu, Simon Baumgartner, and Flip Korn. 2018. Relevant document discovery for fact-checking articles. In *WWW*, pages 525–533.

Benjamin Zapilko, Johann Schaible, Philipp Mayr, and Brigitte Mathiak. 2013. Thesoz: A skos representation of the thesaurus for the social sciences. *Semantic Web*, 4(3):257–263.

Do Transformers Dream of Inference, or
Can Pretrained Generative Models Learn Implicit Inferential Rules?

Zhengzhong Liang and Mihai Surdeanu
Computer Science Department, The University of Arizona
1040 4th St, Tucson, AZ 85721, USA
`{zhengzhongliang, msurdeanu}@email.arizona.edu`

Abstract

Large pretrained language models (LM) have been used successfully for multi-hop question answering. However, most of these directions are not interpretable, as they do not make the inference hops necessary to explain a candidate answer explicitly. In this work, we investigate the capability of a state-of-the-art transformer LM to generate explicit inference hops, i.e., to infer a new statement necessary to answer a question given some premise input statements. Our analysis shows that such LMs can generate new statements for some simple inference types, but performance remains poor for complex, real-world inference types such as those that require monotonicity, composition, and commonsense knowledge.

1 Introduction

The emergence of large pretrained language models (LM) (Devlin et al., 2019; Liu et al., 2019) yielded significant progress in question answering (QA), including complex QA tasks that require multi-hop reasoning (Banerjee et al., 2019; Asai et al., 2019; Yadav et al., 2019). Most of these state-of-the-art (SOTA) approaches address multi-hop reasoning tasks in a discriminative manner: they take the question, the candidate answer, and all the context available as the input, and produce a single score indicating the likelihood of the answer as justified by the provided context (an example is shown in Figure 1). However, *why* that context actually justifies the answer remains unclear to the human end user of the QA system.

In contrast, most of us are likely to answer the question in Figure 1 by building a reasoning chain from the given facts. For example, such a possible chain starts by first combining "metal is a thermal conductor" and "steel is made of metal' to yield "steel is a thermal conductor". Next, combining "steel is a thermal conductor" and "heat travels

Question:
Which of these would let the most heat travel through?
A) a new pair of jeans.
B) a steel spoon in a cafeteria.
C) a cotton candy at a store.
D) a calvin klein cotton hat.

Science Fact:
Metal is a thermal conductor.

Common Knowledge:
Steel is made of metal.
Heat travels through a thermal conductor.

Figure 1: An example of question and candidate answers from OpenbookQA (Mihaylov et al., 2018) (the correct answer is option B). The science fact and the commonsense knowledge facts are needed to explain the correct answer. Usually the large LMs solve this problem by taking the question, the science fact, the common knowledge facts and each candidate answer as the input and producing a single score indicating the probability of the candidate answer being justified by all of the inputs. But *why* the facts explain the answer is normally not covered.

through a thermal conductor" yields "heat travels through steel". And, finally, "heat travels through steel" supports the correct explanation that "a steel spoon in a cafeteria would let the most heat travel through." Generating such reasoning chains can be crucial for the adoption of natural language processing applications such as QA in critical domains such as medical or law.

Motivated by this, in this work we investigate whether a state-of-the-art (SOTA) transformer-based language model is able to generate a valid intermediate statement given two premise statements on a natural language QA dataset, which is fundamental to generating the reasoning chains. Our results show that although the SOTA model investigated can handle some types of inferences well, there remain multiple types of inferences where the LM fails.[1]

---

[1]The code and data for our analysis can be found at `https://github.com/clulab/releases/tree/master/emnlp2020-generative-nli`.

Proceedings of the First Workshop on Insights from Negative Results in NLP, pages 76–81
Online, November 19, 2020. ©2020 Association for Computational Linguistics

Category	Without Hint	With Hint
Perfect	31/87	43/87
Acceptable	11/87	13/87
Unacceptable	45/87	31/87

Table 1: Statistics of the quality of the generated T5 statements on the dev set of QASC. The same randomly sampled 87 examples are manually evaluated for their quality, in both the "without hint" and "with hint" configurations.

2 Related Work

Recently several works have investigated whether deep learning (DL) language models (LM) are able to learn and use the explicit and implicit rules in natural language. (Sinha et al., 2019) build a synthetic dataset containing the relationships between people; their language model needs to predict the unstated relationships between people. The problem can be summarized as: given that "Mike is the child of Kate and Kate is the child of Tom", the model needs to predict "Tom is the *grandparent* of Mike", by learning the implicit rule: "If X is the child of Y and Y is the child of Z, then Z is the grandparent of X". It has been shown that the transformer networks perform well on this task.

Other works have analyzed whether DL language models are able to leverage explicit rules. (Clark et al., 2020) generates a synthetic dataset consisting of facts and rules. The problems can be summarized as: given the facts such as "X is red" and "X is big", as well as rules such as "If X is red and big, then X is strong", the LM trained on this data must be able to judge whether "X is strong" is true. They demonstrate that transformers can fulfill this task well, and are able to generalize to unseen lexicons.

However, all existing works investigate this problem in a discriminative manner: either a single score, a single token, or a single choice is produced as the output. In contrast, we conduct our work in a generative manner: the LM needs to generate a whole natural language statement as the output. We believe this task will eventually give the LM the ability to generate clear and complete explanations, which are necessary in multi-hop reasoning problems. Further, we investigate the capability of transformers to generate inferential statements on a complex, real-world task in the science domain, which relies on much sparser data than other tasks previously investigated.

3 Approach

3.1 Problem Formulation

In this paper, we concentrate on a single-hop inference problem. That is, given the statements $S_1(A, B)$ and $S_2(B, C)$, the model needs to generate the valid and reasonable statement $S_3(A, C)$. Unlike reasoning tasks on structured knowledge bases or ConceptNet where A, B, C are entities, here A, B and C can be any text in natural language: they can be words, phrases, or clauses.

We used the QASC dataset (Khot et al., 2020) for this task. QASC contains approximately $10,000$ questions in the science domain, where each answer is associated with two supporting facts (fact 1 and fact 2). These two supporting facts have tokens in common, which is necessary for our inference task that requires overlap between facts (through B). Importantly, for each answer QASC provides a *combined fact* that explains the answer, and which is directly inferred from the two supporting facts. The first two columns in Tables 2, 3, and 4 show a few examples of the supporting facts and the resulting combined fact. The forms of the combined facts can be very diverse due to the annotation process of QASC, where each annotator is first given fact 1, then the annotator needs to find an arbitrary fact 2 that has overlaps with the fact 1, and composes the combined fact, without other restrictions (Khot et al., 2020). [2] The task we investigate here is whether transformer-based LMs can infer the combined fact when provided with the two initial facts.

3.2 Method

We use the pre-trained Google T5 small model (Raffel et al., 2020) published by huggingface (Wolf et al., 2019), and fine-tune it on the QASC dataset.[3] We explore two types of input format:

fact 1 + fact 2 → combined fact: In this setting, T5 takes the two facts as input to generate the combined fact. The T5 input format is "substitution statement 1: [fact 1] statement 2: [fact 2]", where "substitution", "statement 1:" and "statement 2:" are user-defined keywords for the task.

---

[2] Note that the two supporting facts and the gold combined fact of each question in QASC are annotated by the creators of the QASC dataset, not by the authors of this paper.

[3] We used the Adam optimizer with a learning rate of 1e-4, as recommended in the tutorial. The training stops when the evaluation loss starts to increase; we allowed a maximum of 10 epochs of training.

Input	Target	Prediction	Evaluation
substitution statement 1: if weather is stormy then there is a greater chance of rain. *statement 2:* rain is also known as precipitation.	if weather is stormy then there is a greater chance of precipitation.	if weather is stormy then there is greater chance of precipitation.	Perfect, exactly the same
substitution statement 1: lightning can cause a forest fire. *statement 2:* forest fires are examples of wildfires.	wildfires are caused by lightning.	lightning can cause wildfires.	Perfect, semantically the same
substitution statement 1: whiskers are used for feeling by animals. *statement 2:* whiskers whiskers are the stiff hairs on the dog's face.	stiff hairs on the face are used for feeling by animals.	stiff hairs on the dog's face are used for feeling by animals.	Acceptable
substitution statement 1: lymph is a fluid that leaks out of capillaries into spaces between cells. *statement 2:* bacteria invade lymph nodes, which swell, creating the buboes.	swelling nodes leak fluid out of capillaries into spaces between cells.	bacteria can swell.	Unacceptable, unreasonable or contradicting information
substitution statement 1: absorption of nutrients occurs mainly in the small intestine. *statement 2:* diarrhea reduces the absorption of all nutrients.	diarrhea reduces funtcion that occurs mainly in the small intestine.	diarrhea reduces the absorption of nutrients.	Unacceptable, missing essential elements

Table 2: Output of T5 on QASC in the "without hint" configuration.

Input	Target	Prediction	Evaluation
substitution statement 1: protozoa make humans sick when they become human parasites. *statement 2:* exhibit one-celled animals are called protozoa.	one-celled animals make humans sick when they become parasites.	one-celled animals make humans sick.	w/o hint
substitution statement 1: protozoa make humans sick when they become human parasites. *statement 2:* exhibit one-celled animals are called protozoa. *hint:* animals when become one-celled humans make parasites they sick.	one-celled animals make humans sick when they become parasites.	one-celled animals make humans sick when they become human parasites.	w/ hint, statement improved
substitution statement 1: mutualism is a symbiotic relationship in which both species benefit. *statement 2:* domestication of animals is an example of a symbiotic relationship.	domestication of animals is an example of mutualism.	domestication of animals is an example of mutualism.	w/o hint
substitution statement 1: mutualism is a symbiotic relationship in which both species benefit. *statement 2:* domestication of animals is an example of a symbiotic relationship. *hint:* is animals mutualism of domestication example an.	domestication of animals is an example of mutualism.	mutualism is an example of domestication of animals.	w/ hint, statement harmed

Table 3: Comparison of T5 output in the "without hint" and "with hint" configurations on QASC.

fact 1 + fact 2 + lexical hints → combined fact: During our experiments, we noticed that sometimes multiple valid statements could be inferred from fact 1 and fact 2, which tended to confuse the LM.[4] To mitigate this issue, we added lexical hints to the model input, on what tokens would be best to be included in the generated statement. The terms in the hint are generated as $(\mathcal{Q} \cup \mathcal{A}) \cap (\mathcal{F}_1 \cup \mathcal{F}_2)$, where $\mathcal{Q}$ is the set of unique terms in the question, $\mathcal{A}$ is the set of unique terms in the answer, $\mathcal{F}_1$ and $\mathcal{F}_2$ are the sets of unique terms in fact 1 and fact 2.[5] This is inspired by the fact that each question in QASC is derived from the gold combined fact, so that even when multiple valid statements may be generated from fact 1 and fact 2, paying extra attention on the terms in the question and the correct answer is likely to force the model to make predictions related to the gold combined fact.

3.3 Evaluation Metric

For each configuration, we manually evaluated 100 generated statements against the corresponding gold combined fact on the dev set.[6] All generations are categorized into three classes.

Perfect: The generated statement is (1) exactly the same as the gold combined fact, or (2) semantically the same as the gold combined fact but uses a different expression.

---

[4] E.g., for the first and second row in Table 3, "one-celled animals make humans sick" is a valid generation, but not perfect w.r.t. the target.

[5] Thus, the text containing the lexical hints is simply a bag of words, rather than grammatical correct text.

[6] 13 data points had issues in the raw data, and were removed, leaving the actual number of data points analyzed as 87.

Input	Target	Prediction	Question Type
substitution statement 1: skin color is a polygenic trait. *statement 2:* polygenic traits are the result of the interaction of several genes. *hint:* is genes of the result several skin color interaction.	skin color is the result of the interaction of several genes.	skin color is the result of the interaction of several genes.	Instantiation
substitution statement 1: if weather is stormy then there is a greater chance of rain. *statement 2:* rain is also known as precipitation. *hint:* stormy is greater weather there of a chance precipitation.	if weather is stormy then there is a greater chance of precipitation.	if weather is stormy then there is a greater chance of precipitation.	Equivalence
substitution statement 1: all cnidarians are aquatic. *statement 2:* cnidarians have a hydrostatic skeleton. *hint:* a are aquatic hydrostatic.	some aquatic animals have hydrostatic skeletons.	all aquatic animals have a hydrostatic skeleton.	Monotonicity with quantifier
substitution statement 1: absorption of nutrients occurs mainly in the small intestine. *statement 2:* diarrhea reduces the absorption of all nutrients. *hint:* occurs small mainly the diarrhea reduces in intestine .	diarrhea reduces function that occurs mainly in the small intestine.	diarrhea reduces the amount of food that occurs mainly in the small intestine.	Composition and summarization
substitution statement 1: kidney failure may be treated with dialysis. *statement 2:* kidney failure is a death sentence. *hint:* death dialysis.	a lack of dialysis may lead to death.	death can be treated with dialysis.	Need to rephrase to make the new statement reasonable

Table 4: Output of T5 categorized by the types of the inference (w/ hint).

Acceptable: The generated statement is semantically valid, but its meaning is slightly different from the gold combined fact.

Unacceptable: The generated statement (1) contains contradicting information, or (2) has severe grammatically issues, or (3) is missing essential content from the gold combined fact (e.g., contains information from only fact 1 or only fact 2).

4 Results

Table 1 shows the overall statistics gathered by our analysis. All in all, our analysis shows that this inferential task is far from solved, with most of the inferred statements being not perfect. In particular, for the w/o hints configuration, less than half of the generated statements are perfect. Adding lexical hints to the input boosts the generation quality in general, but leaves 51% of inferences as not perfect. A detailed analysis of the generated statements highlights that T5 performs well in certain situations, and not so in others. We categorize below these situations, discuss some possible solutions, and leave a more systematic analysis of the reason why the model fails on some problems to a future study.

Below "well learned" means most of the predictions on that type of generations are evaluated as "perfect" and "not well learned" means most of the predictions are evaluated as "unacceptable" by the criteria mentioned in 3.3.

Inference types well learned:

Instantiation Here the input statements are $S_1(A, B)$ and $IsA(B, C)$, i.e., C is an instantiation of a more general concept B. The target output is $S_1(A, C)$ (Table 4).

Equivalence Here the input statements are $S_1(A, B)$ and $Equ(B, C)$, i.e., B is equivalent to C. The target output is $S_1(A, C)$ (Table 4).

Inference types not well learned:

Multiple possible statements to generate When the input statements are long and complex, there might be multiple valid statements that could be generated from the input (discussed in 3.2). In this case T5 tends to be confused. Adding lexical hints can relieve this problem to some extent by forcing the model to pay extra attention to certain areas in the input, but problems remain. First, even when adding the lexical hints, some generations are still not reasonable (Table 3). Second, accurately identifying the important fractions to pay attention to is itself a non-trivial problem. We believe this is an exciting area for future research. For example, some specialized architectures such as the pointer generator network (See et al., 2017) might be capable to learn what parts should be copied or ignored.

Composition and summarization As shown in the third to last row of Table 4, the new statement needs the composition of statement 1 and 2, and some summarization is needed (i.e., "absorption of nutrients" $\rightarrow$ "function").

Dealing with quantifiers in natural language As shown in the second to last row of Table 4, the new statement needs complex monotonicity reasoning and the understanding of quantifiers.

Generating statements that comply with commonsense knowledge In several examples, the model generates statements that are grammatically correct but unreasonable regarding commonsense knowledge. In particular, many of these inferences require commonsense knowledge to generate new text and rephrasing to make the new statement reasonable. For example, in the last row of Table 4, "death can be treated with dialysis" is grammatically correct but unreasonable.

There might be multiple reasons why some types of generations are not well learned. For instance, it could be because the biases learned by T5 in the pre-training stage impede it from learning meaningful patterns by fine-tuning on a downstream task with relatively few training samples (e.g., the QASC dataset used in this paper has only about 8,000 training examples). Alternatively, it is possible that the patterns to be learned in this downstream task are too complex to be learned from the small training data available. We leave a more systematic analysis in this direction to future studies.

5   Conclusion

In this work we investigate how well a state-of-the-art transformer language model can generate a valid statement inferred from two given statements. We manually evaluated two fine-tuned T5 models (Raffel et al., 2020) with slightly different inputs (i.e., with and without contextual information) on the Question Answering via Sentence Composition dataset (Khot et al., 2020). Our analysis indicates that the two models can generate good-quality statements, when the inference relies solely on instantiation or equivalence. However, the models perform poorly on more complex inferences such as: (a) multiple valid statements can be generated given the premises, (b) inference that requires non-trivial reasoning of monotonicity (especially with quantifiers in natural language), (c) inference that needs composition and summarization, and (d) statements that require rephrasing based on background commonsense knowledge.

References

Akari Asai, Kazuma Hashimoto, Hannaneh Hajishirzi, Richard Socher, and Caiming Xiong. 2019. Learning to retrieve reasoning paths over wikipedia graph for question answering. In *International Conference on Learning Representations*.

Pratyay Banerjee, Kuntal Kumar Pal, Arindam Mitra, and Chitta Baral. 2019. Careful selection of knowledge to solve open book question answering. In *Proceedings of the 57th Annual Meeting of the Association for Computational Linguistics*, pages 6120–6129, Florence, Italy. Association for Computational Linguistics.

Peter Clark, Oyvind Tafjord, and Kyle Richardson. 2020. Transformers as soft reasoners over language. *arXiv preprint arXiv:2002.05867*.

Jacob Devlin, Ming-Wei Chang, Kenton Lee, and Kristina Toutanova. 2019. BERT: Pre-training of deep bidirectional transformers for language understanding. In *Proceedings of the 2019 Conference of the North American Chapter of the Association for Computational Linguistics: Human Language Technologies, Volume 1 (Long and Short Papers)*, pages 4171–4186, Minneapolis, Minnesota. Association for Computational Linguistics.

Tushar Khot, Peter Clark, Michal Guerquin, Peter Jansen, and Ashish Sabharwal. 2020. Qasc: A dataset for question answering via sentence composition. In *AAAI*, pages 8082–8090.

Yinhan Liu, Myle Ott, Naman Goyal, Jingfei Du, Mandar Joshi, Danqi Chen, Omer Levy, Mike Lewis, Luke Zettlemoyer, and Veselin Stoyanov. 2019. Roberta: A robustly optimized bert pretraining approach. *arXiv preprint arXiv:1907.11692*.

Todor Mihaylov, Peter Clark, Tushar Khot, and Ashish Sabharwal. 2018. Can a suit of armor conduct electricity? a new dataset for open book question answering. In *Proceedings of the 2018 Conference on Empirical Methods in Natural Language Processing*, pages 2381–2391, Brussels, Belgium. Association for Computational Linguistics.

Colin Raffel, Noam Shazeer, Adam Roberts, Katherine Lee, Sharan Narang, Michael Matena, Yanqi Zhou, Wei Li, and Peter J Liu. 2020. Exploring the limits of transfer learning with a unified text-to-text transformer. *Journal of Machine Learning Research*, 21(140):1–67.

Abigail See, Peter J. Liu, and Christopher D. Manning. 2017. Get to the point: Summarization with pointer-generator networks. In *Proceedings of the 55th Annual Meeting of the Association for Computational Linguistics (Volume 1: Long Papers)*, pages 1073–1083, Vancouver, Canada. Association for Computational Linguistics.

Koustuv Sinha, Shagun Sodhani, Jin Dong, Joelle Pineau, and William L. Hamilton. 2019. CLUTRR:

A diagnostic benchmark for inductive reasoning from text. In *Proceedings of the 2019 Conference on Empirical Methods in Natural Language Processing and the 9th International Joint Conference on Natural Language Processing (EMNLP-IJCNLP)*, pages 4506–4515, Hong Kong, China. Association for Computational Linguistics.

Thomas Wolf, Lysandre Debut, Victor Sanh, Julien Chaumond, Clement Delangue, Anthony Moi, Pierric Cistac, Tim Rault, R'emi Louf, Morgan Funtowicz, and Jamie Brew. 2019. Huggingface's transformers: State-of-the-art natural language processing. *ArXiv*, abs/1910.03771.

Vikas Yadav, Steven Bethard, and Mihai Surdeanu. 2019. Quick and (not so) dirty: Unsupervised selection of justification sentences for multi-hop question answering. In *Proceedings of the 2019 Conference on Empirical Methods in Natural Language Processing and the 9th International Joint Conference on Natural Language Processing (EMNLP-IJCNLP)*, pages 2578–2589, Hong Kong, China. Association for Computational Linguistics.

Counterfactually-Augmented SNLI Training Data Does Not Yield Better Generalization Than Unaugmented Data

William Huang
New York University
`will.huang@nyu.edu`

Haokun Liu
New York University
`haokunliu@nyu.edu`

Samuel R. Bowman
New York University
`bowman@nyu.edu`

Abstract

A growing body of work shows that models exploit annotation artifacts to achieve state-of-the-art performance on standard crowdsourced benchmarks—datasets collected from crowdworkers to create an evaluation task—while still failing on out-of-domain examples for the same task. Recent work has explored the use of counterfactually-augmented data—data built by minimally editing a set of seed examples to yield counterfactual labels—to augment training data associated with these benchmarks and build more robust classifiers that generalize better. However, Khashabi et al. (2020) find that this type of augmentation yields little benefit on reading comprehension tasks when controlling for dataset size and cost of collection. We build upon this work by using English natural language inference data to test model generalization and robustness and find that models trained on a counterfactually-augmented SNLI dataset do not generalize better than unaugmented datasets of similar size and that counterfactual augmentation can hurt performance, yielding models that are less robust to challenge examples. Counterfactual augmentation of natural language understanding data through standard crowdsourcing techniques does not appear to be an effective way of collecting training data and further innovation is required to make this general line of work viable.

1 Introduction

While standard crowdsourced benchmarks have helped create significant progress within natural language processing (NLP), a growing body of evidence shows the existence of exploitable annotation artifacts in these datasets (Gururangan et al., 2018; Poliak et al., 2018; Tsuchiya, 2018) and that models can use artifacts to achieve state-of-the-art performance on these benchmarks (McCoy et al., 2019; Naik et al., 2018). The existence of these

artifacts makes it difficult to predict out-of-domain generalization and creates uncertainty around the abilities these tasks are designed to test.

Recent work has explored using counterfactually-augmented datasets to address annotation artifacts with the intent to build more robust classifiers (Kaushik et al., 2020; Khashabi et al., 2020). These datasets are collected by first sampling a set of seed examples and then creating new examples by minimally editing the seed examples to yield counterfactual labels. This type of data collection has been found to mitigate the presence of artifacts in SNLI (Bowman et al., 2015) and is presented as a way to "elucidate the difference that makes a difference" (Kaushik et al., 2020). Further, Khashabi et al. (2020) present this as an efficient method to collect training data yielding models that are "more robust to minor variations and generalize better" (Khashabi et al., 2020). However, they also find that unaugmented datasets yield better performance than datasets with 50-50 original-to-augmented data when controlling for training set size and annotation cost.

In our work, we further study whether training with counterfactually-augmented data collected through standard crowdsourcing methods yields models with better generalization and robustness by focusing on the domain of natural language inference (NLI): the task of inferring whether a *hypothesis* is true given a true *premise*. We train and compare RoBERTa (Liu et al., 2019) trained on three different datasets: (1) the counterfactually-augmented natural language inference (CNLI) training set of 8.3k seed and augmented SNLI examples from Kaushik et al. (2020), (2) a subsampled set of 8.3k unaugmented SNLI examples to control for size, and (3) the 1.7k CNLI seed examples originally sampled from SNLI. We then compare model performances on MNLI (Williams

Proceedings of the First Workshop on Insights from Negative Results in NLP, pages 82–87
Online, November 19, 2020. ©2020 Association for Computational Linguistics

et al., 2018)—a dataset for the same task with examples out-of-domain to SNLI—and two diagnostic sets (Naik et al., 2018; Wang et al., 2019a).

We find that RoBERTa trained on CNLI yields similar performance on out-of-domain MNLI examples when compared to the unaugmented subsampled SNLI training set and that including counterfactually-augmented examples to the CNLI seed set improves generalization. Further, we find that the improvement over seed examples correspond to an increase in n-grams from the addition of augmented examples, roughly doubling the number of 4-grams, and may be a result of improved lexical diversity from a larger training set. While we see similar trends in most of our diagnostic evaluations, we also find evidence that including augmented examples can yield worse performance than only training with seed examples.

While there is evidence of the benefits of using this type of data for model evaluation (Gardner et al., 2020), we find that using counterfactually-augmented data for training yields *less* robust models. We argue that further innovation is required to effectively crowdsource counterfactually-augmented natural language understanding (NLU) data for training more robust models with better generalization.

2 Related Work

Recent works show that several NLI benchmark datasets contain exploitable annotation artifacts. Several studies (Poliak et al., 2018; Gururangan et al., 2018; Tsuchiya, 2018) show that models trained on hypothesis-only examples manage to perform as much as 35 points higher than chance. Gururangan et al. (2018) also find negation words such as *no* or *never* are strongly associated with *contradiction* predictions. Other works (Naik et al., 2018; McCoy et al., 2019) find that models can exploit premise-hypothesis word overlap to achieve state-of-the-art performance on benchmarks by using associations of high overlap with *entailment* predictions and low overlap with *neutral* predictions.

Nie et al. (2020) use an adversarial human-and-model-in-the-loop procedure to address these concerns in Adversarial NLI (ANLI). Using a model in the loop makes ANLI inherently adversarial towards the model used, and we instead focus on naturally collected human-in-the-loop augmented data.

Kaushik et al. (2020) crowdsource counterfactually-augmented NLI examples that reduce the presence of hypothesis-only bias in SNLI by providing a set of seed examples to crowdworkers and prompting them to minimally edit either the hypothesis or premise to yield a counterfactual label. Khashabi et al. (2020) present this type of data collection as an efficient method to build training sets yielding robust models that generalize better by crowdsourcing counterfactually-augmented BoolQ examples. However, they also find that augmented datasets yield similar to worse performance when the cost of augmenting an example is no cheaper than collecting a new one and the datasets are controlled for size. We differ from Kaushik et al. (2020) by focusing on performance on out-of-domain examples and from Khashabi et al. (2020) by focusing on the task of NLI instead of reading comprehension.

Gardner et al. (2020) use contrast sets written manually by NLP researchers to evaluate models on various annotated tasks. They show that most datasets require 1-3 minutes per augmented example, taking 17-50 hours to create 1,000 examples. We differ by using crowdsourced counterfactually-augmented data and focusing on their use for training instead of evaluation.

3 Experimental Setup

We perform two experiments to study the effects of counterfactually-augmented NLI training data. All experiments use RoBERTa trained on SNLI, CNLI, or CNLI seed examples originally sampled from SNLI and compare performances on various tasks. We first compare MNLI performances to evaluate the impact on model generalization to out-of-domain data. We then use the diagnostic examples from Naik et al. (2018) and the GLUE diagnostic set (Wang et al., 2019a) to study model robustness to challenge examples.

Training Data In SNLI, Bowman et al. (2015) prompt crowdworkers with a scene description premise to collect three hypothesis sentences corresponding to *entailment*, *neutral*, and *contradiction* labels, yielding 570k English premise-hypothesis pairs. Kaushik et al. (2020) collect CNLI examples by prompting crowdworkers to minimally edit seed examples sampled from SNLI to yield counterfactual labels.

For our training data, we use a subsampled set

of 8.3k examples of SNLI, the CNLI training set of 8.3k examples, and the 1.7k CNLI seed examples sampled from SNLI that is also included in the CNLI training set. We subsample SNLI to control for the fact that CNLI only consists of 8.3k examples. We subsample five sets of 8.3k SNLI examples and report results across these five.

Out-of-Domain Set　We treat MNLI as our out-of-domain NLI evaluation data. In collecting MNLI examples, Williams et al. (2018) follow a similar data collection framework while expanding the diversity of their premises by sourcing them from ten sources of freely available text, yielding 433k English premise-hypothesis pairs. The data set includes 393k training examples from five of the ten sources, 20k validation examples, and 20k test examples. The validation and test examples are split in half between *matched* and *mismatched* examples, where *matched* examples come from the same five sources as training examples and *mismatched* examples come from the remaining five sources. We report validation accuracy for the combined MNLI validation set.

Diagnostic Sets　Naik et al. (2018) provide NLI diagnostic sets of automatically generated challenge examples based on MNLI. These sets are split into six categories named Antonymy, Numerical Reasoning, Word Overlap, Negation, Length Mismatch, and Spelling Error. As part of GLUE, Wang et al. (2019a) provide NLI diagnostic sets of challenge examples aimed to evaluate reasoning abilities related to four broad categories: Lexical Semantics, Predicate-Argument Structure, Logic, and Knowledge. We use these sets to test model robustness to challenge examples. We refer the reader to Naik et al. (2018) and Wang et al. (2019a) for additional details on each diagnostic set.

McCoy et al. (2019) provide similar adversarial examples, but we find them too difficult for our models, with performance consistently below 3%, so we do not report performance in detail.

Implementation　Our code[1] builds on `jiant v2 alpha` (Wang et al., 2019b). All experiments use `roberta-base`. For each round of training, we perform 20 runs and randomly search the hyperparameter space of learning rate {1e-5, 2e-5, 3e-5}, batch size {32, 64}, and random seed. Given the small training set size and stability benefits from

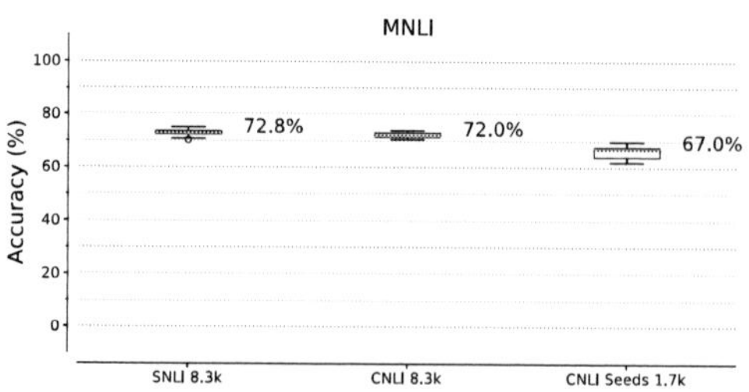

Figure 1: Combined MNLI *matched* and *mismatched* validation accuracy trained on subsampled SNLI, CNLI, and CNLI seed examples. The orange line and label indicate the median score.

longer training found in Mosbach et al. (2020), we train each run for 20 epochs using early stopping based on the respective validation sets.

4　Results

Generalization to MNLI　From the median scores in Figure 1, we see that models trained on CNLI perform no better than models trained on a comparably large sample of unaugmented SNLI examples. This is in line with findings from Khashabi et al. (2020), where training with their minimally perturbed BoolQ dataset of seed and augmented examples yields similar or worse performance on out-of-domain tasks compared to the original BoolQ training set. Additionally, the improvement of CNLI over the 1.7k seed examples shows that counterfactual examples are somewhat helpful when they are strictly additive, as in Khashabi et al. (2020).

Robustness to Diagnostic Sets　Figure 2 presents performances on the diagnostic sets from Naik et al. (2018) and Wang et al. (2019a). For the GLUE diagnostic sets, we follow the authors and use R_3 (Gorodkin, 2004) as our evaluation metric. The distributions of classification accuracy again show that CNLI yields similar performance compared to unaugmented datasets of similar size on most of the categories.

However, we find that training on CNLI yields worse performance than using either unaugmented SNLI or CNLI seed examples for Negation examples. These challenge examples append the phrase *"and false is not true"* to every hypothesis in the MNLI validation set. This construction introduces the strong negation word *"no"* to target the association between negation words and the *contradiction* label without changing the truth condition of the

---

[1] `https://github.com/nyu-mll/ CNLI-generalization`

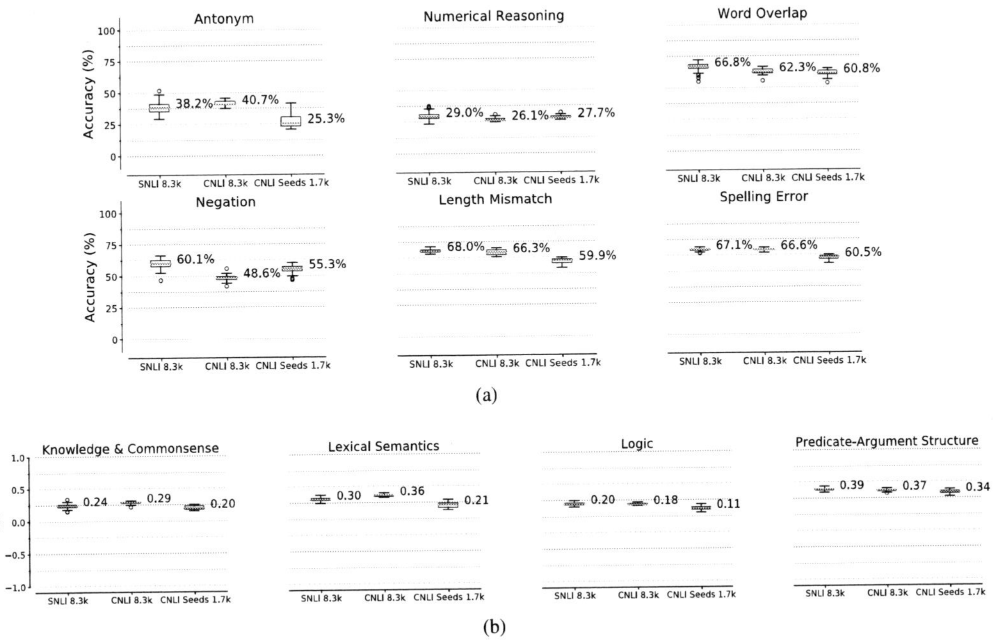

Figure 2: Performance on diagnostic sets using (a) accuracy for Naik et al. (2018) examples and (b) R_3 score on GLUE diagnostic examples trained on subsampled SNLI, CNLI, and CNLI seed examples. Labels and orange lines indicate median scores.

n	SNLI 8.3k	CNLI 8.3k	CNLI Seed 1.7k
1	6.2k	4.8k	3.5k
2	30.4k	21.6k	13.0k
3	52.3k	36.3k	19.9k
4	60.2k	42.5k	21.5k

Table 1: Number of unique n-gram types observed in each training set.

sentence. We speculate that the augmented data may have amplified this association already present among the seed examples. Not only does this show that CNLI can yield models that are less robust to certain challenge examples, but it also provides evidence that adding substantial numbers of counterfactual examples to a dataset can hurt robustness.

Lexical Diversity Given the minimal edits constraint in CNLI, we study the lexical diversity of the training sets to see the effectiveness of this constraint and whether the general improvement of CNLI over seed examples is a result of greater diversity from a larger training set. Table 1 provides the number of n-grams present in each training set with n varying from one to four. We see that including minimally edited examples to CNLI increases

the number of n-grams present, roughly doubling the number of 4-grams, which corresponds to the general improvement over seed examples.

We also observe that CNLI contains roughly 70% of 2-, 3-, and 4-grams compared to similarly large unaugmented training sets. This seems natural given the minimal edits constraint when collecting counterfactually-augmented examples and highlights the fact that this type of data augmentation results in less diversity per example.

5   Conclusion

We follow a similar setup to Khashabi et al. (2020) and use English NLI data to test whether counterfactually-augmented training data yields models that generalize better to out-of-domain data and are more robust to challenge examples. We first find that adding counterfactually-augmented data improves generalization, but provides no advantage over adding similar amounts of unaugmented data. Further, we find that the improvement over seed examples corresponds to an increase in n-gram diversity. We also find that including counterfactually-augmented data can make models less robust to challenge examples. Assuming that crowdworkers take a similar amount of time to make targeted edits to examples and to write new examples (Bowman et al., 2020), there is then no obvious value in crowdsourcing augmentations under current protocols for use as training data.

Despite these findings, we argue that there is still value in naturally collected counterfactually-augmented NLU data. Gardner et al. (2020) show that collecting this type of data can be used as a method to address systematic gaps in testing data. As performances on benchmarks become saturated, we still view this style of augmenting test sets as a viable method to provide longer-lasting benchmarks in addition to standard test set creation.

The success of Gardner et al. (2020) in using expert-designed counterfactual augmentation to target specific phenomena for *evaluation* suggests that it may be possible to target heuristics in training data with expert guidance during the crowdsourcing process. Further, understanding how to identify heuristics to target and the types of useful augmentations to collect, assuming such a thing is possible, are important directions we leave to future work.

Acknowledgements

We thank Clara Vania and Jason Phang for their helpful feedback and Alex Wang for providing the script for n-gram counts that we base our lexical diversity analysis code on. This project has benefited from financial support to SB by Eric and Wendy Schmidt (made by recommendation of the Schmidt Futures program), by Samsung Research (under the project *Improving Deep Learning using Latent Structure*), by Intuit, Inc., and in-kind support by the NYU High-Performance Computing Center and by NVIDIA Corporation (with the donation of a Titan V GPU). This material is based upon work supported by the National Science Foundation under Grant No. 1922658. Any opinions, findings, and conclusions or recommendations expressed in this material are those of the author(s) and do not necessarily reflect the views of the National Science Foundation.

References

Samuel R. Bowman, Gabor Angeli, Christopher Potts, and Christopher D. Manning. 2015. A large annotated corpus for learning natural language inference. In *Proceedings of the 2015 Conference on Empirical Methods in Natural Language Processing, EMNLP 2015, Lisbon, Portugal, September 17-21, 2015*, pages 632–642. The Association for Computational Linguistics.

Samuel R. Bowman, Jennimaria Palomaki, Livio Baldini Soares, and Emily Pitler. 2020. Collecting entailment data for pretraining: New protocols and negative results. In *Proceedings of EMNLP*.

Matt Gardner, Yoav Artzi, Victoria Basmova, Jonathan Berant, Ben Bogin, Sihao Chen, Pradeep Dasigi, Dheeru Dua, Yanai Elazar, Ananth Gottumukkala, Nitish Gupta, Hanna Hajishirzi, Gabriel Ilharco, Daniel Khashabi, Kevin Lin, Jiangming Liu, Nelson F. Liu, Phoebe Mulcaire, Qiang Ning, Sameer Singh, Noah A. Smith, Sanjay Subramanian, Reut Tsarfaty, Eric Wallace, Ally Zhang, and Ben Zhou. 2020. Evaluating models' local decision boundaries via contrast sets.

J. Gorodkin. 2004. Comparing two k-category assignments by a k-category correlation coefficient. *Computational Biology and Chemistry*, 28(5):367 – 374.

Suchin Gururangan, Swabha Swayamdipta, Omer Levy, Roy Schwartz, Samuel R. Bowman, and Noah A. Smith. 2018. Annotation artifacts in natural language inference data. In *Proceedings of the 2018 Conference of the North American Chapter of the Association for Computational Linguistics: Human Language Technologies, NAACL-HLT, New Orleans, Louisiana, USA, June 1-6, 2018, Volume 2 (Short Papers)*, pages 107–112. Association for Computational Linguistics.

Divyansh Kaushik, Eduard H. Hovy, and Zachary Chase Lipton. 2020. Learning the difference that makes A difference with counterfactually-augmented data. In *8th International Conference on Learning Representations, ICLR 2020, Addis Ababa, Ethiopia, April 26-30, 2020*. OpenReview.net.

Daniel Khashabi, Tushar Khot, and Ashish Sabharwal. 2020. More bang for your buck: Natural perturbation for robust question answering. In *Proceedings of EMNLP*.

Yinhan Liu, Myle Ott, Naman Goyal, Jingfei Du, Mandar Joshi, Danqi Chen, Omer Levy, Mike Lewis, Luke Zettlemoyer, and Veselin Stoyanov. 2019. RoBERTa: A robustly optimized BERT pretraining approach. *CoRR*, abs/1907.11692.

Tom McCoy, Ellie Pavlick, and Tal Linzen. 2019. Right for the wrong reasons: Diagnosing syntactic heuristics in natural language inference. In *Proceedings of the 57th Conference of the Association for Computational Linguistics, ACL 2019, Florence, Italy, July 28- August 2, 2019, Volume 1: Long Papers*, pages 3428–3448. Association for Computational Linguistics.

Marius Mosbach, Maksym Andriushchenko, and Dietrich Klakow. 2020. On the stability of fine-tuning BERT: misconceptions, explanations, and strong baselines. *CoRR*, abs/2006.04884.

Aakanksha Naik, Abhilasha Ravichander, Norman M. Sadeh, Carolyn Penstein Rosé, and Graham Neubig.

2018. Stress test evaluation for natural language inference. In *Proceedings of the 27th International Conference on Computational Linguistics, COLING 2018, Santa Fe, New Mexico, USA, August 20-26, 2018*, pages 2340–2353. Association for Computational Linguistics.

Yixin Nie, Adina Williams, Emily Dinan, Mohit Bansal, Jason Weston, and Douwe Kiela. 2020. Adversarial NLI: A new benchmark for natural language understanding. In *Proceedings of the 58th Annual Meeting of the Association for Computational Linguistics, ACL 2020, Online, July 5-10, 2020*, pages 4885–4901. Association for Computational Linguistics.

Adam Poliak, Jason Naradowsky, Aparajita Haldar, Rachel Rudinger, and Benjamin Van Durme. 2018. Hypothesis only baselines in natural language inference. In *Proceedings of the Seventh Joint Conference on Lexical and Computational Semantics, *SEM@NAACL-HLT 2018, New Orleans, Louisiana, USA, June 5-6, 2018*, pages 180–191. Association for Computational Linguistics.

Masatoshi Tsuchiya. 2018. Performance impact caused by hidden bias of training data for recognizing textual entailment. In *Proceedings of the Eleventh International Conference on Language Resources and Evaluation, LREC 2018, Miyazaki, Japan, May 7-12, 2018*. European Language Resources Association (ELRA).

Alex Wang, Amanpreet Singh, Julian Michael, Felix Hill, Omer Levy, and Samuel R. Bowman. 2019a. GLUE: A multi-task benchmark and analysis platform for natural language understanding. In *7th International Conference on Learning Representations, ICLR 2019, New Orleans, LA, USA, May 6-9, 2019*. OpenReview.net.

Alex Wang, Ian F. Tenney, Yada Pruksachatkun, Phil Yeres, Jason Phang, Haokun Liu, Phu Mon Htut, , Katherin Yu, Jan Hula, Patrick Xia, Raghu Pappagari, Shuning Jin, R. Thomas McCoy, Roma Patel, Yinghui Huang, Edouard Grave, Najoung Kim, Thibault Févry, Berlin Chen, Nikita Nangia, Anhad Mohananey, Katharina Kann, Shikha Bordia, Nicolas Patry, David Benton, Ellie Pavlick, and Samuel R. Bowman. 2019b. `jiant` 1.3: A software toolkit for research on general-purpose text understanding models. `http://jiant.info/`.

Adina Williams, Nikita Nangia, and Samuel R. Bowman. 2018. A broad-coverage challenge corpus for sentence understanding through inference. In *Proceedings of the 2018 Conference of the North American Chapter of the Association for Computational Linguistics: Human Language Technologies, NAACL-HLT 2018, New Orleans, Louisiana, USA, June 1-6, 2018, Volume 1 (Long Papers)*, pages 1112–1122. Association for Computational Linguistics.

NMF Ensembles? Not for Text Summarization!

Alka Khurana
Department of Computer Science
University of Delhi
Delhi, India
akhurana@cs.du.ac.in

Vasudha Bhatnagar
Department of Computer Science
University of Delhi
Delhi, India
vbhatnagar@cs.du.ac.in

Abstract

Non-negative Matrix Factorization (NMF) has been used for text analytics with promising results. Instability of results arising due to stochastic variations during initialization makes a case for use of ensemble technology. However, our extensive empirical investigation indicates otherwise. In this paper, we establish that ensemble summary for single document using NMF is no better than the best base model summary.

1 Introduction

Non-negative Matrix factorization (NMF) has demonstrated promise in text analytic tasks like topic modeling (Suh et al., 2017; Qiang et al., 2018; Belford et al., 2018), document summarization (Lee et al., 2009; Khurana and Bhatnagar, 2019) and document clustering (Shahnaz et al., 2006; Shinnou and Sasaki, 2007). The method finds favour due to the presence of non-negative elements in resultant factor matrices, which enhance intuitive understanding of the underlying latent semantic structure of the text (Lee and Seung, 1999).

Recent applications of ensemble methods for NMF based topic modeling has shown considerable promise (Suh et al., 2017; Qiang et al., 2018; Belford et al., 2018). These observations drive our motivation for exploring NMF ensembles for document summarization task.

1.1 NMF for Text Summarization

Consider a (pre-processed) document D consisting of n sentences ($S_1, S_2, \ldots, S_n$) and m terms ($t_1, t_2, \ldots, t_m$) represented by a Boolean term-sentence matrix $A_{m \times n}$. NMF decomposition of A results into two non-negative factor matrices W and H, where W is $m \times r$ term-topic (feature) matrix and H is $r \times n$ topic-sentence (co-efficient) matrix, with $r \ll \min\{m, n\}$.

Columns in W correspond to document topics represented as $\tau_1, \tau_2 \ldots \tau_r$ in the latent semantic space, and columns in H represent sentences in D. Element w_{ij} in W signifies the contribution of term t_i in topic τ_j, and element h_{ij} in H denotes the strength of topic τ_i in sentence S_j. Deft manipulation of the elements of two factor matrices yields distinctive sentence scores (Lee et al., 2009; Khurana and Bhatnagar, 2019). Top scoring sentences are selected to generate summary of desired length.

Instability of NMF for Text Summarization: Even though NMF based automatic text summarization is unsupervised and carries advantages of language, domain and collection independence, yet it has been used sporadically for summarization. The reason can be linked to stochastic variations in factor matrices due to random initialization.

Repeated NMF factorization of the input term-sentence matrix results into different sentence scores, generating different summaries. This ambivalence renders the resulting NMF summaries dubitable. In authors' opinion, this has retarded development in this line of research.

Lee et al. (2009) suggested a simplistic fix to this problem by using static initialization for W and H. Experiment using DUC2002[1] data-set with varying initial seed values for W and H shows that the best initialization value is document specific (Fig. 1). Hence, fixed initialization of factor matrices is not a prudent idea.

Another fix for the problem is to use NNDSVD (Non-negative Double Singular Value Decomposition (Boutsidis and Gallopoulos, 2008)) based initialization for NMF factor matrices. Our earlier work (Khurana and Bhatnagar, 2019) establishes that this initialization method improves the sum-

---

[1] Well studied data-set for single document summarization available at https://duc.nist.gov consisting of 533 unique documents.

Proceedings of the First Workshop on Insights from Negative Results in NLP, pages 88–93
Online, November 19, 2020. ©2020 Association for Computational Linguistics

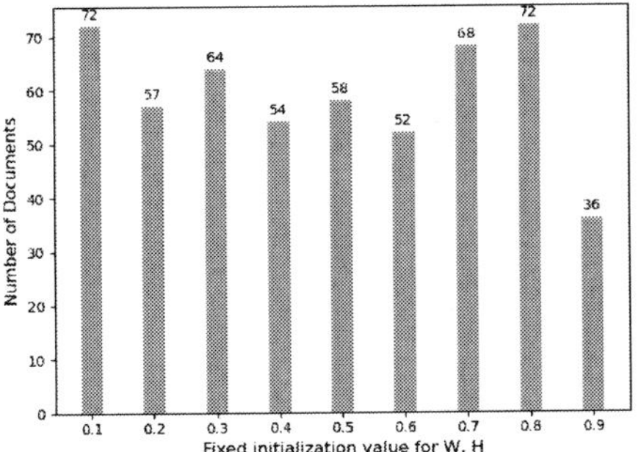

Figure 1: Number of documents with highest ROUGE-L recall score for different initial seed values of NMF factor matrices.

mary quality over fixed initialization for several benchmark data-sets.

1.2 NMF Ensembles

Random initialization has been exploited by clustering and topic modeling researchers to create ensembles (Greene et al., 2008; Belford et al., 2018; Qiang et al., 2018). Ensembling is a machine learning technique, which combines (multiple) varying base models to construct a consensus model, which is expected to perform better than individual base models.

Effectiveness of NMF ensembles in text analytics, specifically in topic modeling (Belford et al., 2018; Qiang et al., 2018), motivated the current research. We initiated the study with the aim to leverage stochastic variations in NMF factors and resulting diverse base summaries, to combine into stable ensemble summary.

Extrapolating earlier studies, we expected that NMF ensemble summary, smoothed over multifarious summaries obtained by randomly initialized NMF factors, will accomplish higher ROUGE scores. However, our investigations establish that NMF ensembles are not effective. Rather, despite heavy overhead of creating multiple base models and combining them, NMF ensemble often perform worse than the best base model for single document extractive summarization.

2 NMF Ensembles for Text Summarization

Ensemble methods are employed in supervised, semi-supervised and unsupervised learning settings. In all scenarios, they comprise two phases.

In the first phase, *diverse* base models are generated. Diversity in models is recognized to be the key factor for improvement (Kuncheva and Hadjitodorov, 2004), which is commonly sourced from variations in base algorithm, algorithmic parameters or data itself.

In second phase, multiple base models are combined using a consensus (aka integration) function. Wide variety of choices for creating diversity and combining base models gives rise to numerous possibilities for creating ensembles (Zhou, 2012).

2.1 Generation of diverse base models

Repeated application of NMF on the term-sentence matrix leads to generation of multiple base models. In the present context, we achieve diversity using two methods.
(i) Repeated factorization[2] of A using NMF with random initial seed values for W and H, and
(ii) Repeated factorization by varying the number of latent topics into which the document is decomposed, as suggested in (Greene et al., 2008). This strategy implicitly embeds variations that arise out of random initialization.

In practice, variation in choice of NMF solvers and initialization methods is also a source of diversity. We however, refrain from following this direction because of weak scientific ground.

2.2 Combining NMF base models

We examine six combining methods, in increasing order of complexities, to generate consensus summaries. First three are simple aggregation methods, where sentence scores are combined directly. Next two methods are based on rank manipulation of the scored sentences. Finally, we use *Stacking*, which is a sophisticated combining method (Zhou, 2012; Belford et al., 2018).
i. **Average:** We calculate the consensus score of each sentence in the document by averaging sentence scores over all base models, and use it for summary sentence selection.
ii. **Median:** Since average is sensitive to outliers, we calculate median score of each sentence across all base models and use it for summary sentence selection.
iii. **Quartile:** We obtain consensus score by considering third quartile of the sentence scores across all base models, and use it for summary sentence

---

[2]We calculate r according to the formula proposed in (Aliguliyev, 2009).

selection.

iv. **Voting:** We rank sentences based on their scores. Consensus rank of a sentence is the most frequent rank (majority) of the sentence amongst base models. Top ranking sentences are selected for summary.

v. **Ranking:** We count the number of times a sentence appears among the top k scoring sentences (k is the desired number of sentences). Finally, sentences are ranked based on the frequency of appearing among top-k ranked sentences. Top scoring sentences are included in summary.

vi. **Stacking:** *Stacking* is a well established combining method, which combines base level models to create a meta-training set (Zhou, 2012). Subsequently, ensemble model is trained on this meta-training set. We stack topic-term (W^T) matrices (base level models) as meta-training set ($\widehat{W}$) for producing the *stacked ensemble* (Belford et al., 2018).

$\widehat{W}$ matrix is factorized using NMF with NNDSVD initialization to obtain ensembled topic-term matrix, which along with A is used for scoring sentences using term-oriented sentence selection method, NMF-TR, proposed in (Khurana and Bhatnagar, 2019). Finally, top-k scoring sentences are included in summary.

3 Performance Evaluation

In this section, we present extensive experimentation[3] carried out to investigate the performance of NMF ensembles for extractive summarization. First, we evaluate the performance based on combining methods described in Sec. 2 and the sizes of ensemble. Next, we study the effect of diversity in base models on ensemble performance. Finally, we test the statistical significance of our results. All experiments are performed on DUC2001[4] data-set consisting of 308 documents and DUC2002[1] data-set. We report macro averaged ROUGE recall scores (R-1: ROUGE-1, R-2: ROUGE-2, R-L: ROUGE-L) (Lin, 2004).

In interest of brevity, all results are reported as performance gain (+) or loss (-) over NMF-TR scores as baseline method. Table 1 shows ROUGE scores of this baseline for DUC2001 and DUC2002 data-sets reported in (Khurana and Bhatnagar, 2019).

	R-1	R-2	R-L
DUC2001	44.7	15.9	39.3
DUC2002	49.0	21.5	44.1

Table 1: Macro-averaged ROUGE recall performance of NMF-TR method (Khurana and Bhatnagar, 2019).

3.1 Examining Combining Methods

Primary objective of this experiment is to examine the comparative performance of model integration methods. However, size of an ensemble is a crucial factor that determines the quantum of performance gain. Oversized ensembles have obvious computational and memory overheads, while undersized ensembles run the risk of little performance gains and reduced stability. Ergo, we evaluate the performance of each combining method on ensembles of varying sizes. We compute macro-averaged ROUGE recall scores, each score averaged over ten executions to combat random variations. Table 2 shows the performance differential for six combining methods for ten different sizes for DUC2002 data-set. A cursory glance is sufficient to conclude that there are more *negs* than *pos'*. Degradation in performance is most unexpected. Macro-level analyses in the bottom row and rightmost column consolidate the surprise.

The bottom row 'Total' shows the number of times the ensemble improves summary quality across all combining methods. For ensemble size 100, there is ≈50% chance (9/18) of improving the summary quality across all methods. The rightmost column 'Total' shows the number of times a combining method improves summary across all sizes for each integration method. It suggests that simple combining methods improve marginally even for large size ensemble.

To confirm the trend, we repeated the same experiment with DUC2001 data-set (Table 3). Apparently there is better chance of improvement for this data-set using NMF ensembles, but the gain is meagre (less than 0.5 in each case) and does not justify the computational overhead.

Consolidating observations from Table 2 & 3, none of the the combining methods yield noticeably better quality summaries than the baseline method. Further, increasing the size of ensemble also does not hold promise.

Since Table 2 & 3 exhibit similar trends, we choose to perform remaining experiments on DUC2002 data-set as it clearly demonstrates infirmity of NMF ensembles.

---

[3]Code is available https://github.com/alkakhurana/NMF-Ensembles

[4]Available at https://duc.nist.gov

DUC2002											
		$\ell = 2$	$\ell = 4$	$\ell = 6$	$\ell = 8$	$\ell = 10$	$\ell = 20$	$\ell = 30$	$\ell = 40$	$\ell = 50$	$\ell = 100$	Total
Average	R-1	-0.572	-0.268	-0.225	-0.098	-0.118	-0.060	+0.040	+0.108	+0.064	+0.151	4
	R-2	-0.727	-0.429	-0.447	-0.293	-0.278	-0.220	-0.123	-0.084	-0.128	-0.027	0
	R-L	-0.557	-0.279	-0.292	-0.164	-0.195	-0.132	-0.039	+0.022	-0.030	+0.069	2
Median	R-1	-	-0.165	-0.048	-0.050	-0.125	+0.047	+0.170	+0.166	+0.159	+0.219	5
	R-2	-	-0.362	-0.248	-0.287	-0.279	-0.123	-0.003	-0.053	-0.043	+0.024	1
	R-L	-	-0.209	-0.098	-0.138	-0.185	-0.021	+0.093	+0.063	+0.069	+0.124	4
Quartile	R-1	-	-0.367	-0.355	-0.145	-0.212	-0.093	+0.029	-0.044	+0.041	+0.154	3
	R-2	-	-0.550	-0.606	-0.406	-0.401	-0.292	-0.212	-0.257	-0.187	-0.057	0
	R-L	-	-0.392	-0.408	-0.227	-0.294	-0.167	-0.073	-0.135	-0.054	+0.066	1
Voting	R-1	-	-0.561	-0.470	-0.295	-0.333	-0.103	-0.125	-0.029	+0.068	+0.138	2
	R-2	-	-1.002	-0.898	-0.669	-0.625	-0.409	-0.328	-0.238	-0.121	-0.102	0
	R-L	-	-0.579	-0.501	-0.345	-0.403	-0.193	-0.214	-0.110	-0.006	+0.046	1
Ranking	R-1	-	-3.078	-2.815	-2.806	-2.829	-2.564	-2.319	-2.192	-2.112	-1.913	0
	R-2	-	-3.485	-3.271	-3.213	-3.247	-3.027	-2.729	-2.625	-2.567	-2.402	0
	R-L	-	-2.735	-2.486	-2.508	-2.551	-2.356	-2.093	-1.992	-1.890	-1.742	0
Stacking	R-1	-0.152	-0.093	-0.076	-0.063	-0.136	-0.202	-0.181	-0.084	-0.208	-0.184	0
	R-2	-0.416	-0.307	-0.285	-0.226	-0.331	-0.322	-0.352	-0.295	-0.383	-0.385	0
	R-L	-0.208	-0.095	-0.113	-0.078	-0.157	-0.212	-0.205	-0.122	-0.248	-0.196	0
Total		0	0	0	0	0	1	4	4	5	9	

Table 2: Performance differential in macro-averaged ROUGE recall scores w.r.t NMF-TR for different ensemble sizes and combining methods. ℓ is the size of ensemble. '-' indicates that the integration method is not meaningful.

DUC2001											
		$\ell = 2$	$\ell = 4$	$\ell = 6$	$\ell = 8$	$\ell = 10$	$\ell = 20$	$\ell = 30$	$\ell = 40$	$\ell = 50$	$\ell = 100$	Total
Average	R-1	-0.328	-0.158	-0.011	+0.066	+0.054	+0.052	+0.177	+0.105	+0.070	+0.135	7
	R-2	-0.076	+0.152	+0.337	+0.324	+0.294	+0.257	+0.338	+0.313	+0.295	+0.341	9
	R-L	-0.118	+0.003	+0.154	+0.208	+0.163	+0.158	+0.255	+0.187	+0.151	+0.191	9
Median	R-1	-	-0.121	+0.037	+0.104	+0.068	+0.043	+0.047	+0.115	+0.180	+0.210	8
	R-2	-	+0.145	+0.301	+0.302	+0.301	+0.252	+0.224	+0.288	+0.340	+0.315	9
	R-L	-	-0.002	+0.188	+0.188	+0.140	+0.112	+0.108	+0.196	+0.230	+0.232	8
Quartile	R-1	-	-0.391	+0.062	-0.168	-0.087	-0.101	-0.001	+0.005	-0.004	+0.073	3
	R-2	-	-0.014	+0.274	+0.205	+0.199	+0.223	+0.226	+0.266	+0.255	+0.273	8
	R-L	-	-0.205	+0.243	+0.003	+0.033	+0.055	+0.100	+0.124	+0.120	+0.150	8
Voting	R-1	-	-0.464	-0.225	-0.093	+0.008	-0.011	+0.007	+0.046	-0.026	+0.009	4
	R-2	-	-0.290	+0.005	+0.210	+0.268	+0.290	+0.360	+0.379	+0.328	+0.428	8
	R-L	-	-0.192	+0.022	+0.130	+0.189	+0.152	+0.159	+0.202	+0.123	+0.184	8
Ranking	R-1	-	-2.299	-2.295	-2.180	-2.158	-1.768	-1.474	-1.607	-1.391	-1.052	0
	R-2	-	-1.659	-1.680	-1.495	-1.497	-1.164	-0.912	-1.032	-0.895	-0.662	0
	R-L	-	-1.619	-1.599	-1.508	-1.535	-1.152	-0.849	-0.945	-0.812	-0.522	0
Stacking	R-1	-0.009	+0.015	-0.032	-0.021	+0.085	+0.092	+0.032	+0.161	+0.042	-0.034	6
	R-2	+0.216	+0.250	+0.228	+0.201	+0.333	+0.271	+0.300	+0.344	+0.311	+0.242	10
	R-L	+0.178	+0.164	+0.115	+0.163	+0.252	+0.217	+0.211	+0.279	+0.211	+0.127	10
Total		2	6	12	12	14	13	14	15	13	14	

Table 3: Performance differential in macro-averaged ROUGE recall scores w.r.t NMF-TR for different ensemble sizes and combining methods. ℓ is the size of ensemble. '-' indicates that the integration method is not meaningful.

3.2 Diversity in Base Models

Since summary scores are sensitive to the number of latent topics into which document is decomposed, varying the number of latent topics while decomposing the term-sentence matrix is a potential source of diversity in NMF base models. We explore two different ways to accomplish this.

Selecting latent topics from range: We create 100 base models with number of latent topics randomly chosen from the range $[r, 2r]$, where r is determined using method proposed by (Aliguliyev, 2009). We expect that random initialization and variation in the number of topics would inject diversity in base models. We do not test this method with *stacking* because it requires stacked matrices to have same number of columns. Results for this experiment (Table 4) belie our expectation. *Thus varying the number of topics does not improve the*

	Avg	Med	Quart	Vote	Rank
R-1	-0.005	+0.170	+0.041	+0.017	-1.745
R-2	-0.095	-0.035	-0.064	-0.126	-2.227
R-L	+0.002	+0.129	0.000	-0.053	-1.622

Table 4: Performance differential for random variation in number of latent topics in the range $[r, 2r]$ for ensemble size 100.

quality of consensus summary.

Varying latent topics over range: Suspecting that repetition in the number of latent topics in previous experiment curb diversity in the ensemble, we attempt to create diversity by generating base models with all values in the range $[r, 2r]$. Hence, the size of ensemble for this experiment is document specific. Here too, it is not possible to create a *stacking* ensemble because of different number of latent topics in each base model. Results for this diversity creation method are presented in Table 5.

Thus systematically varying the number of topics

	Avg	Med	Quart	Vote	Rank
R-1	-0.265	-0.540	+0.029	-0.397	-2.515
R-2	-0.363	-0.597	-0.268	-0.725	-2.935
R-L	-0.271	-0.566	+0.022	-0.503	-2.262

Table 5: Performance gain/loss when the number of latent topics are in generated from the range [r, 2r].

also fails to infuse diversity and shows no promise.

3.3 Comparison with best summary

With no success in injecting diversity in base models, we proceed to perform deeper analysis to diagnose the cause of degradation. We wanted to answer the question *'How many base models are responsible for pulling down the score of consensus summary?'*.

To answer this, we evaluated all base summaries and noted their ROUGE scores. The score of the best base summary was compared against that of ensemble summary and translated to win (if ensemble summary score is higher or equal), and loss otherwise. This exercise was done for all integration methods and ensemble size 30 and 100.

Results shown in Table 6 are almost startling. E.g. 23/510 for ensemble size 30 means that out of 533 total documents, for 23 documents the ensemble summary was atleast as good as the best base summary. For 510 documents, ensemble summary score was worse than that of the base summary. *Thus NMF ensemble summaries fail miserably to improve quality over the best base summary.*

size = 30						
	Avg	Med	Quart	Vote	Rank	Stk
R-1	23/510	23/510	28/505	22/511	42/491	27/506
R-2	28/505	25/508	26/507	24/509	52/481	28/505
R-L	23/510	21/512	22/511	18/515	41/492	20/513
size = 100						
	Avg	Med	Quart	Vote	Rank	Stk
R-1	11/522	10/523	11/522	6/527	20/513	12/521
R-2	16/517	17/516	18/515	11/522	26/507	16/517
R-L	11/522	11/522	12/521	7/526	18/515	13/520

Table 6: Wins/losses for ensemble summary compared with best base model summary for DUC2002 corpus.

3.4 Statistical Significance of Combining methods

We investigate the statistical significance of our results for all combining methods. We employ bootstrap approach recommended in (Dror et al., 2018), and test the null hypothesis

H0: *NMF ensemble method performs no worse than the baseline NMF-TR,* against the alternative hypothesis,

H1: *NMF ensemble method performs worse than NMF-TR.*

For each combining method, we generate one million bootstrap samples from the ROUGE scores of 533 ensemble summaries. We compute the difference in performance w.r.t baseline and estimate *p-value* as the ratio of number of times ensemble method beats NMF-TR by twice the margin on the bootstrap samples, to the total number of samples. For *p-value* > 0.05, we reject the null hypothesis. Table 7 shows p-values obtained for each ROUGE metric and combining method. According to the computed p-values (Table 7), we fail to accept null hypothesis for each combining method and each ROUGE metric. *Therefore, NMF ensemble meth-*

	Avg	Med	Quart	Vote	Rank	Stk
R-1	0.37	0.13	0.31	0.23	0.99	0.82
R-2	0.59	0.45	0.66	0.44	1	0.90
R-L	0.45	0.19	0.39	0.34	0.99	0.84

Table 7: Probability values for bootstrap sampling based test of ensemble performance w.r.t baseline.

ods are not statistically significantly better than the baseline method.

4 Discussion and Conclusion

Extensive empirical investigation shows that leveraging stochastic variations due to random initialization of NMF factor matrices for extractive document summarization is not straight-forward. We experimented with different NMF solvers available in (Pedregosa et al., 2011) and found no change in results. In absence of any concrete explanation for degraded performance, we forward two plausible reasons.

First, apparently simple combining methods fail to tease apart the differences in term-topic and topic-sentence strengths in the latent space. Possible future investigation in this direction include projection of these matrices in higher dimension, and drawing from the cluster ensemble research to design more sophisticated combining methods.

Second reason is related to the maxim of *sentence ranking and selection* for extractive document summarization. Combining scores from base models alters sentence ranking, and probably less important sentence get pulled *up* in the summary. This is most likely to happen with the lowest ranked sentence in the summary. A single *bad* sentence in the summary can lower down the score substantially. Achieving stable ranks in ensemble technology could be another direction of research.

References

Ramiz M Aliguliyev. 2009. A new sentence similarity measure and sentence based extractive technique for automatic text summarization. *Expert Systems with Applications*, 36(4):7764–7772.

Mark Belford, Brian Mac Namee, and Derek Greene. 2018. Stability of topic modeling via matrix factorization. *Expert Systems with Applications*, 91:159–169.

Christos Boutsidis and Efstratios Gallopoulos. 2008. Svd based initialization: A head start for nonnegative matrix factorization. *Pattern Recognition*, 41(4):1350–1362.

Rotem Dror, Gili Baumer, Segev Shlomov, and Roi Reichart. 2018. The hitchhiker's guide to testing statistical significance in natural language processing. In *Proceedings of the 56th Annual Meeting of the Association for Computational Linguistics (Volume 1: Long Papers)*, pages 1383–1392.

Derek Greene, Gerard Cagney, Nevan Krogan, and Pádraig Cunningham. 2008. Ensemble non-negative matrix factorization methods for clustering protein–protein interactions. *Bioinformatics*, 24(15):1722–1728.

Alka Khurana and Vasudha Bhatnagar. 2019. Extractive document summarization using non-negative matrix factorization. In *International Conference on Database and Expert Systems Applications*, pages 76–90. Springer.

L. I. Kuncheva and S. T. Hadjitodorov. 2004. Using diversity in cluster ensembles. In *2004 IEEE International Conference on Systems, Man and Cybernetics (IEEE Cat. No.04CH37583)*, volume 2, pages 1214–1219 vol.2.

Daniel D Lee and H Sebastian Seung. 1999. Learning the parts of objects by non-negative matrix factorization. *Nature*, 401(6755):788.

Ju-Hong Lee, Sun Park, Chan-Min Ahn, and Daeho Kim. 2009. Automatic generic document summarization based on non-negative matrix factorization. *Information Processing & Management*, 45(1):20–34.

Chin-Yew Lin. 2004. Rouge: A package for automatic evaluation of summaries. *Text Summarization Branches Out*.

F. Pedregosa, G. Varoquaux, A. Gramfort, V. Michel, B. Thirion, O. Grisel, M. Blondel, P. Prettenhofer, R. Weiss, V. Dubourg, J. Vanderplas, A. Passos, D. Cournapeau, M. Brucher, M. Perrot, and E. Duchesnay. 2011. Scikit-learn: Machine learning in Python. *Journal of Machine Learning Research*, 12:2825–2830.

Jipeng Qiang, Yun Li, Yunhao Yuan, and Wei Liu. 2018. Snapshot ensembles of non-negative matrix factorization for stability of topic modeling. *Applied Intelligence*, pages 1–13.

Farial Shahnaz, Michael W Berry, V Paul Pauca, and Robert J Plemmons. 2006. Document clustering using nonnegative matrix factorization. *Information Processing & Management*, 42(2):373–386.

Hiroyuki Shinnou and Minoru Sasaki. 2007. Ensemble document clustering using weighted hypergraph generated by nmf. In *Proceedings of the 45th Annual Meeting of the Association for Computational Linguistics Companion Volume Proceedings of the Demo and Poster Sessions*, pages 77–80.

Sangho Suh, Jaegul Choo, Joonseok Lee, and Chandan K Reddy. 2017. Local topic discovery via boosted ensemble of nonnegative matrix factorization. In *Proceedings of the 26th International Joint Conference on Artificial Intelligence*, pages 4944–4948. AAAI Press.

Zhi-Hua Zhou. 2012. *Ensemble methods: foundations and algorithms*. Chapman and Hall/CRC.

If You Build Your Own NER Scorer, Non-replicable Results Will Come

Constantine Lignos   **Marjan Kamyab**
Brandeis University
415 South St.
Waltham, MA, 02453, USA
{lignos,marjankamyab}@brandeis.edu

Abstract

We attempt to replicate a named entity recognition (NER) model implemented in a popular toolkit and discover that a critical barrier to doing so is the inconsistent evaluation of improper label sequences. We define these sequences and examine how two scorers differ in their handling of them, finding that one approach produces F1 scores approximately 0.5 points higher on the CoNLL 2003 English development and test sets. We propose best practices to increase the replicability of NER evaluations by increasing transparency regarding the handling of improper label sequences.

1   Introduction

The goal of this paper is to demonstrate an issue that complicates the comparison and replication of named entity recognition (NER) systems. Standard F1-based evaluation of NER models in the manner made popular by the CoNLL 2002–3 shared tasks (Tjong Kim Sang, 2002; Tjong Kim Sang and De Meulder, 2003) requires decoding a sequence of per-token labels into entity mentions and computing precision and recall by evaluating the types and spans of the mentions. While there are popular scorer implementations and popular NER toolkits, there is little transparency regarding the *exact* process that scorers use to decode label sequences.

In the case where all label sequences are properly formed, this lack of transparency should have no impact; all correct decoding processes should produce the same result. However, many systems can produce what we call *improper* label sequences (see Section 3.2), and different approaches to decoding improper label sequences for evaluation produce different scores. As the processes for label decoding have not been standardized and are often undocumented, comparisons between reported scores may not be fair, and replication of those scores can prove difficult.

2   Our negative result

We did not intend to begin a project on NER evaluation reproducibility. The discovery process for our negative result began with three separate research projects encountering the same issue: higher-than-expected F1 scores for a certain class of models implemented in a popular NER toolkit, NCRF++ (Yang et al., 2018; Yang and Zhang, 2018).

One of the authors of this paper attempted to reimplement NCRF++'s models as a learning exercise. The reimplementation yielded similar F1 scores to NCRF++ when a CRF output layer was used but produced lower F1 scores when using softmax output. After the other author found the same result in an independent reimplementation, we turned our attention to the only commonality between our implementations: an open-source external scorer. We consulted with researchers in our lab using NCRF++ for two other projects, and a consistent story began to emerge: when scoring softmax models, NCRF++'s internal scorer produced higher scores than other NER scorers.

Our negative result was a failure to replicate the performance of NCRF++, and the cause of this failure was that we did not understand its approach to evaluation. NCRF++'s scorer differs from others in how it treats improper label sequences, and its approach consistently produces higher F1 scores for softmax-output models. The handling of these sequences is effectively undefined behavior for an NER scorer; there is no single correct strategy. In this paper, we quantify the impact of those strategies and propose an evaluation approach that would improve reproducibility by requiring explicit, transparent handling of improper label sequences.

Supplemental material and the resources needed to replicate this study are available at https://lignos.org/repro-ner.

94

Proceedings of the First Workshop on Insights from Negative Results in NLP, pages 94–99
Online, November 19, 2020. ©2020 Association for Computational Linguistics

3 Entity encoding and decoding

3.1 Proper label sequences

As the focus of this venue is on insights from negative results and not the finer points of NER systems, we will first review the process of entity encoding and decoding. Consider the following sentence fragment from the CoNLL 2003 English NER data:

> [Australian]MISC [Davis Cup]MISC captain [John Newcombe]PER.

In this fragment, three entity mentions are annotated. Table 1 shows three well-known approaches to encoding these tokens as a label sequence.

Encoding	Labels					
IOB	I-MISC	B-MISC	I-MISC	O	I-PER	I-PER
BIO	B-MISC	B-MISC	I-MISC	O	B-PER	I-PER
BIOES	S-MISC	B-MISC	E-MISC	O	B-PER	E-PER

Table 1: Proper entity encodings for the tokens of the string *Australian Davis Cup captain John Newcombe*.

Note that in BIO (Begin, Inside, Outside) encoding, every mention begins with a B label; in IOB encoding, mentions begin with I except where necessary to differentiate from the continuation of a preceding same-type mention by using a B label (e.g., I-PER B-PER for two adjacent single-token names). In the BIOES encoding, single-token entities use a single S label, and multi-token entities begin with B, end with E, and use I for everything but the first and last tokens.[1]

3.2 Improper label sequences

This paper is concerned with the implications for evaluation in NER when unexpected label sequences are produced. While there does not appear to be any standard term for this phenomenon, we define an *improper* label sequence as one where the label sequence does not conform to a sequence of labels allowed by the encoding. Consider the improper label sequences given in Table 2.

In all three cases, it is possible to infer the likely "intent" of the system that produced these

---

[1]Historically, it has not been possible to identify *with certainty* the entity encoding an NER study uses based on the acronym used. In early work there was confusion between the IOB (IOB1, Ramshaw and Marcus, 1995; Tjong Kim Sang and Veenstra, 1999) and BIO (IOB2) encodings, and later similar confusion between BIOES and IOBES. Readers may disagree regarding precisely what entity encodings are signified by these acronyms. We do not discuss BMES and BILOU in this paper and consider them isomorphic to BIOES.

Encoding	Labels					
IOB	I-MISC	B-MISC	I-MISC	O	**B-PER**	I-PER
BIO	B-MISC	B-MISC	I-MISC	O	**I-PER**	I-PER
BIOES	S-MISC	B-MISC	**I-MISC**	O	B-PER	E-PER

Table 2: Improper entity encodings for the tokens of the string *Australian Davis Cup captain John Newcombe*, with improper labels identified using bold.

label sequences. For IOB and BIO encodings, the `conlleval` scorer (Tjong Kim Sang, 2004) used for the CoNLL 2002–3 NER evaluations (Tjong Kim Sang, 2002; Tjong Kim Sang and De Meulder, 2003) would effectively "repair"[2] these label sequences, such that they would produce the same entity mentions as the proper encodings in Table 1. We refer to this approach to interpreting improper label sequences as *CoNLL-style* in this paper.

An alternative would be to interpret the label sequence more strictly. An obvious approach for BIO encoding would be to *only* begin a mention when a B label was encountered. In this example, only two mentions would be created, as the final two tokens do not have a proper beginning label.

The `conlleval` scorer does not support the BIOES/IOBES encodings, but `seqeval` (chakki, 2019), a Python library that replicates `conlleval`'s BIO decoding, supports them and uses similar CoNLL-style repair logic for improper BIOES/IOBES sequences. We return to the issue of BIOES/IOBES decoding in Section 5.1.

3.3 Softmax output

Since at least HMM-based NER systems of the late 90s, sequence NER models have identified the most likely label sequence by taking into account the relationship between a label and preceding labels. The most common modern approach to modeling this relationship is to use a conditional random field (CRF), which can learn to avoid producing improper label sequences or be forced to, either through manual manipulation of its weights or forbidding improper transitions entirely.

With the advent of neural models capable of capturing substantial contextual information before the output layer, it is now feasible to create relatively good NER models without a CRF by using softmax to select the highest-scoring label for each

---

[2]It is not clear whether it was an explicit design goal to repair these sequences or they are simply the consequence of implementing a universal decoder for IOB and BIO encodings. Readers interested in examining the decoding logic should inspect the `startOfChunk` and `endOfChunk` functions.

token independently, which is significantly faster. While the model will still indirectly learn to prefer proper label sequences, there is no explicit representation of the sequential relationship between labels. When sufficiently trained, a model with CRF output rarely produces improper label sequences, but softmax-output models do so more frequently.

4 Results

The goal of our experiments is to estimate the increase in F1 scores that can be attributed to use of NCRF++'s internal decoding compared to CoNLL-style decoding when evaluating softmax-output models. We trained models using NCRF++ after modifying it to additionally use an external CoNLL-style scorer, `seqeval`.[3] We report scores from the internal and external scorer. We use a bidirectional LSTM architecture at the word level and test multiple character-level architectures: a bi-LSTM, CNN, and no character-level representation. We use the same hyperparameters, pretrained word embedding (GLoVe 100d), and data (CoNLL 2003 English) used by Yang et al. (2018). Each configuration was run ten times using different random initializations (seeds 0–9). The test set was evaluated using the model from the epoch that attained the highest development set F1 (as scored internally by NCRF++) during training.

Table 3 gives F1 scores for entity mentions for BIOES and BIO encodings across all character-level architectures, including values previously reported by Yang et al. (2018). When using NCRF++'s internal scorer, our results are close to the those previously reported. However, evaluating the same output with an external scorer leads to lower scores.

Table 4 reports the distribution of the increase in F1 scores (NCRF++'s internal score minus the external score) for each system output across encodings and evaluation sets. We computed how much NCRF++'s scoring procedure increases F1 for each run's output and then average across all runs (character-level architectures and random initializations). To demonstrate the statistical reliability of this increase, we performed a Wilcoxon signed-rank test—a non-parametric version of the paired t-test—for each combination of encoding

---

[3]We selected `seqeval` after reviewing its label decoding procedure and confirming that produces the same scores for BIO as `conlleval`. We chose it because it supports both BIO and BIOES encoding and provides greater numerical precision than `conlleval`.

and evaluation set. All four p-values were below 0.0001, and the 95% confidence intervals of the differences were .49–.58 (BIOES) and .38–.43 (BIO) for development, .54–63 (BIOES) and .48–.56 (BIO) for test. In summary, for softmax models, the NCRF++ internal scorer produces scores approximately half a point of F1 higher.

All scores reported so far have been from converged models. It is also of interest to explore what the increase in scores looks like during training. Figure 1 gives the increase in development set F1 scores across all training epochs for all configurations we ran, displaying 3,000 points per encoding. Early in training, NCRF++'s internal scorer can produce F1 scores several points higher than a CoNLL-style scorer, presumably due to producing a high number of improper label sequences preconvergence. Crucially, in all 6,000 development set epochs we evaluated, NCRF++'s internal scorer *always* reported a higher F1 than `seqeval` in our evaluation of softmax-output models.

5 Discussion

5.1 Analysis

Before we discuss the insights gained from our study, it is important contextualize our findings. Our goals are to motivate the establishment of standard evaluation practices for NER, explain the impact of improper label sequence decoding, and encourage authors to be transparent about their approach to evaluation.

We must emphasize that we are not claiming that the way that NCRF++'s scorer decodes improper label sequences is incorrect; it is one of many possible ways of doing so, and we do not wish to single out NCRF++ or its authors specifically for criticism. NCRF++'s approach to decoding improper label sequences is, however, different than the popular approach defined by the widely-used `conlleval` scorer for the CoNLL 2002–3 NER shared tasks (later faithfully reimplemented and extended by `seqeval`), and thus one must exercise caution when comparing scores it generates to those of other scorers.

While we find the NCRF++ entity mention decoder difficult to fully understand, our inspection of the code leads us to believe that it will only begin a mention when the proper tag—B for BIO, B or S for BIOES—is supplied. It is effectively removing some improper label sequences by treating some labels as if they were O.

Source	N	Scorer	BIOES			BIO		
			No Char.	Char. LSTM	Char. CNN	No Char.	Char. LSTM	Char. CNN
Reported	5	NCRF++	$88.49 \pm .17$	$90.77 \pm .06$	$90.60 \pm .11$	-	-	-
Reproduction	10	NCRF++	$88.78 \pm .28$	$90.76 \pm .12$	$90.62 \pm .15$	$88.41 \pm .21$	$90.49 \pm .15$	$90.46 \pm .58$
Reproduction	10	External	$88.21 \pm .27$	$90.20 \pm .09$	$89.99 \pm .19$	$87.98 \pm .21$	$89.93 \pm .19$	$89.88 \pm .21$

Table 3: Means and standard deviation of test set F1 for each tested configuration and from previously reported results (Yang et al., 2018, Table 4). Empty cells indicate configurations without previously reported scores. N gives the number of runs used to compute each value in the row (e.g., each mean was computed over N values).

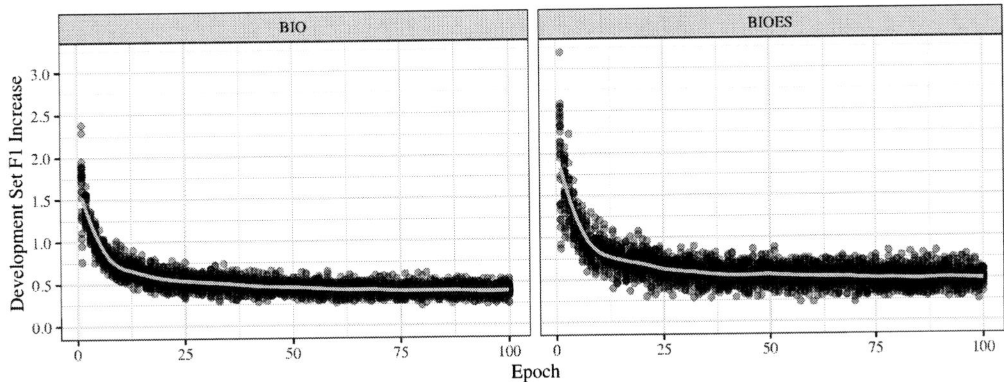

Figure 1: Increase in development set F1 due to NCRF++'s internal scorer for softmax output models across all training epochs, with a local regression (LOESS) fit line.

Data Set	N	BIOES	BIO
Development	30	0.53 ± 0.11	0.40 ± 0.06
Test	30	0.58 ± 0.12	0.52 ± 0.11

Table 4: Means and standard deviations for softmax models of the increase in F1 due to using NCRF++'s internal scorer.

Why would it be advantageous for a system to decode in this way? Unlike in Table 2, where repairing the improper sequences would result in correct answers, many improper sequences represent generalization errors. For example, consider a system using a BIO encoding that observed *Pat Jones* as `B-PER I-PER` frequently in training and must predict labels for *Charity Jones*, annotated as a person in the gold standard. If it has never seen the token *Charity* with the label `B-PER` and has seen *Jones* frequently with the label `I-PER`, it might predict the tag sequence `O I-PER`. A lenient CoNLL-style decoder would decode this as a mention of type `PER` for the token *Jones*, which would result in a false alarm (precision error) and a miss (recall error).

However, a stricter BIO decoder like NCRF++'s

would predict no mentions, resulting in a miss but no false alarm. For softmax output, it appears to be universally advantageous to decode this way; for the 6,000 epochs we scored using the development set, NCRF++'s scorer always gave a higher F1.

Our examples have focused on decoding BIO sequences, partly because `conlleval` set a standard approach to doing so almost two decades ago. Repairing improper BIOES label sequences is much more complex; for example, in the sequences `B-PER E-PER E-PER` and `S-PER I-PER E-PER`, how many entity mentions should be created? There is not a single answer, but `seqeval` implements an approach in the spirit of what `conlleval` does for BIO, and NCRF++ appears to implement a stricter decoder.

While we were not able to find any published or unpublished papers specifically discussing the effect of decoding improper label sequences on F1, as we prepared this paper for submission we discovered a closed GitHub issue[4] opened by Mike Kroutikov pointing out that the way NCRF++ decodes label sequences does not match other NER

[4] `https://github.com/jiesutd/NCRFpp/issues/87`

systems. Reviewing this issue and other issues opened against NCRF++, it is clear that we are not the first to identify its departure from CoNLL-style label decoding. In addition to opening an issue, Kroutikov (2019) blogged about the many potential ways to decode BIOES and examined the approaches taken by other NER implementations.

Our findings raise the question of whether NCRF++'s internal scorer also differs from the external scorer when evaluating models that use CRF output. We performed a post-hoc study where we repeated the same set of experiments we performed for softmax-output models with ones that used a CRF. While NCRF++'s scorer does not give the exact same scores as the external scorer, the increase in F1 attributable to NCRF++'s scoring procedure is quite small when measured on the development set (BIOES 0.0032 ± 0.0040; BIO 0.0072 ± 0.0073), and test set (BIOES -0.015 ± 0.020; BIO 0.0040 ± 0.0051). The experiments using BIOES encoding and evaluating on the test set are the only ones we performed in which on average NCRF++'s internal scorer produced lower scores than the external one.

5.2 Insights

What insights have we gained from our negative result? First, we have clarified how well softmax-output NER models perform when evaluated using CoNLL-style label decoding, which gives lower scores than NCRF++'s internal scorer. The issue of improper label decoding is unlikely to significantly affect any state of the art results, which do not generally use softmax output, but may affect decision-making for NER system designers exploring whether adding a CRF to a system is worth the performance penalty.

Second, we believe our study will help users of a popular toolkit—which received the COLING 2018 "Most reproducible" best paper award—understand how it computes scores and why attempts at replication will fail if they do not also replicate NCRF++'s approach to improper label sequence decoding.

More broadly, the insights from this negative result highlight for all NLP researchers the importance of using a standard evaluation procedure. When possible, using widely-used, well-documented scorers enables fair comparisons of scores across systems.

6   A vision for NER evaluation

Our study leads us to propose a vision for NER evaluation as follows:
1. We should have a well-tested, well-documented, open-source scorer which has been developed independently of any particular model. This scorer should only accept properly-formed label sequences, avoiding the question of the "right" way to decode improper label sequences.
2. The scorer should be accompanied by implementations of standard processes for converting improper label sequences into proper ones. These approaches should include the CoNLL-style approach and a more strict one, like NCRF++'s.
3. Work which wants to use an alternative approach to converting improper label sequences to proper ones should contain a documented, replicable process for doing so.

This procedure separates the process of scoring from the process of interpreting improper label sequences. It also suggests a new research avenue of designing methods for optimally converting improper label sequences into proper ones.

Until the tools required for our vision—perhaps something like SacreBLEU (Post, 2018)—are developed, we recommend `seqeval` as the best solution for NER scoring. It is an easy-to-inspect, faithful reimplementation of `conlleval`. Unlike `conlleval`, it can be called directly from Python and does not truncate scores, avoiding systematic downward bias when aggregating them.

Regarding extensions to this study, while we evaluated on the CoNLL 2003 English data to compare with Yang et al. (2018), evaluating in more languages is essential. Looking beyond the other CoNLL 2002–3 languages, testing against smaller annotated data sets and in lower-resourced languages may reveal more complexity to the problem of decoding improper sequences.

Acknowledgments

Thanks to Elena Álvarez Mellado and Jingxuan Tu, whose usage of NCRF++ for other projects helped us identify the negative result featured here. Thank you to Chester Palen-Michel and three anonymous reviewers for providing feedback on this paper.

References

chakki. 2019. seqeval. Version 0.0.12, `https://github.com/chakki-works/seqeval`.

Mike Kroutikov. 2019. 7776 ways to compute F1 for an NER task. `http://blog.innodatalabs.com/7776_ways_to_compute_f1_for_ner_task/`.

Matt Post. 2018. A call for clarity in reporting BLEU scores. In *Proceedings of the Third Conference on Machine Translation: Research Papers*, pages 186–191, Brussels, Belgium. Association for Computational Linguistics.

Lance Ramshaw and Mitch Marcus. 1995. Text chunking using transformation-based learning. In *Third Workshop on Very Large Corpora*.

Erik Tjong Kim Sang. 2004. conlleval. Version 2004-01-26, `https://www.clips.uantwerpen.be/conll2002/ner/bin/conlleval.txt`.

Erik F. Tjong Kim Sang. 2002. Introduction to the CoNLL-2002 shared task: Language-independent named entity recognition. In *COLING-02: The 6th Conference on Natural Language Learning 2002 (CoNLL-2002)*.

Erik F. Tjong Kim Sang and Fien De Meulder. 2003. Introduction to the CoNLL-2003 shared task: Language-independent named entity recognition. In *Proceedings of the Seventh Conference on Natural Language Learning at HLT-NAACL 2003*, pages 142–147.

Erik F. Tjong Kim Sang and Jorn Veenstra. 1999. Representing text chunks. In *Ninth Conference of the European Chapter of the Association for Computational Linguistics*, pages 173–179, Bergen, Norway. Association for Computational Linguistics.

Jie Yang, Shuailong Liang, and Yue Zhang. 2018. Design challenges and misconceptions in neural sequence labeling. In *Proceedings of the 27th International Conference on Computational Linguistics*, pages 3879–3889, Santa Fe, New Mexico, USA. Association for Computational Linguistics.

Jie Yang and Yue Zhang. 2018. NCRF++: An open-source neural sequence labeling toolkit. In *Proceedings of ACL 2018, System Demonstrations*, pages 74–79, Melbourne, Australia. Association for Computational Linguistics.

HINT3: Raising the bar for Intent Detection in the Wild

Gaurav Arora
Jio Haptik
gaurav@haptik.ai

Chirag Jain
Jio Haptik
chirag.jain@haptik.ai

Manas Chaturvedi
Jio Haptik
manas.chaturvedi@haptik.ai

Krupal Modi
Jio Haptik
krupal@haptik.ai

Abstract

Intent Detection systems in the real world are exposed to complexities of imbalanced datasets containing varying perception of intent, unintended correlations and domain-specific aberrations. To facilitate benchmarking which can reflect near real-world scenarios, we introduce 3 new datasets created from live chatbots in diverse domains. Unlike most existing datasets that are crowdsourced, our datasets contain real user queries received by the chatbots and facilitates penalising unwanted correlations grasped during the training process. We evaluate 4 NLU platforms and a BERT based classifier and find that performance saturates at inadequate levels on test sets because all systems latch on to unintended patterns in training data.

1 Introduction

Over the last few years, task-oriented dialogue systems have gained increasing traction for applications like personal assistants, automated customer support agents, etc. This has led to the availability of several commercialised and/or open conversational bot building platforms. Most popular systems today involve intent detection as a vital part of their Natural Language Understanding (NLU) pipeline. Recent advances in transfer learning (Howard and Ruder, 2018; Peters et al., 2018; Devlin et al., 2019) has enabled systems that perform quite well on existing benchmarking datasets (Larson et al., 2019; Casanueva et al., 2020).

Definitions of intent often vary across users, tasks and domains. Perception of intent could range from a generic abstraction such as "Ordering a product" to extreme granularity such as "Enquiring for a discount on a specific product if ordered using a specific card". Additionally, factors such as imbalanced data distribution in the training set, assumptions during training data generation, diverse

background of domain experts involved in defining the classes make this task more challenging. During inference, these systems may be deployed to users with diverse cultural backgrounds who might frame their queries differently even when communicating in the same language. Furthermore, during inference, apart from correctly identifying in-scope queries, the system is expected to accurately reject out-of-scope (Larson et al., 2019) queries, adding on to the challenge.

Most existing datasets for intent detection are generated using crowdsourcing services. To accurately benchmark in real-world settings, we release 3 new single-domain datasets, each spanning multiple coarse and fine grain intents, with the test sets being drawn entirely from actual user queries on the live systems at scale instead of being crowdsourced. On these datasets, we find that the performance of existing systems saturates at unsatisfactory levels because they end up learning spurious patterns from the training dataset instead of generalising to the perceived meanings of intents.

We evaluate 4 NLU platforms - Dialogflow[1], LUIS[2], Rasa NLU[3], Haptik[4][5] and a BERT (Devlin et al., 2019) based classifier on all 3 datasets and highlight gaps in language understanding. We further probe into queries where all the current systems fail and question the efficacy of the current approach of learning. Additionally, we repeat all our experiments on the subset of training data and show a performance drop in all the systems despite retaining relevant and sufficient utterances in the training subset. We've made our datasets and code freely accessible on GitHub to promote

---

[1] https://cloud.google.com/dialogflow
[2] https://www.luis.ai/
[3] https://github.com/RasaHQ/rasa/
[4] https://haptik.ai
[5] Access requests for signup on Haptik are processed via contact form at https://haptik.ai/contact-us/

Proceedings of the First Workshop on Insights from Negative Results in NLP, pages 100–105
Online, November 19, 2020. ©2020 Association for Computational Linguistics

Dataset	Example Intents		Example Queries		
	Type	Label	Train	Test	
				In-scope	Out-of-Scope
SOF Mattress	Generic	OFFERS	What are the available offers	Any other offers	If I order now do i get 20% discount in lockdown period
			Give me some discount		
	Specific	100_NIGHT_TRIAL_OFFER	What is the 100-night offer	Free 100 days trial	
			Trial offer on customisation		I need try
Curekart	Generic	RECOMMEND_PRODUCT	Sir I want to fast gain weight.	I need Beginners hair multivitamin	Role of electrolytes powder
			i'm beginner in gym	Which is the best whey protein	Is it help for sperm count
			For biceps and tricep muscle growth supplements	Can i get rivamal 120 ml at my home	Can diabetic patient have it
Power play11	Generic	CHAT_WITH_AN_AGENT	Connect with agent	chat with customer service agent	Application is not responding during team joining
			My transaction is incorrect	PowerPlay11 rummy issue	
			My sign up bonus is incorrect	Suddenly balance gone	Why my current basketball teams being shown??
			Did not receive my amount	Why it is showing wrong balance	

Table 1: Few examples of Intents and Queries in Train and Test set in HINT3 dataset

transparency and reproducibility[6].

2 Prior Work

Despite intent detection being an important component of most dialogue systems, very few datasets have been collected from real users. Web Apps, Ask Ubuntu and Chatbot datasets from (Braun et al., 2017) contain a limited number of intents ($<$10), oversimplifying the task. More recent datasets like HWU64 from (Liu et al., 2019) and CLINC150 from (Larson et al., 2019) span a large number of intents in multiple domains but are generated using crowd sourcing services hence are limited in diversity in user expressions which arise from but not limited to domain specific presumptions, context from how and where the bot is made available, paraphrases emerging from cultural and ethnic diversity of user base, conversational slang, etc. Our work has some similarity with CLINC150, in that they also highlight the problem of out-of-scope intent detection and with BANKING77 from (Casanueva et al., 2020) that focuses on a single domain. However, all three - HWU64, CLINC150,

---

[6]https://github.com/hellohaptik/HINT3

Dataset	#Intent	#Queries			
		Train		Test	
		Full	Subset	in-scope	oos
SOFMattress	21	328	180	231	166
Curekart	28	600	413	452	539
Powerplay11	59	471	261	275	708

Table 2: Statistics of the 3 datasets in HINT3

BANKING77 offer relatively large and well balanced training set which might not be always feasible to collect for every new domain. For all datasets mentioned so far, recent works have reported a reasonably high performance ($>$90% average) for in-scope queries. Despite this, gaps in language understanding become apparent when such systems are deployed. Datasets introduced in this paper and further analysis of results attempts to recognise critical gaps in language understanding and calls for further research into more robust methods.

3 Datasets

We introduce HINT3, a collection of datasets shown in Table 2 - **SOFMattress**, **Curekart** and **Powerplay11** each containing diverse set of intents in a single domain - mattress products retail, fitness

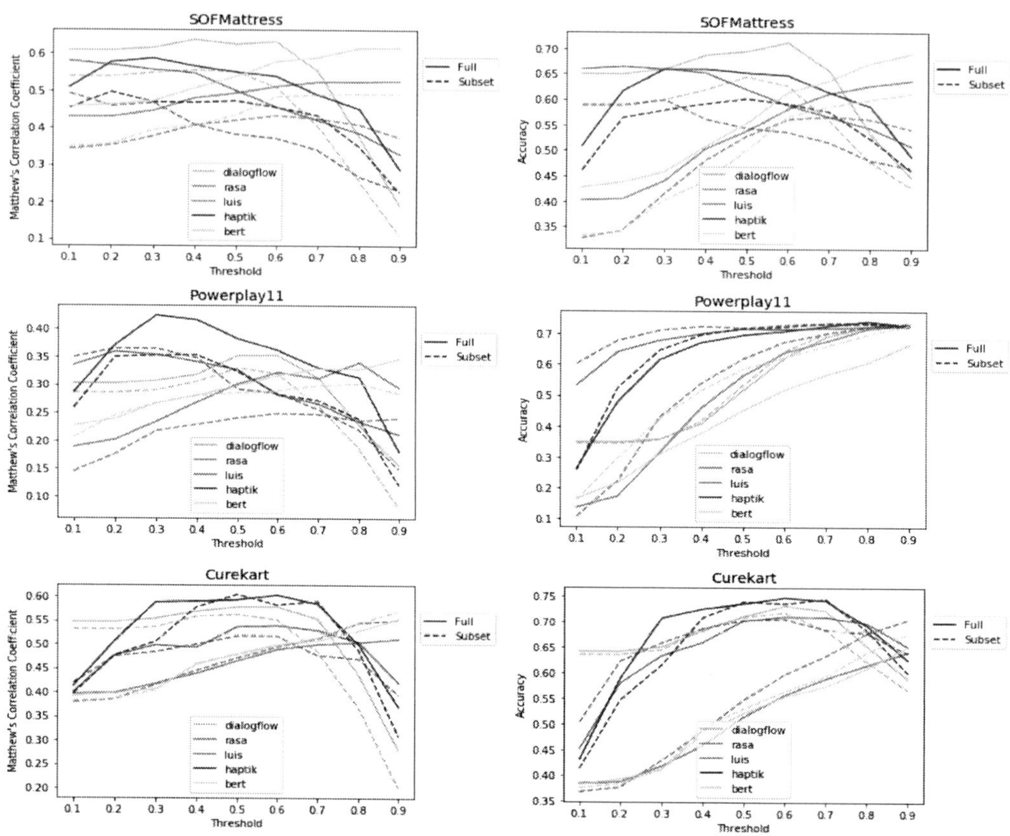

Figure 1: Matthew's Correlation Coefficient and Accuracy across all datasets and platforms

supplements retail and online gaming respectively. Table 1 shows few example intents of varying granularity in HINT3 dataset, along with examples of training queries created by domain experts and in-scope, out-of-scope queries received from real users.

3.1 Training Data Collection

Training data is prepared by a team of domain experts trying to emulate real users after in-depth research of historical user queries. The experts do not create an explicit set of out of scope queries primarily because the universe of such queries is infinitely big. Training datasets show class imbalance, occurrence of domain specific words, acronyms[7]. All training data queries are in English.

Dataset Variants

In addition to **Full** training sets, we create **Subset** versions for each training set. For each class, after retaining the first query we iterate over the

rest, discarding a query if it has an entailment score (Bowman et al., 2015) greater than 0.6 in both directions with any of the queries retained so far i.e. the subset version has the following property

$$E(x_a, x_b) \leq 0.6 \;\wedge\; E(x_b, x_a) \leq 0.6;$$
$$a \neq b, a \in [1, |\hat{X}_i|], b \in [1, |\hat{X}_i|] \,\forall\, I$$

where I is the set of all intents, $\hat{X}_i$ is the set of queries retained for class i, $E(h, p)$ is the entailment scoring function with h as hypothesis and p as premise. We use ELMo model trained on SNLI (Peters et al., 2018; Parikh et al., 2016) [8] for $E(h, p)$. These are intended to evaluate performance with only semantically different sentences in the training set as ideally systems should already understand semantically similar queries to the ones present in the training set.

	SOFMattress		Curekart		Powerplay11	
	Full	**Subset**	**Full**	**Subset**	**Full**	**Subset**
Dialogflow	73.1	**65.3**	75.0	71.2	59.6	55.6
RASA	69.2	56.2	**84.0**	80.5	49.0	38.5
LUIS	59.3	49.3	72.5	71.6	48.0	44.0
Haptik	72.2	64.0	80.3	79.8	**66.5**	**59.2**
BERT	**73.5**	57.1	83.6	**82.3**	58.5	53.0

Table 3: Inscope Accuracy at low threshold=0.1 for Full and Subset data variants

3.2 Test Data Collection and Annotation

Our test sets contain the first message received by live systems from real users over a period of 15 days. Inter-annotator agreement was 75.8%, 80.0% and 73.4% for SOFMattress, Curekart and Powerplay11 respectively and conflicts were resolved by domain experts. One major reason for low inter-annotator agreement was unclear criteria for defining an intent which sometimes lead to overlapping intents of different levels of granularity, even after we had made sure to manually merge any conflicting or highly similar intents in the training data.

Directly coming from real users our test set queries also contain messaging slangs, acronyms, spelling mistakes, grammatical mistakes and usage of code-mixed languages[7]. Queries in non-Latin script or code-mixed languages were marked as out of scope (labelled as NO_NODES_DETECTED). Since live chat systems don't cater all the queries related to a brand, our test set contains relevant out-of-scope queries received from users about that domain. Any identifiable information of users, brands was replaced with made-up values in both train and test sets.

4 Benchmark Evaluation

We evaluated the performance of our datasets on platforms like Dialogflow, LUIS, RASA and Haptik in addition to evaluating performance on BERT. All layers of BERT were fine-tuned with a learning rate of 4e-5 for up to 50 epochs with a warmup period of 0.1 and early stopping.

4.1 Out-Of-Scope (OOS) prediction

We use thresholds on the model's probability estimate for the task of predicting whether a query is OOS. We show performance on thresholds ranging from 0.1 to 0.9 at an interval of 0.1 to show the maximum performance a model can achieve irrespective of how we choose the threshold.

4.2 Metrics

We consider Accuracy and Matthew's Correlation Coefficient[9] as overall performance metrics for the systems. We use OOS recall (Larson et al., 2019) to evaluate performance on OOS queries and accuracy of in-scope queries to evaluate performance on in-scope queries.

5 Results

Figure 1 presents results for all systems, for both Full and Subset variations of the dataset. Best Accuracy on all the datasets is in the early 70s. Best MCC for the datasets varies from 0.4 to 0.6, suggesting the systems are far from perfectly understanding natural language.

In Table 3, we consider in-scope accuracy at a very low threshold of 0.1, to see if false positives on OOS queries would not have mattered, what's the maximum in-scope accuracy that current systems are able to achieve. Our results show that even with such a low threshold, the maximum in-scope accuracy which systems are able to achieve on Full Training set is pretty low, unlike the 90+ in-scope accuracies of these systems which have been reported on other public datasets like CLINC150 in (Larson et al., 2019). And, the in-scope accuracy is even worse for the Subset of the training data.

Table 5 shows percentage drop in in-scope accuracy on subset data across all systems as compared to in-scope accuracy on full data. The drop varies from 0.6% to 22.3% across datasets and platforms. In an ideal world, this drop should be close to 0 across all datasets, as if the system understands the meaning of queries in training data, its performance should not get affected at all by removing queries in training data which are semantically similar to the ones already present.

Analyzing few example queries which failed on all platforms in Table 4 suggests that these models

---

[9]https://scikit-learn.org/stable/modules/model_evaluation

Test query	True label	Top predicted label	Sample training queries for True label	Sample training queries for predicted label
Ergo 7272 inches price?	MATTRESS_COST	**L,H,D,R**: ERGO_FEATURES	• Price of mattress • Custom size cost	• Features of Ergo mattress • Tell me about SOF Ergo mattress
Trail option are there	100_NIGHT_TRIAL_OFFER	**L,H,D**: COD **R**: EMI	• Trial details • How to enroll for trial	• Can I get COD option? • Can it deliver by COD
I require 75 inch 57 inch. Is it available?	SIZE_CUSTOMIZATION	**L**: DISTRIBUTORS **H,D,R**: WHAT_SIZE_TO_ORDER	• Will I get an option to Customise the size • How can I order a custom sized mattress	• Want to know the custom size chart • Show me all available sizes
20 % discount available on emi	OFFERS	**L,H,D,R**: EMI	• Want to know the discount • Tell me about the latest offers	• You guys provide EMI option? • No cost EMI is available?
How will u deliver with this LockDown in place ?	NO_NODES_DETECTED	**L,H,D,R**: CHECK_PINCODE	-	• Do you deliver to my pincode
Covid19 how can you deliver	NO_NODES_DETECTED	**L,H,D,R**: CHECK_PINCODE		• Will you be able to deliver here

Table 4: Few examples of test queries in SOFMattress which failed on all platforms, **L**: LUIS, **H**: Haptik, **D**: Dialogflow, **R**: Rasa. NO_NODES_DETECTED is the out-of-scope label.

	SOF Mattress	Curekart	Power play11
Dialogflow	**10.6**	5.0	**6.7**
RASA	18.7	4.1	10.5
LUIS	16.8	1.2	8.3
Haptik	11.3	**0.6**	10.9
BERT	22.3	1.5	9.4

Table 5: Percentage **drop** in Inscope Accuracy at low threshold=0.1 in Subset data as compared to Full

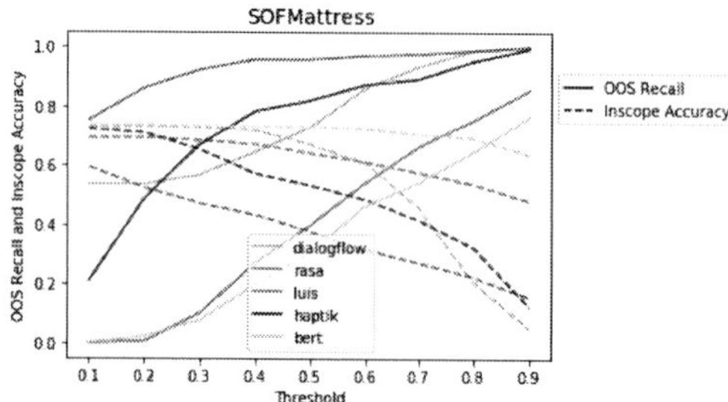

Figure 2: Out-of-Scope (OOS) Recall at the cost of Inscope Accuracy for SOFMattress Full dataset

aren't actually "understanding" language or capturing "meaning", instead capturing spurious patterns in training data, as was also pointed in (Bender and Koller, 2020). Predicting based on these spurious patterns, which models latch on to during training, leads to models having high confidence even on OOS queries. Figure 2 shows this behaviour on SOFMattress Full dataset, as significant percentage of OOS queries have high confidence scores on all systems, except LUIS, for which it is at the cost of in-scope accuracy.

6   Conclusion

This paper analyzed intent detection on 3 new datasets consisting of both in-scope and out-of-scope queries received on 3 live chat bots over a period of 15 days. Our findings indicate that

there's a significant gap in performance on crowd-sourced datasets vs in a real world setup. NLU systems don't seem to be actually "understanding" language or capturing "meaning". We believe our analysis and dataset will lead to developing better, more robust dialogue systems.

Acknowledgments

We are grateful to Bot Analysts at Haptik, especially Aaron Dsouza[10], who helped us open-source HINT3 datasets. We also want to thank clients of Haptik who allowed us to share queries received on their bots with the research community.

References

Emily M. Bender and Alexander Koller. 2020. Climbing towards NLU: On meaning, form, and understanding in the age of data. In *Proceedings of the 58th Annual Meeting of the Association for Computational Linguistics*, pages 5185–5198, Online. Association for Computational Linguistics.

Samuel R. Bowman, Gabor Angeli, Christopher Potts, and Christopher D. Manning. 2015. A large annotated corpus for learning natural language inference. In *Proceedings of the 2015 Conference on Empirical Methods in Natural Language Processing*, pages 632–642, Lisbon, Portugal. Association for Computational Linguistics.

Daniel Braun, Adrian Hernandez Mendez, Florian Matthes, and Manfred Langen. 2017. Evaluating natural language understanding services for conversational question answering systems. In *Proceedings of the 18th Annual SIGdial Meeting on Discourse and Dialogue*, pages 174–185, Saarbrücken, Germany. Association for Computational Linguistics.

Iñigo Casanueva, Tadas Temčinas, Daniela Gerz, Matthew Henderson, and Ivan Vulić. 2020. Efficient intent detection with dual sentence encoders. In *Proceedings of the 2nd Workshop on Natural Language Processing for Conversational AI*, pages 38–45, Online. Association for Computational Linguistics.

[10]Reachable at aaron.dsouza@haptik.ai

Jacob Devlin, Ming-Wei Chang, Kenton Lee, and Kristina Toutanova. 2019. BERT: Pre-training of deep bidirectional transformers for language understanding. In *Proceedings of the 2019 Conference of the North American Chapter of the Association for Computational Linguistics: Human Language Technologies, Volume 1 (Long and Short Papers)*, pages 4171–4186, Minneapolis, Minnesota. Association for Computational Linguistics.

Jeremy Howard and Sebastian Ruder. 2018. Universal language model fine-tuning for text classification. In *Proceedings of the 56th Annual Meeting of the Association for Computational Linguistics (Volume 1: Long Papers)*, pages 328–339, Melbourne, Australia. Association for Computational Linguistics.

Stefan Larson, Anish Mahendran, Joseph J. Peper, Christopher Clarke, Andrew Lee, Parker Hill, Jonathan K. Kummerfeld, Kevin Leach, Michael A. Laurenzano, Lingjia Tang, and Jason Mars. 2019. An evaluation dataset for intent classification and out-of-scope prediction. In *Proceedings of the 2019 Conference on Empirical Methods in Natural Language Processing and the 9th International Joint Conference on Natural Language Processing (EMNLP-IJCNLP)*, pages 1311–1316, Hong Kong, China. Association for Computational Linguistics.

Xingkun Liu, Arash Eshghi, Pawel Swietojanski, and Verena Rieser. 2019. Benchmarking natural language understanding services for building conversational agents. In *Proceedings of the Tenth International Workshop on Spoken Dialogue Systems Technology (IWSDS)*, pages xxx–xxx, Ortigia, Siracusa (SR), Italy. Springer.

Ankur Parikh, Oscar Täckström, Dipanjan Das, and Jakob Uszkoreit. 2016. A decomposable attention model for natural language inference. In *Proceedings of the 2016 Conference on Empirical Methods in Natural Language Processing*, pages 2249–2255, Austin, Texas. Association for Computational Linguistics.

Matthew Peters, Mark Neumann, Mohit Iyyer, Matt Gardner, Christopher Clark, Kenton Lee, and Luke Zettlemoyer. 2018. Deep contextualized word representations. In *Proceedings of the 2018 Conference of the North American Chapter of the Association for Computational Linguistics: Human Language Technologies, Volume 1 (Long Papers)*, pages 2227–2237, New Orleans, Louisiana. Association for Computational Linguistics.

The Extraordinary Failure of Complement Coercion Crowdsourcing

Yanai Elazar   Victoria Basmov   Shauli Ravfogel   Yoav Goldberg   Reut Tsarfaty
Computer Science Department, Bar Ilan University
Allen Institute for Artificial Intelligence
{yanaiela,vikasaeta,shauli.ravfogel}@gmail.com
{yoav.goldberg,reut.tsarfaty}@gmail.com

Abstract

Crowdsourcing has eased and scaled up the collection of linguistic annotation in recent years. In this work, we follow known methodologies of collecting labeled data for the *complement coercion* phenomenon. These are constructions with an *implied* action — e.g., "I started a new book I bought last week", where the implied action is *reading*. We aim to collect annotated data for this phenomenon by reducing it to either of two known tasks: Explicit Completion and Natural Language Inference. However, in both cases, crowdsourcing resulted in low agreement scores, even though we followed the same methodologies as in previous work. Why does the same process fail to yield high agreement scores? We specify our modeling schemes, highlight the differences with previous work and provide some insights about the task and possible explanations for the failure. We conclude that specific phenomena require tailored solutions, not only in specialized algorithms, but also in data collection methods.

1   Introduction

Crowdsourcing has become extremely popular in recent years for annotating datasets. Many works use frameworks like Amazon Mechanical Turk (AMT) by converting complex linguistic tasks into easy-to-grasp presentations which make it possible to crowdsource linguistically-annotated data at scale (Bowman et al., 2015; FitzGerald et al., 2018; Dasigi et al., 2019; Wolfson et al., 2020).

In this work, we attempt to use existing methodologies for crowdsourcing linguistic annotations in order to collect annotations for *complement coercion* (Pustejovsky, 1991, 1995), a phenomenon involving an implied action triggered by an event-selecting verb. Specifically, certain **verb classes** require an *event-denoting* complement, as in: "I **started** *reading* a book", "I **finished** *eating* the

Task	Annotations
Explicit	
After a heartfelt vow, she agrees and the two begin kissing as the preacher tries to **continue** __ the ceremony.	{officiating}, ϕ
Entailment	
Hunter waited for max to **finish** his burger before asking him again. $\rightsquigarrow$ Hunter waited for max to **finish swallowing** his burger before asking him again.	ENT NEU CON

Table 1: Examples for the two modeling and annotation schemes used in this work. Both examples are labeled with different (disagreeing) answers. In the Explicit modeling, each label is a set, which can be empty (ϕ) (meaning that no event is implied), or not (and thus the context suggests an implied event). The second modeling follows the NLI scheme, a standard approach for evaluating language understanding. The ENT, NEU and CON labels refer to the entail, neutral and contradict labels accordingly.

cake", etc. However, such *event-denoting* complements might remain implicit, not appearing in the surface form. Consider for instance, the sentence "I **started** __ a new book." Here the event that was started remains implicit. Our task is then, first, to detect that the verb '**started**' in this context implies some unmentioned event, and that probable events in this context are *reading* or *writing*. Furthermore, we wish to predict that for "I **started** __ the book I bought yesterday", the more probable event is *reading*, rather than *writing*.

This phenomenon (described in detail in Section 2) seems intuitive at first, and easy-to-grasp by non-experts. However, we find that collecting annotated data for this task via crowdsourcing is very challenging, achieving low agreement scores between annotators (§3), despite using two common collection methods in frequently used setups. The two framings we use for data collection along with examples for them are presented in Table 1.

Proceedings of the First Workshop on Insights from Negative Results in NLP, pages 106–116
Online, November 19, 2020. ©2020 Association for Computational Linguistics

These low agreement scores come as a surprise, given the large body of previous work on crowd-sourcing linguistic annotations. Why do such issues arise when collecting data for *complement coercion*, while for similar phenomena the same approaches yield successful results? Although it is difficult to answer this question, we aim to high-light the similarities and the differences with other tasks, and provide some insights into this question.

2 Background

Complement Coercion We are interested in the linguistic phenomenon of *complement coercion*.[1] In complement coercion, there is a clash between an expectation for a verb argument denoting an event, and the appearance of a noun argument de-noting an entity. Uncovering the covert event re-quires the comprehender to infer the implied event by invoking the comprehender's lexical semantics and/or world knowledge (Zarcone et al., 2017).

Consider Examples 1 and 2 below, with an im-plicit event of *reading* or *writing* missing in the surface form. Inferring the implicit event (marked __) is necessary in order to construe the full se-mantics of this sentence.

1. I **started** __ a new book.

2. I **started** __ a new book I bought last week.

The reconstruction of the covert event requires an interplay between semantics[2] and world knowl-edge. In example 1 above, the prefix "I started __ " with the event-selecting verb *started* triggers ex-pectations for some event-denoting object (*reading*, *writing*, *eating*, *watching*, etc). The object that fol-lows, "a new book", narrows down the expectations — based on world knowledge. As McGregor et al. (2017) puts it, "Different nouns grant privileged ac-cess to different activities, particularly those which are most frequently performed with the entities they denote". Although the entity narrows down the set of possible events, the implied event might remain ambiguous (in Example 1, both *reading* and *writing* are plausible, but *eating* is not). As can be seen in Example 2, additional context, as in "I bought last week", provides further world-knowledge cues, to-wards accessing a more specific event (in this case

reading is more likely than *writing*), thus resolving the remaining ambiguity.

Complement coercion is particularly frequent with certain verb classes, including *aspectual verbs* — verbs that "describe the initiation, termination, or continuation of an activity" (Levin, 1993) — such as: 'start', 'begin', 'continue' and 'finish' (McGre-gor et al., 2017). This set of verbs is the focus of our work. Note however, that such verbs may appear in similar constructions that do *not* imply any covert action or event. For instance, in the following sentence:

3. I **started** a new company.

Here, the verb 'start' is used as an entity-selecting (and not event-selecting) verb, a synonym of 'found' or 'establish'. See more examples of simi-lar non-coercive constructions in Appendix B.

Annotated data for complement coercion (Puste-jovsky et al., 2010) was collected in the past, based on a tailor-made annotation methodology (Puste-jovsky et al., 2009), consisting of a multi-step pro-cess that includes word-sense disambiguation by experts. The annotation focused on coercion de-tection (as well as labeling the arguments type) and did not involve identifying the implied action. Here, we aim to collect complement coercion data via non-expert annotation, at scale, to test whether models can recover the implicit events and resolve the emerging ambiguities.

Crowdsourcing NLI NLI, originally framed as Recognizing Textual Entailment (RTE), has be-come a standard framework for testing reasoning capabilities of models. It originated from the work by Dagan et al. (2005), where a small dataset was curated by experts using precise guidelines with a specific focus on lexical and syntactic variability rather than delicate logical issues, while dismissing cases of disagreements or ambiguity. Bowman et al. (2015); Williams et al. (2018) then scaled up the task and crowdsourced large-scale NLI datasets. In contrast to Dagan et al. (2005), the task definitions were short and loose, relying on the annotators' common sense understanding. Many works since have been using the NLI framework and the crowd-sourcing procedure associated with it to test models for different language phenomena (Marelli et al., 2014; Lai et al., 2017; Naik et al., 2018; Ross and Pavlick, 2019; Yanaka et al., 2020).

---

[1]Complement coercion has been studied in linguistics from many theoretical viewpoints. See Appendix A for background.

[2]E.g., understanding the difference between entity-denoting and event-denoting elements.

3 Copmlement Coercion Crowdsourcing

3.1 Explicit Completion Attempt

We begin by directly modeling the phenomenon. For a set of sentences containing possibly-coercive verbs, we wish to determine for each verb if it entails an implicit event, and if so, to figure out what the event is. This direct task-definition approach is reminiscent of studies that collected annotated data for other missing elements phenomena, such as Verb-Phrase Ellipsis (Bos and Spenader, 2011), Numeric Fused-Heads (Elazar and Goldberg, 2019), Bridging (Roesiger, 2018; Hou et al., 2018) and Sluicing (Hansen and Søgaard, 2020). However, when attempting to crowdsource and label complement coercion instances, we reach very low agreement scores in the first step: determining whether there is an implied event or not. We discuss this experiment in greater detail in Appendix C.

3.2 NLI for Complement Coercion

In light of the low agreements on explicit modeling of the task of complement coercion, we turn to a different crowdsourcing approach which was proven successful for many linguistic phenomena – using NLI as discussed above (§2). NLI was used to collect data for a wide range of linguistic phenomena: Paraphrase Inference, Anaphora Resolution, Numerical Reasoning, Implicatures and more (White et al., 2017; Poliak et al., 2018; Jeretic et al., 2020; Yanaka et al., 2020; Naik et al., 2018) (see Poliak (2020)). Therefore, we take a similar approach, with similar methodologies, and make use of NLI as an evaluation setup for the complement coercion phenomenon.

Here we do not directly model the identification and recovery of event verbs, but rather, we reduce it to an NLI task. Intuitively, if in Example 2 the semantically plausible implied event is *reading*, we expect the sentence "I **started** a book I bought last week" to *entail* a sentence that contains the event explicitly: "I **started** *reading* a book I bought last week" (Table 2).[3] In contrast, we expect "I **started** a book" to be *neutral* with respect to "I **started** *reading* a book", since both *reading* and *writing* are plausible in that context, and there is no reason to prefer one of these complements over the other. Examples of this format, along with the different labels we employ, are shown in Table 2.

Example	Label
I started a book I bought last week. ↝ I started reading a book I bought last week.	ENT
I started a book. ↝ I started reading a book. I started eating a book.	NEU CON

Table 2: Examples for NLI pairs with a complement coercion structure. The ENT, NEU and CON labels refers to entail, neutral and contradict accordingly.

Corpus Candidates In order to keep the task simple, we avoid complexities of lexical, semantic and grammatical differences. Each example is composed of a minimal-pair (Kaushik et al., 2019; Warstadt et al., 2020; Gardner et al., 2020) consisting of two sentences; one as the premise and the other as the hypothesis. We construct minimal pairs as follows: First, we extract dependency-parsed sentences from the Book Corpus (Zhu et al., 2015) containing the lemma of one of the verbs: 'start', 'begin', 'continue' and 'finish'.[4] Then, we keep sentences where the anchor verb is attached to another verb with an 'xcomp' dependency[5] (e.g. 'started' in "started reading"). These sentences are used as the hypotheses. To construct the premises, we remove the dependent verb (e.g. 'read'), as well as all the words between the anchor and the dependent verb (e.g. 'to' in the infinitive form: "to read"). Additional examples are provided in Appendix D.

Note that this procedure sometimes generates ungrammatical or implausible sentences, which are flagged by the annotators.

Crowdsourcing Procedure We follow the standard procedure of collecting NLI data with crowdsourcing and collect annotations from Amazon Mechanical Turk (AMT). Specifically, we follow the instruction from Glockner et al. (2018), which involves three questions:

1. Do the sentences describe the same event?

2. Does the new sentence add new information to the original sentence?

3. Is the new sentence incorrect/ungrammatical?

We discard any example which at least one worker marked as incorrect/ungrammatical. If the answer

---

[3] We follow Bowman et al. (2015), who modeled entailment based on event coreference.

[4] These are frequent verbs that often appear in complement coercion constructions (McGregor et al., 2017).

[5] We use spaCy's parser (Honnibal and Johnson, 2015; Honnibal and Montani, 2017).

to the first question was negative, we considered the label as contradict. Otherwise, we considered the label as entail if the answer to the second question was negative, and neutral if it was positive. A screenshot of the interface is displayed in Figure 2 in the Appendix.

We require an approved rate of at least 99%, at least 5000 completed HITs, and filter workers to be from English-speaking countries. We also condition the turkers to pass a validation test with a perfect score. We pay 8 cents per HIT.

Results We collect 76[6] pairs (after filtering ungrammatical sentences), each labeled by three different annotators. The Fleiss Kappa (Fleiss, 1971) agreement is $k = 0.24$. This score is remarkably low, compared to previous work that similarly collected NLI labels and achieved scores between 0.61 and 0.7. Why does this happen? Consider the following examples, along with their labels:

4. "We **finished** Letterman and I got up from the couch and said, I'm going to bed." ⤳
"We **finished** *watching* Letterman and I got up from the couch and said, I'm going to bed."
ENT ENT ENT

5. "Flo set the sack of sausage and egg biscuits on the counter right as the young man **finished** his case." ⤳
"Flo set the sack of sausage and egg biscuits on the counter right as the young man **finished** *pleading* his case."
ENT NEU CON

6. "We **start** the interviews later today." ⤳
"We **start** *shooting* the interviews later today."
NEU CON CON

Example 4 was labeled by all three annotators as *entail*. However, annotators were in disagreement on examples 5, 6. Example 5 was annotated with all three possible labels (entail, contradict and neutral). Indeed, different readings of this phrase are possible — more formally, different readers *construe* the meaning of the utterance differently; "*[Construal] is a dynamic process of meaning construction, in which speakers and hearers encode and decode, respectively*" (Trott et al., 2020). An annotator who understands the word 'case' as a legal case, will choose *entail*, while an annotator

who interprets 'case' as a bag and imagines a different background story (for example, a young man packing a brief-case), will choose *contradict*. Finally, an annotator who thinks of both scenarios will choose *neutral*, which can be argued to be the correct answer. However, we find that for a human hearer, holding both scenarios in mind at the same time is hard, which we attribute to the *construal* of meanings. When a human construes an interpretation, they construes it in a single fashion until primed otherwise. So, it is not natural to conceive competing meaning scenarios when one is already "locked in" on a specific construal.

Although the sentence pairs were carefully built to exclude lexical and syntactic variances, ambiguous sentences such as the above recur throughout the dataset. We believe that these disagreements are inherent to this type of problem, and are not due to other factors such as poor annotations. As evidence, the authors of this work also annotated a subset of these examples and reached a similar (low) agreement.

4   Discussion

Inherent Disagreements in Human Textual Inferences Recently, Pavlick and Kwiatkowski (2019) discussed a similar trend of disagreements in five popular NLI datasets (RTE (Dagan et al., 2005), SNLI (Bowman et al., 2015), MNLI (Williams et al., 2018), JOCI (Zhang et al., 2017) and DNC (Poliak et al., 2018)). In their study, annotators had to select the degree to which a premise entails a hypothesis, on a scale (Chen et al., 2020) (instead of discrete labels). Pavlick and Kwiatkowski (2019) show that even though these datasets are reported to have high agreement scores, specific examples suffer from inherent disagreements. For instance, in about 20% of the inspected examples, "there is a nontrivial second component" (e.g. entailment and neutral). Our findings are related to theirs, although not identical: while the disagreements they report are due to the individuals' interpretations of a situation, in our case, disagreements are due to the difficulty in imagining a different scenario. While some works propose to collect annotator disagreements and use them as inputs (Plank et al., 2014; Palomaki et al., 2018) (see Pavlick and Kwiatkowski (2019) for an elaborated overview), this will not hold in our case, because only one of the labels is typically correct.

However, the bottom-line is the same: these dis-

---

[6]We stopped at 76 examples since we did not see fit to annotate more data with the low agreements we obtained.

agreements cannot be dismissed as 'noise', they are more profound. We hypothesize that when tackling specific phenomena like the one we address in this work, which involve sources of disagreements that are often 'ignored' (not intentionally) during the collection of large datasets,[7] these sources of disagreements are highlighted and manifest themselves more clearly. This results in low agreement scores as we see in our study.

Scale Annotations Recent works have proposed to collect labels for NLI pairs on a scale (Pavlick and Kwiatkowski, 2019; Chen et al., 2020; Nie et al., 2020). Although we agree that this technique may produce a more fine-grained understanding of human judgments, Pavlick and Kwiatkowski (2019); Nie et al. (2020) observed that scale annotations may result in a multi-modality of the distribution. The different distributions can be viewed as different construals, where each individual interprets the example differently.

Task Definition Another issue might arise from the task definition itself. As opposed to annotation efforts for linguistic tasks such as parsing (Marcus et al., 1993) and semantic role labeling (Carreras and Màrquez, 2005) that are carried out by expert annotators and often have annotation guidelines of dozens of pages, the transition to crowdsourcing has reduced the guidelines to a few phrases, and expert annotators have been replaced by laymen. This transition required to simplify the guidelines and to avoid complex definition and corner-cases. Even though crowdsourcing enabled an easier annotation process and collection of huge amounts of data, it also came with a cost: lack of refined definitions and relying on people's "common sense" and "intuition". However, as we see in this work, such intuitions are not consistent across individuals and are not sufficient for some tasks. We believe that, similar to the issues mentioned above, the lack of proper definitions tends to amplify disagreements when dealing with specific phenomena, which was often the reason behind the elaborated and long guidelines in classic datasets (Kalouli et al., 2019).

Possible Solution As we approach "solving" current NLP dataset, which were once perceived as complicated, we also reach an understanding that the datasets at hand do not reflect the full capacity of language, and specific linguistic phenomena, which may posses specific challenges, are lost in

the crowds. Some phenomena turn out to be more complex, and require specific solutions. In this work we show that, like we do with algorithmic solutions we need to reconsider the data collection process. We hold that data collection for these phenomena also require training of the annotators (Roit et al., 2020; Pyatkin et al., 2020), whether experts or crowdsourcing workers, and may also require coming up with novel annotation protocols.

Another potential solution is to use deliberation between the workers as a mean to improve agreement (Schaekermann et al., 2018). With respect to the disagreements we observed, a deliberation between workers would allow them to share the construals each individual had imagined, thus reaching a consensus on the labels. It would also serve as a training for recovering more construals, allowing them to better identify the *neutral* cases.

5 Conclusions

In this work, we attempt to crowdsource annotations for complement coercion constructions. We use two modeling methods, which were successful in similar settings, but resulted in low agreement scores in our setup. We highlight some of the issues we believe are causing the disagreements. The main one being different construals (Trott et al., 2020) of the utterances by different people — as well as the difficulty to consider a different one, once fixating on a specific construal — that led to different answers. We connect our findings to previous work that observed some inherent disagreement in human judgments in popular datasets, such as SNLI and MNLI (Pavlick and Kwiatkowski, 2019). Although this issue is less prominent in these datasets (which is manifested as higher agreement scores), we notice that when tackling a *specific* phenomenon, e.g. involving implicit elements, these issues may arise.

We also argue that the *lack* of detailed definitions in the commonly used NLI tasks may lead to poor performance on small buckets of language-specific phenomena. This drop might be lost in large-scale datasets, but may have critical effects when modeling and studying specific phenomena. As a community, we claim, we should seek to identify those buckets and further investigate them, using more profound approaches for data collection, with clear and grounded definitions. We hope that our attempted trial in data collection will allow others to learn from our failure.

---

[7] Due to large scale annotations, 'marginal' phenomena might be ignored to keep the instructions clear and concise.

Acknowledgments

We would like to thank Adam Poliak and Abhilasha Ravichander for providing valuable feedback on this paper. Moreover, we would like to thank the reviewers, as well as the workshop organizers for their constructive reviews. Yanai Elazar is grateful to be partially supported by the PBC fellowship for outstanding Phd candidates in Data Science. This project has received funding from the Europoean Research Council (ERC) under the Europoean Union's Horizon 2020 research and innovation programme, grant agreement No. 802774 (iEXTRACT) and grant agreement No. 677362 (NLPRO).

References

Roberto G. de Almeida and Roberto G. Veena D. Dwivedi. 2008. Coercion without lexical decomposition: Type-shifting effects revisited. *The Canadian Journal of Linguistics / La revue canadienne de linguistique*, 53:301 – 326.

Johan Bos and Jennifer Spenader. 2011. An annotated corpus for the analysis of vp ellipsis. *Language Resources and Evaluation*, 45(4):463–494.

Samuel R. Bowman, Gabor Angeli, Christopher Potts, and Christopher D. Manning. 2015. A large annotated corpus for learning natural language inference. In *Proceedings of the 2015 Conference on Empirical Methods in Natural Language Processing (EMNLP)*. Association for Computational Linguistics.

Xavier Carreras and Lluís Màrquez. 2005. Introduction to the conll-2005 shared task: Semantic role labeling. In *Proceedings of the ninth conference on computational natural language learning (CoNLL-2005)*, pages 152–164.

Tongfei Chen, Zhengping Jiang, Adam Poliak, Keisuke Sakaguchi, and Benjamin Van Durme. 2020. Uncertain natural language inference. In *Proceedings of The 58th Annual Meeting of the Association for Computational Linguistics (ACL)*.

Ido Dagan, Oren Glickman, and Bernardo Magnini. 2005. The pascal recognising textual entailment challenge. In *Machine Learning Challenges Workshop*, pages 177–190. Springer.

Pradeep Dasigi, Nelson F Liu, Ana Marasovic, Noah A Smith, and Matt Gardner. 2019. Quoref: A reading comprehension dataset with questions requiring coreferential reasoning. In *Proceedings of the 2019 Conference on Empirical Methods in Natural Language Processing and the 9th International Joint Conference on Natural Language Processing (EMNLP-IJCNLP)*, pages 5927–5934.

Yanai Elazar and Yoav Goldberg. 2019. Where's my head? definition, data set, and models for numeric fused-head identification and resolution. *Transactions of the Association for Computational Linguistics*, 7:519–535.

Nicholas FitzGerald, Julian Michael, Luheng He, and Luke Zettlemoyer. 2018. Large-scale qa-srl parsing. In *Proceedings of the 56th Annual Meeting of the Association for Computational Linguistics (Volume 1: Long Papers)*, pages 2051–2060.

Joseph L Fleiss. 1971. Measuring nominal scale agreement among many raters. *Psychological bulletin*, 76(5):378.

Matt Gardner, Yoav Artzi, Victoria Basmova, Jonathan Berant, Ben Bogin, Sihao Chen, Pradeep Dasigi, Dheeru Dua, Yanai Elazar, Ananth Gottumukkala, Nitish Gupta, Hanna Hajishirzi, Gabriel Ilharco, Daniel Khashabi, Kevin Lin, Jiangming Liu, Nelson F. Liu, Phoebe Mulcaire, Qiang Ning, Sameer Singh, Noah A. Smith, Sanjay Subramanian, Reut Tsarfaty, Eric Wallace, Ally Zhang, and Ben Zhou. 2020. Evaluating nlp models via contrast sets. *arXiv preprint*.

Max Glockner, Vered Shwartz, and Yoav Goldberg. 2018. Breaking NLI systems with sentences that require simple lexical inferences. In *Proceedings of the 56th Annual Meeting of the Association for Computational Linguistics (Volume 2: Short Papers)*, pages 650–655, Melbourne, Australia. Association for Computational Linguistics.

Daniele Godard and Jacques Jayez. 1993. Towards a proper treatment of coercion phenomena. In *Sixth Conference of the European Chapter of the Association for Computational Linguistics*, Utrecht, The Netherlands. Association for Computational Linguistics.

A. E. Goldberg. 1995. *Constructions: A construction grammar approach to argument structure.* Chicago: University of Chicago Press.

Victor Petrén Bach Hansen and Anders Søgaard. 2020. What do you mean 'why?': Resolving sluices in conversations. In *AAAI*, pages 7887–7894.

Matthew Honnibal and Mark Johnson. 2015. An improved non-monotonic transition system for dependency parsing. In *Proceedings of the 2015 conference on empirical methods in natural language processing*, pages 1373–1378.

Matthew Honnibal and Ines Montani. 2017. spacy 2: Natural language understanding with bloom embeddings, convolutional neural networks and incremental parsing. *To appear*, 7(1).

Yufang Hou, Katja Markert, and Michael Strube. 2018. Unrestricted bridging resolution. *Computational Linguistics*, 44(2):237–284.

E. Matthew Husband, Lisa A. Kelly, and David C. Zhu. 2011. Using complement coercion to understand the neural basis of semantic composition: Evidence from an fmri study. *Journal of Cognitive Neuroscience*, 23:3254–3266.

Ray Jackendoff. 1996. The architecture of the language faculty. MIT Press.

Ray Jackendoff. 2002. Foundations of language: Brain, meaning, grammar, evolution.

Paloma Jeretic, Alex Warstadt, Suvrat Bhooshan, and Adina Williams. 2020. Are natural language inference models IMPPRESsive? Learning IMPlicature and PRESupposition. In *Proceedings of the 58th Annual Meeting of the Association for Computational Linguistics*, pages 8690–8705, Online. Association for Computational Linguistics.

Aikaterini-Lida Kalouli, Annebeth Buis, Livy Real, Martha Palmer, and Valeria dePaiva. 2019. Explaining simple natural language inference. In *Proceedings of the 13th Linguistic Annotation Workshop*, pages 132–143.

Divyansh Kaushik, Eduard Hovy, and Zachary Lipton. 2019. Learning the difference that makes a difference with counterfactually-augmented data. In *International Conference on Learning Representations*.

Zoltán Kövecses and Günter Radden. 1998. Metonymy: Developing a cognitive linguistic view. *Cognitive linguistics*, 9(1):37–77.

Gina R. Kuperberg, Arim Choi, Neil Cohn, Martin Paczynski, and Ray Jackendoff. 2010. Electrophysiological correlates of complement coercion. *Journal of Cognitive Neuroscience*, 22:2685–2701.

Alice Lai, Yonatan Bisk, and Julia Hockenmaier. 2017. Natural language inference from multiple premises. In *Proceedings of the Eighth International Joint Conference on Natural Language Processing (Volume 1: Long Papers)*, pages 100–109.

Beth Levin. 1993. *English Verb Classes and Alternations*. The University of Chicago Press.

Mitchell Marcus, Beatrice Santorini, and Mary Ann Marcinkiewicz. 1993. Building a large annotated corpus of english: The penn treebank.

Marco Marelli, Stefano Menini, Marco Baroni, Luisa Bentivogli, Raffaella Bernardi, Roberto Zamparelli, et al. 2014. A sick cure for the evaluation of compositional distributional semantic models. In *LREC*, pages 216–223.

Brian McElree, Liina Pylkkänen, Martin J. Pickering, and Matthew J. Traxler. 2006. A time course analysis of enriched composition. *Psychonomic Bulletin & Review*, 13:53–59.

Stephen McGregor, Elisabetta Jezek, Matthew Purver, and Geraint Wiggins. 2017. A geometric method for detecting semantic coercion. In *IWCS 2017 - 12th International Conference on Computational Semantics - Long papers*.

Aakanksha Naik, Abhilasha Ravichander, Norman Sadeh, Carolyn Rose, and Graham Neubig. 2018. Stress test evaluation for natural language inference. In *Proceedings of the 27th International Conference on Computational Linguistics*, pages 2340–2353.

Yixin Nie, Xiang Zhou, and Mohit Bansal. 2020. What can we learn from collective human opinions on natural language inference data?

Jennimaria Palomaki, Olivia Rhinehart, and Michael Tseng. 2018. A case for a range of acceptable annotations. In *SAD/CrowdBias@ HCOMP*, pages 19–31.

Ellie Pavlick and Tom Kwiatkowski. 2019. Inherent disagreements in human textual inferences. *Transactions of the Association for Computational Linguistics*, 7:677–694.

Maria Mercedes Piñango and Ashwini Deo. 2016. Reanalyzing the complement coercion effect through a generalized lexical semantics for aspectual verbs. *J. Semantics*, 33:359–408.

Maria Piñango and Ashwini Deo. 2014. Reanalyzing the complement coercion effect through a generalized lexical semantics for aspectual verbs. *Journal of Semantics*, 33.

Barbara Plank, Dirk Hovy, and Anders Søgaard. 2014. Learning part-of-speech taggers with inter-annotator agreement loss. In *Proceedings of the 14th Conference of the European Chapter of the Association for Computational Linguistics*, pages 742–751.

Adam Poliak. 2020. A survey on recognizing textual entailment as an nlp evaluation.

Adam Poliak, Aparajita Haldar, Rachel Rudinger, J Edward Hu, Ellie Pavlick, Aaron Steven White, and Benjamin Van Durme. 2018. Collecting diverse natural language inference problems for sentence representation evaluation. In *Proceedings of the 2018 Conference on Empirical Methods in Natural Language Processing*, pages 67–81.

James Pustejovsky. 1991. The generative lexicon. *Comput. Linguistics*, 17:409–441.

James Pustejovsky. 1995. *The Generative Lexicon*. MIT Press, Cambridge, MA.

James Pustejovsky and Pierrette Bouillon. 1994. On the proper role of coercion in semantic typing. In *COLING 1994 Volume 2: The 15th International Conference on Computational Linguistics*.

James Pustejovsky, Jessica Moszkowicz, Olga Batiukova, and Anna Rumshisky. 2009. Glml: Annotating argument selection and coercion. In *Proceedings of the Eight International Conference on Computational Semantics*, pages 169–180.

James Pustejovsky, Anna Rumshisky, Alex Plotnick, Elisabetta Jezek, Olga Batiukova, and Valeria Quochi. 2010. Semeval-2010 task 7: Argument selection and coercion. In *Proceedings of the 5th international workshop on semantic evaluation*, pages 27–32.

Valentina Pyatkin, Ayal Klein, Reut Tsarfaty, and Ido Dagan. 2020. Qadiscourse – discourse relations as qa pairs: Representation, crowdsourcing and baselines.

Ina Roesiger. 2018. BASHI: A Corpus of Wall Street Journal Articles Annotated with Bridging Links. In *Proceedings of the Eleventh International Conference on Language Resources and Evaluation (LREC 2018)*, Miyazaki, Japan. European Language Resources Association (ELRA).

Paul Roit, Ayal Klein, Daniela Stepanov, Jonathan Mamou, Julian Michael, Gabriel Stanovsky, Luke Zettlemoyer, and Ido Dagan. 2020. Controlled crowdsourcing for high-quality qa-srl annotation. In *Proceedings of the 58th Annual Meeting of the Association for Computational Linguistics*, pages 7008–7013.

Alexis Ross and Ellie Pavlick. 2019. How well do nli models capture verb veridicality? In *Proceedings of the 2019 Conference on Empirical Methods in Natural Language Processing and the 9th International Joint Conference on Natural Language Processing (EMNLP-IJCNLP)*, pages 2230–2240.

Mike Schaekermann, Joslin Goh, Kate Larson, and Edith Law. 2018. Resolvable vs. irresolvable disagreement: A study on worker deliberation in crowd work. *Proceedings of the ACM on Human-Computer Interaction*, 2(CSCW):1–19.

Sean Trott, Tiago Timponi Torrent, Nancy Chang, and Nathan Schneider. 2020. (re)construing meaning in NLP. In *Proceedings of the 58th Annual Meeting of the Association for Computational Linguistics*, pages 5170–5184, Online. Association for Computational Linguistics.

Alex Warstadt, Alicia Parrish, Haokun Liu, Anhad Mohananey, Wei Peng, Sheng-Fu Wang, and Samuel R Bowman. 2020. Blimp: The benchmark of linguistic minimal pairs for english. *Transactions of the Association for Computational Linguistics*, 8:377–392.

Aaron Steven White, Pushpendre Rastogi, Kevin Duh, and Benjamin Van Durme. 2017. Inference is everything: Recasting semantic resources into a unified evaluation framework. In *Proceedings of the Eighth International Joint Conference on Natural Language Processing (Volume 1: Long Papers)*, pages 996–1005.

Adina Williams, Nikita Nangia, and Samuel Bowman. 2018. A broad-coverage challenge corpus for sentence understanding through inference. In *Proceedings of the 2018 Conference of the North American Chapter of the Association for Computational Linguistics: Human Language Technologies, Volume 1 (Long Papers)*, pages 1112–1122. Association for Computational Linguistics.

Tomer Wolfson, Mor Geva, Ankit Gupta, Matt Gardner, Yoav Goldberg, Daniel Deutch, and Jonathan Berant. 2020. Break it down: A question understanding benchmark. *Transactions of the Association for Computational Linguistics*.

Hitomi Yanaka, Koji Mineshima, Daisuke Bekki, and Kentaro Inui. 2020. Do neural models learn systematicity of monotonicity inference in natural language? In *Proceedings of the 58th Annual Meeting of the Association for Computational Linguistics (ACL2020)*, pages 6105—-6117.

Lai Yao-Ying. 2017. *The complement coercion phenomenon: Implications for models of sentence processing*. Ph.D. thesis, Yale University.

Soyeon Yoon. 2012. Constructions, semantic compatibility, and coercion: An empirical usage-based approach.

Alessandra Zarcone, Ken McRae, Alessandro Lenci, and Sebastian Padó. 2017. Complement coercion: The joint effects of type and typicality. *Frontiers in Psychology*, 8:1987.

Sheng Zhang, Rachel Rudinger, Kevin Duh, and Benjamin Van Durme. 2017. Ordinal common-sense inference. *Transactions of the Association for Computational Linguistics*, 5:379–395.

Yukun Zhu, Ryan Kiros, Rich Zemel, Ruslan Salakhutdinov, Raquel Urtasun, Antonio Torralba, and Sanja Fidler. 2015. Aligning books and movies: Towards story-like visual explanations by watching movies and reading books. In *Proceedings of the IEEE international conference on computer vision*, pages 19–27.

A Linguistic Background

Complement coercion has been studied in linguistics from many theoretical viewpoints. Lexical semantic accounts (such as Pustejovsky 1991, 1995 and others) and Construction Grammar accounts (e.g. Goldberg 1995) "attempt to formalize what semantic features of a lexical item have been changed to conform to those of the construction" (Yoon, 2012). One of the main approaches is the Type-Shifting analysis (Pustejovsky, 1991, 1995; Jackendoff, 1996, 2002), "which asserts that complement coercion involves a type-shifting operation that coerces the entity-denoting complement to an event"(Yao-Ying, 2017). Another approach (de Almeida and Dwivedi 2008 and others) "claims that complement coercion involves a hidden VP structure with an empty verb head, which is saturated by pragmatical inference in context" (Yao-Ying, 2017). Cognitive linguistics accounts (such as Kövecses and Radden 1998) exploit metonymy as the mechanism behind coercion constructions (Yoon, 2012). Complement coercion has been also extensively investigated in the framework of neurolinguistic research (for example, Kuperberg et al. 2010) and psycholinguistic studies (e.g., McElree et al. 2006). The latter often show that "coercion sentences elicit increased processing times" (Husband et al., 2011) compared with non-coercion sentences. Such theories as the Type-Shifting Hypothesis mentioned above and the Structured-Individual Hypothesis (Piñango and Deo, 2016) suggest different explanations for this associated processing cost (Yao-Ying, 2017).

B Complement Coercion: Counter Examples

Here we provide some additional examples of constructions that are similar to the ones in Examples 1,2 (the verb 'start' is followed by a non-event-denoting complement) but do *not* function as complement coercion constructions. Consider the following sentences:

7. I **started** a new company.

8. His name **started** the list.

9. Her wedding dress **started** a new tradition among brides.

In example 7 the verb 'start' is used as an entity-selecting (and not event-selecting) verb, a synonym of 'found', 'establish', so that there is no type clash.

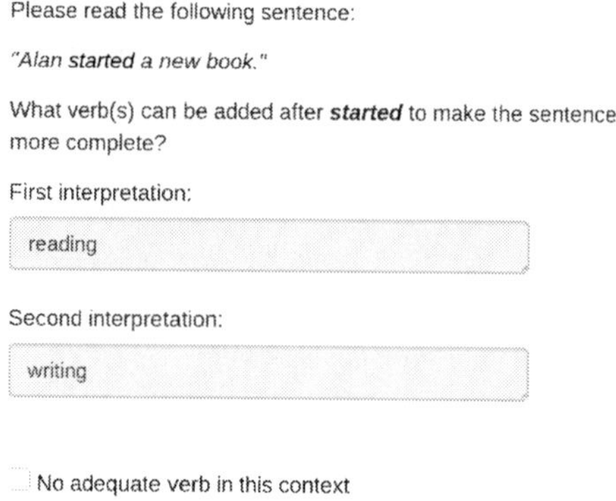

Figure 1: A screenshot of the explicit task presented to the annotators.

In example 8 the verb 'start' is used in its 'non-eventive' (Zarcone et al., 2017) or 'stative' (Piñango and Deo, 2014) sense ('constitute the initial part of something'). When used this way, the verb 'start' does not exclusively select for eventive complements, so, again, there is no type clash. Also, some authors (Godard and Jayez, 1993; Yao-Ying, 2017; Pustejovsky and Bouillon, 1994) argue that in coercion constructions the subject should be an "intentional controller of the event" (Godard and Jayez, 1993). In example 9 this condition does not hold, therefore there is no coercion.

C Explicit Modeling

In the *Explicit Completion* approach, the goal is to add the implicit argument of the coercion construction, if such completion exists. For instance, in the sentence "I started ___ a new book", possible completions are 'reading' and 'writing', and in Example 7 no completion fits. Concretely, given a sentence with a complement coercion verb candidate, the task is to complete it with a set of possible verbs that describe the covert event. As not all candidates function as parts of complement coercion constructions, annotators can mark that no additional verb is adequate in the context. In cases where there is more than one semantically plausible answer (e.g. Ex. 1), we ask annotators to provide two completion sets, each consisting of a group of semantic equivalent verbs, which correspond to different possible understandings of the text. A screenshot of the task presented to the turkers is shown in Figure 1.

This approach to task definition is reminiscent of those used for other missing elements phenomena, such as Verb Phrase Ellipsis (Bos and Spenader, 2011), Numeric Fused-Heads (Elazar and Goldberg, 2019), Bridging (Roesiger, 2018; Hou et al., 2018) and Sluicing (Hansen and Søgaard, 2020). However, in contrast to these tasks, where the answers can usually be found in the context,[8] the answers in our case are more open-ended (although still bounded by some restrictions (Godard and Jayez, 1993; Pustejovsky and Bouillon, 1994)). This makes this task more challenging for annotation.

Corpus Candidates In the *explicit completion* setting, we look for natural sentences that contain one of the following anchor verbs: 'start', 'begin', 'continue' and 'finish', - immediately followed by a direct object without any dependent verb in between.

Annotation Procedure We use the same restrictions from the previous procedure and create a new validation test, tailored for the new task. We pay 4 cents per Hit.

Results We collect annotations for 200 sentences, with two annotations per sentence. We compute the Fleiss Kappa (Fleiss, 1971) after a relaxation of the annotations into two labels: added a complement or not. Similarly to the previous modeling, the agreement score is $k = 0.18$, which is considered to be low. Consider the following examples:

9. "In 2011, Old Navy **began** __ a second rebranding to emphasize a family-oriented environment, known as Project ONE.", — $\{advertising, promoting, endorsing\}, \phi$

10. "After he had **finished** __ his studies Sadra began to explore unorthodox doctrines and as a result was both condemned and excommunicated by some Shi'i 'ulamā'.", — $\{pursuing, doing\}, \phi$

According to the definition of complement coercion, these examples do not require a complement. However, as can be seen from these examples, the proposed complements do contribute to an easier understanding of the sentence. We note that this concept of 'missing' is hard to explain and can be also subjective. Another obstacle is that strict adherence to the linguistic definition does not always

---

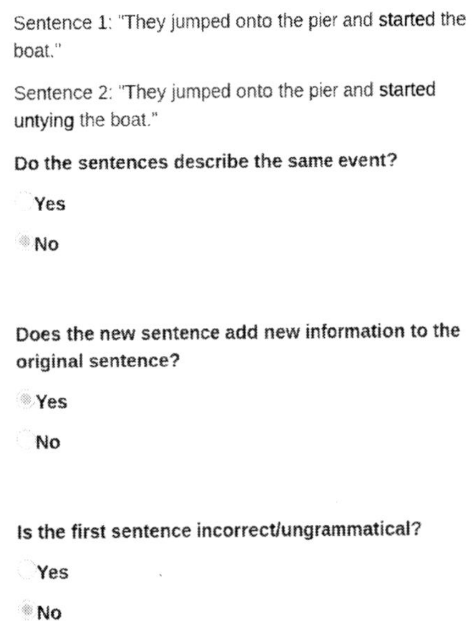

Figure 2: Screenshot of the interface shown to the turkers for collecting labels. This setup follows the instructions used for labeling NLI data in Glockner et al. (2018).

contribute to potential usefulness of the task for downstream applications. For this phenomenon, we did not follow the strict linguistic definition and used a more relaxed one. Additional examples along with their annotations are provided in Table 4.

D NLI Framing: Additional Material

We provide a screenshot of the NLI interface shown to the turkers in Figure 2.

NLI Data We provide additional examples for the original and the modified sentences (hypotheses and premises accordingly) used in the NLI framing (§3.2), along with the three obtained labels, in Table 3.

---

[8]Although not always. Some of the answers in the NFH work by Elazar and Goldberg (2019) are also open-ended, but those are relatively rare. Furthermore, the answers in sluicing are sometimes a modification of the text.

Premise	Hypothesis	Annotations
that gives us something to work with if he starts trouble.	that gives us something to work with if he starts making trouble.	ENT ENT ENT
I do hope you will continue mrs. cox's incredible hospitality.	I do hope you will continue to enjoy mrs. cox's incredible hospitality.	CON CON CON
he asked me as he continued a tune.	he asked me as he continued to strum a tune.	NEU NEU CON
how would she continue questions like this?	how would she continue to answer questions like this?	CON CON CON
he finished a sip of coffee and replied, not surprised.	he finished taking a sip of coffee and replied, not surprised.	ENT ENT NEU
it was pike's idea to start these games.	it was pike's idea to start playing these games.	ENT NEU CON
I started deep breaths and tried to cleanse my mind.	I started taking deep breaths and tried to cleanse my mind.	ENT ENT NEU
I would like to finish this movie sometime in this year!	I would like to finish watching this movie sometime in this year!	ENT ENT CON

Table 3: Examples for NLI pairs with a complement coercion structure. The ENT, NEU and CON labels refers to the entail, neutral and contradict accordingly.

Text	Annotations
... it will likely travel in a parabola, *continuing* its stabilizing spin, ...	ϕ, ϕ
Afterwards, they decide to *continue* the pub crawl to avoid attracting suspicion.	$\{doing\}, \{doing\}$
I was surprised he did not *continue* his openness at the RFPERM.	$\{embue\}, \{showing, displaying, ...\}$
In 1994, he joined Motilal Oswal to *start* their institutional desk before moving to UBS in 1996.	$\{employ\}_1, \{work\}_2, \{working\}$
In 1943 she *started* a career as an actress with the stage name Sheila Scott a name ...	$\phi, \{pursuing\}$
..., giving him the opportunity to *continue* the work left by his predecessors as well as ...	$\phi, \{researching, studying\}$
In the Middle Ages it was a battle cry , which was used to *start* a Feud or a Combat reenactment.	$\phi, \{fighting\}$
In addition, deductions are taken if the man *finishes* the element on two feet ...	$\phi, \{competing\}$

Table 4: Examples for the Explicit modeling. ϕ denotes the empty set, meaning no event is implied. When a subscript is present it denotes the different interpretation of the sentence, by the same annotator.

Embedding Structured Dictionary Entries

Steven R. Wilson[1], Walid Magdy[1,2], Barbara McGillivray[2,3], and Gareth Tyson[2,4]
[1]The University of Edinburgh, Edinburgh, UK
[2]The Alan Turing Institute, London, UK
[3]University of Cambridge, Cambridge, UK
[4]Queen Mary University of London, London, UK
steven.wilson@ed.ac.uk, wmagdy@inf.ed.ac.uk
bmcgillivray@turing.ac.uk, g.tyson@qmul.ac.uk

Abstract

Previous work has shown how to effectively use external resources such as dictionaries to improve English-language word embeddings, either by manipulating the training process or by applying post-hoc adjustments to the embedding space. We experiment with a multi-task learning approach for explicitly incorporating the structured elements of dictionary entries, such as user-assigned tags and usage examples, when learning embeddings for dictionary headwords. Our work generalizes several existing models for learning word embeddings from dictionaries. However, we find that the most effective representations overall are learned by simply training with a skip-gram objective over the concatenated text of all entries in the dictionary, giving no particular focus to the structure of the entries.

1 Introduction

While word embedding models are typically trained using large text corpora with objectives based on distributional semantics, recent work has shown how to take advantage of external resources like WordNet (Miller, 1995) and other manually created dictionaries in order to better capture word-level semantic relationships of interest. For example, previous work has used the graph structure of external resources to post-process pre-trained word embeddings, enforcing that the similarity between embeddings reflects the similarity inferred from the graph structure of lexicons like WordNet (Faruqui et al., 2015). Following in a similar principle, others use known synonymy and antonymy relationships between words to adjust the distance between word embeddings (Mrkšić et al., 2016). Other work uses traditional dictionaries to improve the overall coverage of word embedding models by creating embeddings for rare words be leveraging information from their definitions (Bahdanau et al., 2017).

While dictionaries have been shown to be useful, most previous work has focused only on using the text of the definitions in order to learn word representations. However, many dictionaries include additional structural elements such as usage examples, quotations containing the headword, tags, labels, and more. For some online crowd-built dictionaries, information such as the contributing users and even upvotes and downvotes are available.

We conjecture that such meta information may prove useful and, therefore, we seek to leverage all of this additional information to *build improved representations of the words defined in a given dictionary*. To do this, we generalize the Consistency-Penalized Autoencoder (CPAE) (Bosc and Vincent, 2018) to allow for not only the reconstruction of dictionary definitions, but also for making predictions about the other structural elements available, such as usage examples and user-assigned tags.

We make the following contributions in this paper: (1) we propose a flexible, multi-task learning extension to the CPAE model that can be used to produce embeddings from structured dictionary entries, (2) we evaluate the applicability of this extended model to three English-language dictionary datasets, each with their own unique characteristics and sets of structural elements, and (3) we demonstrate the a simple baseline approach for learning word embeddings, based on the popular skip-gram with negative sampling framework, can often lead to representations that better capture word-level semantic similarity according to a range of commonly used evaluation tasks.

2 Data & Baseline

2.1 Structured Dictionary Data

We consider three manually constructed, machine-readable, English-language dictionaries: English

Proceedings of the First Workshop on Insights from Negative Results in NLP, pages 117–125
Online, November 19, 2020. ©2020 Association for Computational Linguistics

Wordnet[1] (Miller, 1995), English Wiktionary[2], and Urban Dictionary (UD)[3], each containing definitions for each word in addition to one or more structural elements such as usage examples, tags, or votes (Table 1). We find that many of the terms that are defined in Urban Dictionary are not commonly used in everyday language, and so we choose to further filter the set of headwords from Urban Dictionary to those that have been used at least 10,000 times in a sample of tweets sampled over a five-year period as identified in (Wilson et al., 2020b).

2.2 Baseline Approach

To provide a simple baseline for later evaluation, we train word embeddings using the entire text of each dictionary, including all structured elements, by treating each structural element as a short document and prepending the entry headword to each. We use a standard skip-gram model with negative sampling (SGNS), trained using the FastText library (Mikolov et al., 2018).

3 Auto-encoding Structured Entries with Multi-task Learning

Next, we present an approach for learning word embeddings that implicitly encode a wide range of the elements that are present in a dictionary entry. Given a word defined in a dictionary, the objective of the model is to accurately recover as much structural information as possible, including the word's definition, usage examples, tags, and authors. We also leverage user provided votes as a means of sorting and filtering the dictionary entries. The model takes a word's definition as input, and learns a transformation from the words in the definition to an embedding that contains features that describe the structural elements of the dictionary entry for the word. We treat the prediction of each type of structural element as a separate task within a multi-task learning framework.

3.1 Model Architecture

Our model (Figure 1; a more formal, detailed description of the model is given in Appendix A) can be seen as a generalization of several others: a simple auto-encoder, Hill's model (Hill et al., 2016), and the consistency penalized auto-encoder

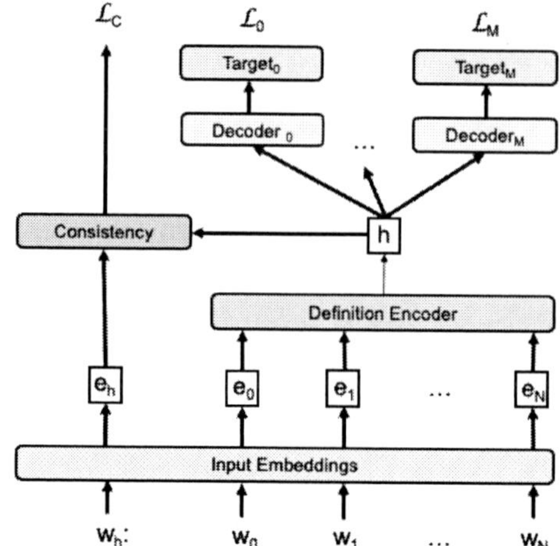

Figure 1: Model architecture for multi-task learning autoencoder for embedding words from their structured dictionary entries. Input tokens are embedding using the Input Embeddings layer, and the n tokens in the definition of headword w_h are passed to the Definition Encoder to produce the definition embedding h. This embedding should be consistent (low distance) with the embedding of the definition headword e_h. M possible output tasks can be used, each with its own decoder which needs to reconstruct the Target.

(CPAE). In each case, the input for the model is a definition[4] for the target headword, w_h. The input tokens are converted into a sequence of embeddings using a learnable word embedding layer, and these embeddings are passed to the definition encoder, which produces a single embedding, h, which is used as the representation for w_h.

This embedding is then fed to any number of decoders, each with their own specific objective and loss function (details in the subsections of Appendix A). The goal of each decoder's loss is to influence the weights of the encoder to produce an embedding h that is most useful for capturing a specific structural element of the dictionary entry for w_h, or to retain some other important property of the embedding h. The decoders that we use and their associated losses become components in the overall loss function for our model: $\mathcal{L} = \lambda_0 \mathcal{L}_0 + \lambda_1 \mathcal{L}_1 \ldots + \lambda_n \mathcal{L}_m$ for up to m objectives, each with its own associated weight term. These weights can be used to control the overall influence of the objective in the final loss computation.

---

[1]To make our results directly comparable with (Bosc and Vincent, 2018), we use the filtered version of WordNet included at: https://github.com/tombosc/cpae

[2]https://en.wiktionary.org/

[3]https://www.urbandictionary.com/

[4]Or, in the case of polysemous words, the concatenation of all tokens in all definitions, separated by a SEP token

	defs	examples	tags	votes	headwords	definitions	tokens
Wordnet	✓	✓			83K	159K	2.4M
Wiktionary	✓	✓	✓		214K	380K	4.6M
Urban Dictionary	✓	✓	✓	✓	2M	3.5M	195M
UD (Filtered)	✓	✓	✓	✓	22K	104K	59M

Table 1: Structural elements present in three machine-readable dictionaries, and number of headwords, definitions, and total tokens present in each. UD (Filtered) is the filtered version of Urban Dictionary which doesn't contain words that are not commonly used or definitions for which the difference between the number of upvotes and downvotes is negative. This is the version of Urban Dictionary that is used when training our proposed model.

The target of each decoder is dependent on the structural element that it is meant to encoder. For the definitions, the goal of the decoder is to reproduce the definition itself (making the use of this task alone equivalent to a simple autoencoder). For the usage examples and tags, the target task is the predict the context in which the headword appears using a skip-gram learning objective. We also experiment with using the user-provided votes to filter and sort the data, as well as to provide weights for the input definitions.

An additional loss term can be used in order to enforce the consistency between the learned embedding h and the input embedding for the headword e_h. This is similar to the main objective of Hill's model (Hill et al., 2016) and is the consistency penalty that is used in the CPAE model (Bosc and Vincent, 2018). This forces the model to produce embeddings for headwords that are consistent to the embeddings produced for the same words when they appear in the definitions of *other* headwords.

4 Evaluation and Results

We evaluate all produced embeddings[5] across a range of intrinsic evaluation tasks as used in (Jastrzebski et al., 2017).[6] For these word-level semantic similarity tasks, the machine generated scores (cosine similarity between the produced word embeddings) are compared against human-labeled similarity scores by computing the correlation between the two sets of scores.

The tasks involved include the Marco, Elia and Nam (MEN) annotated word pairs based on image captioning data (Bruni et al., 2014), the SimVerb (SV) verb similarity dataset (Gerz et al., 2016), both of which have standardized development and testing splits. We use the development splits of

these datasets in order to tune our models. The WordSim-353 (WS) dataset contains both similarity (WS-S) and relatedness (WS-R) annotations for the same sets of words, allowing us to examine the ability of our models to capture each of these semantic relations. We also evaluate using the SimLex-999 dataset and a subset of that data, SimLex-333 (SL999 and SL333) (Hill et al., 2015). The SL333 subset contains only the 333 most related pairs according to the human annotations. Stanford's Contextual Word Similarities (SCWS) dataset (Huang et al., 2012), the 65 word pairs studied by Rubenstein and Goodenough (RG65) 1965, the Mechanical Turk (MT) dataset (Radinsky et al., 2011), and the Rare Words (RW) dataset (Luong et al., 2014) round out the rest of our evaluatoin tasks.

For models that use our proposed architecture, we initialize the input embeddings using the baseline pre-trained skip-gram embeddings. We train these embeddings ourselves in the case of WordNet and Wiktionary, and use the `ud-basic` embeddings released by (Wilson et al., 2020a) for Urban Dictionary.[7] Table 2 shows the similarity and relatedness scores achieved when using various combinations of objectives in our model.[8]

We observe that for WordNet, the simple SGNS embeddings are always outperformed by the other approaches, which is in line with the results reported in (Bosc and Vincent, 2018) where the CPAE-P model was found to achieve the best results when using WordNet. We can see that adding structure, which, for the case of WordNet, only includes usage examples, leads to an improvement over the base CPAE-P model in many cases. The overall trend is similar for the Wiktionary data, yet we see a stronger performance from the SGNS baseline. In fact, SGNS achieves the best results for

---

[5]Details of the experimental setup are in Appendix C.

[6]We used code from the *web* package, located at: `https://github.com/kudkudak/word-embeddings-benchmarks` to run the intrinsic evaluation tasks.

[7]These embeddings were trained on the entirety of Urban Dictionary rather than just the subset that we use in this study.

[8]Only best performing models are shown; the full set of results can be found in Appendix B.

		dev		test									
	Model	MEN	SV	MEN	WS-R	WS-S	SL999	SL333	SV	SCWS	RG65	MT	RW
WordNet	SGNS	58.6	34.7	56.2	45.6	62.9	35.0	20.4	34.4	54.0	63.1	52.8	23.2
WordNet	Hill's Model	61.1	45.6	59.9	42.3	59.5	43.8	__35.8__	44.2	59.0	73.6	56.0	30.3
WordNet	CPAE-P	**68.3**	49.4	67.3	50.6	66.4	**47.4**	34.1	45.3	**61.5**	76.7	61.4	**31.5**
WordNet	+ Structure	68.0	__52.0__	**67.8**	**54.4**	**67.6**	45.8	33.5	__47.4__	61.3	**76.8**	**61.9**	28.5
Wikt.	SGNS	65.1	**43.2**	65.0	56.5	68.7	**42.1**	22.4	38.0	56.6	72.8	**63.3**	25.1
Wikt.	Hill's Model	63.8	33.5	66.3	53.8	70.6	37.6	**27.4**	33.2	**58.7**	80.7	57.9	**30.3**
Wikt.	CPAE-P	65.1	33.4	64.1	60.4	**73.0**	35.5	18.4	33.1	56.9	**87.7**	58.2	21.4
Wikt.	+ Structure	**65.2**	38.0	**67.0**	**61.4**	72.8	39.5	21.6	**38.2**	57.3	85.6	60.4	25.4
UD	SGNS	__79.1__	42.1	__78.0__	__65.7__	__74.2__	__47.9__	30.2	__35.5__	__62.5__	__89.3__	__74.3__	__39.2__
UD	Hill's Model	72.5	38.9	70.0	61.4	69.6	44.3	32.8	29.5	60.1	75.8	68.4	34.2
UD	CPAE-P	71.4	38.4	68.5	61.3	69.6	44.7	29.2	30.0	59.2	71.1	65.1	32.7
UD	+ Structure	74.6	**42.6**	72.3	64.1	71.1	47.8	**33.9**	30.4	60.4	78.9	69.2	34.9

Table 2: Correlation (Spearman's ρ) with gold standard similarity and relatedness scores for development and evaluation datasets. Hill's model (Hill et al., 2016) is the structured dictionary encoder with only the consistency penalty, CPAE-P is the Consistency Penalized Autoencoder (Bosc and Vincent, 2018) with pre-trained word embedding targets, and the version with Structure is our proposed extension to the model, making use of additional training objectives based on any available structural elements. SGNS is the skip-gram with negative sampling baseline word embedding model. **Bold** indicates the best result for a given dictionary, __underlined__ numbers are also the overall best.

two of the test datasets and achieves competitive results across the board, making it a viable alternative to the more complex dictionary auto-encoding approaches. Finally, for the Urban Dictionary data, we see the baseline SGNS approach overtaking the other methods in almost every evaluation set, also leading to many of the best overall scores found in this study. This shift in performance may be related to the overall size of each dataset: Urban Dictionary dataset contains approximately 200 million total tokens, compared to the 1.7 million in WordNet and 4.6 million in English Wiktionary. Further, as Urban Dictionary's definitions contain a mixture of noisy submissions, jokes, and opinions, they are likely to be less closely tied to the true meanings of the headwords (Nguyen et al., 2018). This could make the auto-encoding objective less useful overall in comparison to learning representations of the words simply based on their usage contexts.

5 Conclusions

We show that the extension of the CPAE model to include additional structural elements can provide some gains in word-level semantic similarity tasks, however, the the extra complexity of this approach is unnecessary for learning useful word embeddings, and in many cases, leads to degradation in the scores across a range of standard word embedding evaluation metrics in comparison to simpler approaches. To build general purpose word embeddings from a sufficiently large dictionary (i.e., containing at least several hundred million tokens of

text), our recommendation is to simply concatenate all of the structural elements together as a single text, inserting the entry headword between each element, and applying the widely popular skip-gram architecture to this text to learn traditional distribution embeddings. This approach requires only a single learning objective, trains in much less time, and achieves competitive results in many cases, making it an easier alternative to explicitly leveraging structural information from dictionary entries while still creating useful embeddings.

Future work should explore how these approaches would work when applied to more English dictionaries such as the Oxford English Dictionary[9] in order to better understand the effects of using a more standardized dictionary to learn embeddings. Further, dictionaries in other languages, particularly lower-resource languages, should be considered, since our results suggest that the approaches described in this paper outperform the baseline approach mostly in settings where the total amount of text in the dictionary is small.

Acknowledgments

This work was supported by The Alan Turing Institute under the EPSRC grants EP/N510129/1, and EP/S033564/1. We also acknowledge support via EP/T001569/1.

---

[9]https://www.oed.com/

References

Dzmitry Bahdanau, Tom Bosc, Stanisław Jastrzebski, Edward Grefenstette, Pascal Vincent, and Yoshua Bengio. 2017. Learning to compute word embeddings on the fly. *arXiv preprint arXiv:1706.00286*.

Tom Bosc and Pascal Vincent. 2018. Auto-encoding dictionary definitions into consistent word embeddings. In *Proceedings of the 2018 Conference on Empirical Methods in Natural Language Processing*, pages 1522–1532.

Elia Bruni, Gemma Boleda, Marco Baroni, and Nam-Khanh Tran. 2012. Distributional semantics in technicolor. In *Proceedings of the 50th Annual Meeting of the Association for Computational Linguistics (Volume 1: Long Papers)*, pages 136–145.

Elia Bruni, Nam-Khanh Tran, and Marco Baroni. 2014. Multimodal distributional semantics. *Journal of Artificial Intelligence Research*, 49:1–47.

Laura Burdick, Jonathan K Kummerfeld, and Rada Mihalcea. 2018. Factors influencing the surprising instability of word embeddings. In *Proceedings of the 2018 Conference of the North American Chapter of the Association for Computational Linguistics: Human Language Technologies, Volume 1 (Long Papers)*, pages 2092–2102.

Manaal Faruqui, Jesse Dodge, Sujay Kumar Jauhar, Chris Dyer, Eduard Hovy, and Noah A Smith. 2015. Retrofitting word vectors to semantic lexicons. In *Proceedings of the 2015 Conference of the North American Chapter of the Association for Computational Linguistics: Human Language Technologies*, pages 1606–1615.

Daniela Gerz, Ivan Vulić, Felix Hill, Roi Reichart, and Anna Korhonen. 2016. Simverb-3500: A large-scale evaluation set of verb similarity. In *Proceedings of the 2016 Conference on Empirical Methods in Natural Language Processing*, pages 2173–2182.

Felix Hill, KyungHyun Cho, Anna Korhonen, and Yoshua Bengio. 2016. Learning to understand phrases by embedding the dictionary. *Transactions of the Association for Computational Linguistics*, 4:17–30.

Felix Hill, Roi Reichart, and Anna Korhonen. 2015. Simlex-999: Evaluating semantic models with (genuine) similarity estimation. *Computational Linguistics*, 41(4):665–695.

Eric H Huang, Richard Socher, Christopher D Manning, and Andrew Y Ng. 2012. Improving word representations via global context and multiple word prototypes. In *Proceedings of the 50th Annual Meeting of the Association for Computational Linguistics (Volume 1: Long Papers)*, pages 873–882.

Stanisław Jastrzebski, Damian Leśniak, and Wojciech Marian Czarnecki. 2017. How to evaluate word embeddings? on importance of data efficiency and simple supervised tasks. *arXiv preprint arXiv:1702.02170*.

Diederik P Kingma and Jimmy Ba. 2014. Adam: A method for stochastic optimization. *arXiv preprint arXiv:1412.6980*.

Minh-Thang Luong, Ilya Sutskever, Quoc V Le, Oriol Vinyals, and Wojciech Zaremba. 2014. Addressing the rare word problem in neural machine translation. *arXiv preprint arXiv:1410.8206*.

Tomáš Mikolov, Édouard Grave, Piotr Bojanowski, Christian Puhrsch, and Armand Joulin. 2018. Advances in pre-training distributed word representations. In *Proceedings of the Eleventh International Conference on Language Resources and Evaluation (LREC 2018)*.

George A Miller. 1995. Wordnet: a lexical database for english. *Communications of the ACM*, 38(11):39–41.

N Mrkšić, D Séaghdha, B Thomson, M Gašić, L Rojas-Barahona, PH Su, D Vandyke, TH Wen, and S Young. 2016. Counter-fitting word vectors to linguistic constraints. In *2016 Conference of the North American Chapter of the Association for Computational Linguistics: Human Language Technologies, NAACL HLT 2016-Proceedings of the Conference*, pages 142–148.

Dong Nguyen, Barbara McGillivray, and Taha Yasseri. 2018. Emo, love and god: making sense of urban dictionary, a crowd-sourced online dictionary. *Royal Society open science*, 5(5):172320.

Kira Radinsky, Eugene Agichtein, Evgeniy Gabrilovich, and Shaul Markovitch. 2011. A word at a time: computing word relatedness using temporal semantic analysis. In *Proceedings of the 20th international conference on World wide web*, pages 337–346.

Herbert Rubenstein and John B Goodenough. 1965. Contextual correlates of synonymy. *Communications of the ACM*, 8(10):627–633.

Steven R. Wilson, Walid Magdy, Barbara McGillivray, Kiran Garimella, and Gareth Tyson. 2020a. Urban dictionary embeddings for slang nlp applications. In *Proceedings of The 12th Language Resources and Evaluation Conference*, pages 4764–4773.

Steven R. Wilson, Walid Magdy, Barbara McGillivray, and Gareth Tyson. 2020b. Analyzing temporal relationships between trending terms on twitter and urban dictionary activity. In *12th ACM Conference on Web Science*, WebSci '20, page 155–163, New York, NY, USA. Association for Computing Machinery.

Appendix

A   Detailed Model Description

Formally, let $\mathcal{D} = \{w_{in}^0, w_{in}^1, \ldots, w_{in}^n\}$ be a sequence of tokens in the definition for w_h. The elements of $\mathcal{D}$ belong to the vocabulary of all words that appear in definitions, $\mathcal{V}_{in}$, and w_h belongs to the vocabulary of all headwords, $\mathcal{V}_h$. In the case of polysemous words which have more than one meaning, we concatenate the tokens from all definitions together into a single sequence, and separate them by a special `SEP` token.

Given the full sequence of input words, $E_{in}(\mathcal{D}) = \{e_{in}^0, e_{in}^1, \ldots, e_{in}^n\}$ is the set of d_{in}-dimensional embeddings representing words in the definition. These embeddings can be learned during training, or pre-initialized and frozen, as discussed later in this section. The embeddings are passed into an encoder layer in order to produce a single d_h-dimensional embedding $h = \mathrm{enc}(E_{in}(\mathcal{D}))$. The encoder can be any type of model that takes a variable-length sequence of embeddings as input and produces a single, fixed-length embedding as output.

This embedding is then fed to any number of decoders, each with their own specific objective and loss function. The goal of each decoder's loss is to influence the weights of the encoder to produce an embedding h that is most useful for capturing a specific structural element of the dictionary entry for w_h, or to retain some other important property of the embedding h. In the following subsections, we describe the decoders that we use and their associated loss, which become components in the overall loss function for our model:

$$\mathcal{L} = \lambda_0 \mathcal{L}_0 + \lambda_1 \mathcal{L}_1 \ldots + \lambda_n \mathcal{L}_n$$

for up to n objectives, each with its own associated weight term. These weights can be used to control the overall influence of the objective in the final loss computation.

A.1   Definitions as reconstruction targets

The words in a well-formed definition should provide a precise encapsulation of one of the meanings of the headword being defined. So, we expect that a combination of the meanings of the words in the definition should provide a reasonable approximation for the meaning of the word itself. Since the input to our encoder is the set of embeddings of the definition words, a decoder objective based on the intermediate representation, h, will lead to a simple auto-encoder for the definition itself.

The definition decoder with learned parameters θ produces a set of predictions of the words belonging to the original definition $\hat{\mathcal{D}} = \mathrm{dec}_\theta(h)$, and this decoder is used to compute the definition reconstruction loss $\mathcal{L}_R$. We use a simple conditional unigram language modeling loss as our reconstruction loss

$$\mathcal{L}_\mathcal{R} = -\log p(\mathcal{D}|\theta) = \sum_{w \in \mathcal{D}} -\log p(w|\theta)$$

where $p(w|\theta)$ is determined by the decoder dec_θ. For the decoder, the auto-encoder model uses a single linear layer with input size d_h and output size $|\mathcal{V}_{def}|$, followed by a softmax operation, providing a probability $p(w)$ for all words in the output vocabulary $\mathcal{V}_{def}$. The output vocabulary $\mathcal{V}_{def}$ is equal to $\mathcal{V}_{in}$ for the traditional auto-encoder setting, since the objective is to reproduce the set of input words. However, in practice, we can speed up computation with minimal impact on performance by reducing $\mathcal{V}_{def}$ to only contain the m_{def} most common words, and treating all others as out-of-vocabulary. The out-of-vocabulary words are represented by a single token `UNK` which is ignored for the purposes of the loss computation. Including only this objective (which can be achieved by setting $\lambda_t = 0$ for every other task t) is equivalent to a simple definition auto-encoder: given the word in the headword's definition, produce an intermediate embedding h which can then be used to reconstruct the original set of words from the definition.

A.2   Usage examples and tags as context

While widely used distribution word embeddings rely on examples of words in context in order to learn representations of those words, hundreds of examples of usage of each word are usually required in order to build stable representations (Burdick et al., 2018). We experiment with using only the few prototypical examples that are provided in the dictionary definitions themselves as training samples for the term. This has several advantages: first, no data outside of the dictionary itself is needed to train the embeddings, and second, usage examples should, by nature, be written in a way that a specific meaning of the term is emphasized, providing a potentially stronger semantic signal than randomly sampled occurrences of a term in a text corpus. Usage contexts may help to capture aspects of meaning that correspond to general semantic relatedness between words. Similarly, tags provide high-level category information related to words, and we expect that words with similar sets of tags will be related in meaning.

To incorporate this information into our model, we use a skip-gram language modeling objective similar to the one used by the word2vec model for learning word embeddings from word-in-context samples. That is, given the embedding for a word, h, we train a new feedforward output layer to predict the set of words that appear in the usage example context *around* the target word, or in the case of tags, the output layer should predict all tags. In the case of the usage examples, we replace the word and its morphological variations with a special MASK token so that the model does not learn to simply predict the word itself. Then, we define new vocabularies $\mathcal{V}_{use}$ and $\mathcal{V}_{tag}$ for all words that appear in usage examples in the dictionary and all tags, respectively, and we train linear layers to predict the set of usage words and tags given h. The loss $\mathcal{L}_{use}$ is then the cross-entropy between the predicted distribution over $\mathcal{V}_{use}$ and the equally sized vector of counts representing the number of times each word actually appeared in a usage example, and the same is done with the tag distribution to compute the tag prediction loss, $\mathcal{L}_{tag}$. As with the definition decoder, we allow for the size of the output vocabulary to be restricted to the most common m_{use}/m_{tag} words.

A.3 Consistency between embeddings

The consistency penalized auto-encoder model (CPAE) adapted an additional constraint, based on Hill's model (Hill et al., 2016), to minimize the distance between the input embedding $e_h = E_{in}(w_h)$ and the learned encoder embedding h. To achieve this, the Euclidean distance between the two embeddings is minimized as an additional component of the loss, the consistency penalty: $\mathcal{L}_C = (h - e_h)^2$ which can only be computed for for the set of words which are both *defined* (headwords) and used within definitions of other words, i.e., $\mathcal{V}_h \cap \mathcal{V}_{in}$. When setting $\lambda_t = 0$ for all other tasks t, we can approximately recover Hill's model (Hill et al., 2016). It was previously shown (Bosc and Vincent, 2018) that initializing the weights of the input embeddings E_{in} with pre-trained word embeddings, paired with this type of consistency constraint, can lead to improved performance on

a number of word relatedness tasks (we label this setting as CPAE-P).

A.4 Votes as signals of importance

User-provided information can be used in several ways in our method. In our current setup, there may often be too many entries for a given headword to be able to adequately focus on all of them at once using our models which rely on a recurrent encoder for the concatenation of all tokens in all definitions. In Urban Dictionary, we can rely on the signal of user-provided votes, which are applied at the *entry*-level. This information can help sort the set of entries by importance: when training our concatenated lists of definitions, entries, and tags, we try sorting[10] them by their net number of votes (up-votes − down-votes) so that the top scoring entries will be processed by the model first, giving them priority over the other entries. We also remove any entries that received negative net votes from the concatenated list of entries. Empirically, we found that using the voting information in this way resulted in either a minor improvement or no change in the results, and so all results presented reflect the use of votes as signals of importance where votes are available.

B Additional Results

Table 3 shows the full set of results across all three dictionaries using the same evaluation tasks as before. AE/Autoencoder is the simple autoencoder model in which the loss term only consists of the definition reconstruction penalty. CPAE is the Consistency Penalized Autoencoder (Bosc and Vincent, 2018) which is the same as the AE model with the addition of the consistency penalty. Model names ending with "-P" use pre-trained embeddings (the same used for the SGNS baseline) to initialize the input embedding layer of the model. Hill's model (Hill et al., 2016) only uses the consistency penalty and always uses pre-trained embeddings to initialize the input embedding layer. SGNS is the skip-gram with negative sampling baseline, and "+Structure" is the same as the previous row, but using out multi-task learning framework to train the model to use the structural elements available in the dictionary. For the Urban Dictionary data, for models that use pre-trained embeddings to initialize the input layer, "Full" indicates that those embeddings

---

[10]We also explore using votes to weight the loss for each example, but find no significant differences in the results.

		dev		test									
	Model	MEN	SV	MEN	WS-R	WS-S	SL999	SL333	SV	SCWS	RG65	MT	RW
WordNet	Autoencoder	48.9	38.7	49.0	31.3	50.7	36.2	22.4	33.8	54.0	61.4	44.0	21.8
	+ Structure	45.0	42.7	45.7	28.6	41.4	32.9	22.3	38.7	50.1	65.8	40.1	21.9
	CPAE	51.1	41.6	48.9	34.5	47.8	39.7	29.0	37.2	53.2	60.0	40.5	23.4
	+ Structure	51.0	44.1	51.5	36.6	52.2	36.3	23.6	37.6	54.0	63.6	47.0	21.9
	AE-P	55.8	45.9	52.8	39.2	59.7	41.8	28.2	40.4	56.8	68.2	49.4	24.4
	+ Structure	55.8	45.3	55.9	39.9	62.1	42.2	27.2	43.5	57.3	66.8	50.8	23.8
	CPAE-P	**68.3**	49.4	67.3	50.6	66.4	**47.4**	34.1	45.3	**61.5**	76.7	61.4	**31.5**
	+ Structure	68.0	<u>**52.0**</u>	**67.8**	**54.4**	**67.6**	45.8	33.5	<u>**47.4**</u>	61.3	**76.8**	**61.9**	28.5
	Hill's Model	61.1	45.6	59.9	42.3	59.5	43.8	<u>35.8</u>	44.2	59.0	73.6	56.0	30.3
	SGNS	58.6	34.7	56.2	45.6	62.9	35.0	20.4	34.4	54.0	63.1	52.8	23.2
Wiktionary	Autoencoder	45.8	27.3	49.2	44.4	60.3	29.4	9.8	25.4	47.9	77.2	45.5	22.4
	+ Structure	43.3	14.1	45.8	35.5	62.3	20.9	-2.9	16.3	42.3	50.7	40.7	17.7
	CPAE	53.3	27.4	53.1	52.4	61.6	34.6	15.8	29.3	54.2	75.2	49.7	16.8
	+ Structure	38.6	18.3	46.1	32.3	53.3	20.2	-1.3	19.9	43.1	56.1	33.6	13.9
	AE-P	51.3	31.2	51.1	43.5	59.8	32.9	15.8	27.5	49.8	82.7	43.5	25.8
	+ Structure	54.0	31.2	54.0	49.2	64.0	33.6	20.3	27.3	49.3	78.1	48.6	24.2
	CPAE-P	65.1	33.4	64.1	60.4	**73.0**	35.5	18.4	33.1	56.9	**87.7**	58.2	21.4
	+ Structure	**65.2**	38.0	**67.0**	**61.4**	72.8	39.5	21.6	**38.2**	57.3	85.6	60.4	25.4
	Hill's Model	63.8	33.5	66.3	53.8	70.6	37.6	**27.4**	33.2	**58.7**	80.7	57.9	**30.3**
	SGNS	65.1	**43.2**	65.0	56.5	68.7	**42.1**	22.4	38.0	56.6	72.8	**63.3**	25.1
Urban Dictionary	Autoencoder	8.7	9.3	13.2	3.4	7.9	10.3	9.3	10.3	25.2	15.8	8.3	4.1
	+ Structure	14.1	11.7	16.0	8.3	20.7	11.2	11.0	8.0	25.2	32.8	10.5	6.2
	CPAE	1.7	7.4	5.9	-2.2	5.6	3.9	-0.1	4.5	23.4	-1.4	0.6	2.8
	+ Structure	20.0	15.8	22.9	17.8	17.4	10.1	9.8	5.5	27.3	21.3	13.1	3.8
	AE-P (Part)	20.9	7.5	16.1	6.7	18.6	10.0	3.6	5.5	31.8	2.5	12.2	7.1
	+ Structure	26.3	9.8	18.6	9.5	22.1	11.0	6.0	4.7	33.1	-3.5	7.0	7.9
	CPAE-P (Part)	54.9	26.1	51.7	42.4	55.6	31.8	23.1	20.4	48.1	47.4	46.9	11.8
	+ Structure	57.1	24.9	52.0	40.5	52.7	30.4	24.5	19.2	48.4	45.7	51.3	11.6
	Hill's (Part)	57.4	24.7	55.1	43.7	57.0	31.4	24.4	19.3	49.9	47.8	49.2	12.7
	SGNS (Part)	65.8	28.2	63.6	51.7	58.2	36.8	20.5	27.6	55.4	50.9	59.6	17.1
	AE-P (Full)	21.1	8.6	17.1	8.0	18.3	10.4	4.8	5.0	30.4	0.3	12.7	12.1
	+ Structure	25.4	9.4	18.4	12.2	20.8	12.0	12.4	6.6	32.2	8.2	11.4	9.3
	CPAE-P (Full)	71.4	38.4	68.5	61.3	69.6	44.7	29.2	30.0	59.2	71.1	65.1	32.7
	+ Structure	74.6	**42.6**	72.3	64.1	71.1	47.8	**33.9**	30.4	60.4	78.9	69.2	34.9
	Hill's (Full)	72.5	38.9	70.0	61.4	69.6	44.3	32.8	29.5	60.1	75.8	68.4	34.2
	SGNS (Full)	<u>79.1</u>	42.1	<u>78.0</u>	<u>65.7</u>	<u>74.2</u>	<u>47.9</u>	30.2	<u>35.5</u>	<u>62.5</u>	<u>89.3</u>	<u>74.3</u>	<u>39.2</u>

Table 3: Full similarity and relatedness evaluation results for each dictionary.

have been trained on the entirety of Urban Dictionary, while "Part" means that the embeddings were only trained on the filtered subset (only commonly used words, no words receiving negative total votes) of Urban Dictionary that was used to train the main dictionary embedding model.

The models presented in the Results section of the main paper are those that achieved the best result for at least one evaluation task for any dictionary dataset. However, from this full set of results, we can observe that the addition of structural elements through multi-task learning does lead to improvements in some cases, especially for the Urban Dictionary. This may be due to the fact that the definitions in Urban Dictionary are not always strictly providing direct meanings of the words and sometimes include jokes and opinions (Nguyen et al., 2018), so the usage examples and tags can be used to help provide more useful signals when training the model. This phenomenon can be seen even more closely from the very poor results achieved by the plain autoencoder and CPAE models on Urban Dictionary, which achieve no better than random results on some of the evaluation tasks, indicating that the signal from the definitions in Urban Dictionary is extremely noisy, even within the filtered subset of the dictionary.

C Experimental details

We train our models for a maximum of 150 epochs, implementing early-stopping using two of the intrinsic evaluation tasks which have readily available development sets: MEN (Bruni et al., 2012) and SimVerb-999 (Hill et al., 2015). When the model average performance on these two tasks does not increase for 10 epochs in a row, we stop training and save the embeddings produced by the model which achieved the maximum average score on these development tasks. We initialize our input embeddings with the baseline FastText embeddings trained on the concatenation of all structural dictionary elements treated as plain text.

For our definition encoder, we use a 300-dimensional, bidirectional GRU[11] layer followed by a single feedforward layer. We set the dimension d_h to match the size of whichever pre-trained embeddings we use with that model (usually 300) so that the consistency penalty can be properly computed. We limit the size of each output vocabulary to the most common 10,000 words, and we limit the size of the input vocabulary to the most common 50,000 words.

We use Adam (Kingma and Ba, 2014) as the optimizer with a learning rate of 3×10^{-4}. Following (Bosc and Vincent, 2018), we set the λ value for the reconstruction task to 1 and modify the other weights proportionally. Given the previously reported importance of the consistency penalty, we set this to 64. In order to focus our search on the possible combinations of objectives, we also leave the λ values for the tags and examples at 1.

---

[11]We also experimented with several other simple encoder types, including the LSTM that was used in (Bosc and Vincent, 2018), but found the bi-GRU to give consistently better or equal results with a smaller number of parameters.